The Legend of

GW00374612

Sutcl

Special thanks go to: Bob Bee for the loan of his Wisden collection;

Andy Collier for his photos and both Frank O'Gorman and George

Karger for gifting me their autographs.

Dedicated to Rhody x

Contents

Jack Hobbs   Herbert Sutcliffe

Introduction
Thursday 9th September 1976, Canterbury Kent

The old Annexe Stand at Canterbury's St Lawrence Cricket ground had the warmth of late summer radiating from its timbers but despite this an elderly gentleman in a tweed jacket, puffing away on his pipe, reckoned 1911 was hotter. From memory, it was September 1976, the year of the great drought that had all England and Wales bathed in desiccating conditions, from June through to the end of August, followed by torrential downpours that moved cars down streets and, after all that, the sun shone again, the final ember from a flame-coated summer, the one we all got hideously sunburnt from with the skin on our shoulders blistered into bubbles, that one.

Anyway, the scene is day two of the Kent versus Sussex County game and Javed Miandad, in the course of his 164, eclipsed even the savage majesty of Alan Knott's 144 the day before.

Taking no pleasure watching Kent's bowlers suffer a hiding from some Pakistan protégé, I engaged the elderly gentleman on a topic of his earliest cricket memories. Turned out the octogenarian had seen the likes of Gilbert Jessop and F.S. Jackson. He was there at the Oval in 1909 when Archie MacLaren over-bowled D.W. Carr on debut but, in all his cricketing life, the day that gave him greatest pleasure was attending the third day's play at the Oval in 1926 between England and Australia.

''You see'', he stressed, ''Hobbs and Sutcliffe that morning were *so* good that.''. There was a pause as we watched Underwood try to curb Miandad. When I looked back at him again the old boy tried desperately to suppress tears, eyes watery as a flood of memories and emotions hurtled back at him, ''. that they conquered not only the Aussies but also the sticky wicket. Heroes they were, proper heroes''. His voice faded to a silent nod for added authenticity.

I never asked his name. I was 10 at the time, a mad keen Kent and England cricket fan, living only a five-minute walk from the St Lawrence cricket ground. Mum would give me the entrance money, Father approved because anything to do with cricket was obviously good for the soul. Here I was, engulfed in cricket history, creaking and worn-out timber boards underfoot, sitting down, drinking my orange squash, soaking in the ambience for life, tasting it for ever more in the memory and all in a wooden stand built 69 years earlier and weathered into an atmospheric Edwardian relic, deep in conversation with a set of grandfather figures all of whom spoke about the first great flush of Kent trophies back before the First World War. They revered the tall, splendour of left-hander Frank Woolley, the Pride of Kent, they longed for the slow-left-arm of highly strung Colin Blyth, warmed to the comical spirit of Patsy Hendren from Middlesex, admired Walter Hammond and no one ever bowled faster than Harold Larwood. Hobbs was a greater batsman than Bradman on bad wickets. They couldn't decide who was better between Sutcliffe and Hutton and the original elderly gentleman, the one who wept a little, announced that his father had watched Dr W.G. Grace, Ranjitsinhji and Richardson at Old Trafford back in 1896.

Those men, and one looked like the former US President Franklin D. Roosevelt, are silent now. I never saw them again but the majesty of Javed Miandad's batting and those anecdotes remain vivid.

''Miandad are over there and me and mum are over here'' quipped one of them, chuckling to himself.

The memory of that gentleman, the very venerable but unknown cricket fan, recalling Hobbs and Sutcliffe at the Oval fifty years earlier, is a thread to the present. Those famous openers secured mellifluous moments that reminded the unknown cricket fan of his distant prime. Perhaps he was there with his father?

Maybe he and his old cronies were the fashion statement of the *roaring twenties*? A mere scratch of the surface reveals the 1920s as a time of rapid economic growth, of greater independence for women most manifestly the rise of so-called 'flappers'; these free spirited, short-haired young women, poo-pooed by older generations as immoral, liked showing off their legs while dancing to the can-

can. The explosion of jazz, the rise of vehicular traffic jams across London's bridges, the massive overuse of car horns polluting the noise and the maximum extent of the British Empire, all symbols of the 1920s, became a time when young adults, too young to have served in the war, frolicked in their burgeoning wages, greater freedoms and tobacco clouds.

Hideous and obvious racism existed in British society back then. According to a recent and rare visit to a London pub, I was told by a lawyer, in his fifties, that London is the most tolerant and multi-cultural city in the world. One Englishman's view was that the 'feel' of London is something to be proud of and should be exported around the world. I posed the Englishman's view to a black bouncer, biceps the size and shape of Napoleonic cannon balls, and do you know what? He asked me to drink up and leave.

The reason was rather blurred. I did exactly as he said, added him as a Facebook friend, and he did, actually, agree with the Englishman's statement. Back in the 1920s Blacks and Asians were considered savages and jokes involving the n-word were appreciated by most. Few Englishmen regarded racism of this kind in anyway offensive.

Part of the explanation must come from genuine ignorance through lack of contact with people of different races.

Sex before marriage was completely and utterly frowned upon. Anybody born out of wedlock was known as an illegitimate, or more specifically: a bastard. Being 'gay' was considered a very attractive trait in a human being. Often bowlers displayed very obvious signs of gayness on the field of play when they took a wicket. The winning team, especially in a big game at the end of the season, often embarked on gay events that involved drinking lots of alcohol. You see: being 'gay' in the 1920s meant being jolly and homosexuality was punishable with a custodial sentence, although this law was finally ditched in 1967. A considerable majority of people smoked. It was considered very much in vogue. Even Hobbs and Sutcliffe, the most famous sporting stars of the decade, smoked.

Yet the 1920s also represented the aftermath of deep, residual pain, of people forced to cope with emotional hardship and loss. English cricket had been broken. Her opening bowling resources depleted beyond immediate repair. Either aged like the 46-year-old Sydney Barnes, or injured beyond repair like his opening partner on the triumphant Ashes tour of 1911/12, Frank Foster, or killed during the Great War as fallen heroes such as Major Booth and Percy Jeeves; both of whom would have jostled to the top of England's opening bowling queue come 1919.

Without any heavy artillery of fast bowlers, England lost the first eight Tests against Warwick Armstrong's massive squad of talent in the first two post-war Ashes series and so a cloud of inferiority and depression descended upon the landscape.

Immediately prior to the Great War, England had played 16 Tests, won 12 and drawn the other four. Given that these Tests were against Australia and South Africa (no other Test teams existed), both opponents got crushed home and away, the yearning to cheer an England team of comparable standard pervaded every nook and cranny from grass-roots to the MCC Committee room at Lord's. To return to winning ways would alleviate the trauma, partially eradicate the sense of loss and raise morale, not to mention spawn the next generation of super stars.

The Legend of Hobbs and Sutcliffe aims to uncover the truth behind their status as undeniably the greatest opening partnership Test cricket has known. The bare statistics reveal a conspicuous dominance over all rivals to a greater degree than, say, Sydney Barnes in the bowling camp; indeed, their superiority as the most celebrated opening partnership in history falls not far short of Don Bradman's astonishing outlier as the greatest batsman of all time. Statistics are at the back but let the story unfold and wait until the end.

Chapter One: 1882 to 1918

Where to start? One could plum for the first time Jack Hobbs opened the batting with Herbert Sutcliffe: 1922 Scarborough Festival, playing for C.I. Thornton's XI - at the request of Sir Henry Leveson-Gower - against the MCC Touring Party soon to sail for a Test series in South Africa; 'twas the final curtain-call of the 1922 first-class season in England. Yet the first seed sprouted as early as the 21st December 1882 with the birth of the first child for Flora and John Hobbs, a boy christened John Berry Hobbs, Berry being his mother's maiden name.

John and Flora were honest, upstanding, God-fearing folk who had the misfortune of living in the most squalid eastern section of Cambridge and struggled to make ends meet. This financial situation was partly because, as a roof slater, John brought home a low salary and Flora was blessed with such extraordinary fertility she produced no fewer than twelve children over the next 19 years. Jack was the eldest of six brothers and six sisters. They never went hungry; his parents did all they could and drilled manners and diligence into their offspring. The result brought that humble dignity to Hobbs, later so revered across the cricketing world.

They moved to a two-up, two-down 1870s built, red-brick terrace house while Jack was still a toddler and his father John, a keen club cricketer, turned out for the Anchor's Pub team; his father's cricket skills and humble nature attracted the attention of Cambridge University who invited him to become a groundsman. This was also low-paid, one of servitude to the educated elite, yet John Hobbs loved his job.

Jack had cricket in his DNA, as soon as he could stand up, his father gave him a cricket bat and fed him balls to hit. He made a heck of a noise, as a toddler of two, in front of the 1884 Australians at Fenners against Cambridge. Even as a two-year-old, he marvelled at how far the cricket ball could be hit. As he grew older, Jack spent many long hours helping his father with his duties whenever he could, immersing himself in cricket and watching the net sessions of the Cambridge cricketers. He stood beyond the back of the net, sizing up the top bowlers and batsmen, taking on board their techniques.

Jack was just short of his twelfth birthday and about to leave school when a further seismic jolt in deference to English cricket happened up North in the Nidderdale valley in Yorkshire, with the birth of Herbert Sutcliffe. Herbert's start was a spartan, grim tragedy. His father died from a rugby accident when he was four; by the time Herbert was 10 his mother had passed from tuberculosis. He moved with his brothers into Aunt Harriet's house, some fifty miles South-West in Pudsey; thus, the Sutcliffe brothers deprived a good woman the chance of a full life of happiness. Harriet never could attract a suitor, not with three boys in toe. Given a strict, religious upbringing, Herbert hated his childhood which led him along an austere tapestry, full of discipline, impeccable manners and aloofness. Like Jack, Herbert came from the humblest of backgrounds.

Around the time Herbert's mother died, the 22-year-old Jack had raised the antennae of about the best professional batsman in the country: Tom Hayward from Surrey. The heavy-set, handlebar-moustachioed, Cambridge-born Surrey and England opener was on his way to becoming the second batsman, after W.G. Grace, to score a hundred hundreds. Hayward was also young Jack's number one idol. Jack's stepping stones included debuting, aged 11, in men's cricket, representing a college choir XI, where he made 'one or two runs'.

Jack coached himself as a batsman, practising the shots of the finest undergraduates. Like Bradman a quarter of a century later, he used a stump and a tennis ball to fine-tune his technique and would hurry the domestic chores his mother demanded from him before running off to join some impromptu game on Parker's Piece, a vast open green field designated for recreation. As a teenager, he scored 90 for the Ivy Club, out to such an abominable LBW decision that the young reporter for a local paper, printed in defiance: 'J. Hobbs, not out 90'.

As his cricket skills developed Hobbs became a netball bowler to the undergraduates. He delivered accurate away-swingers but found it a chore. The Ivy Club disbanded so Jack played for Ainsworth and also for the Cambridge Liberals, not that in any way could Jack be described as political. One time, when both clubs faced each other in a fixture, both wanted Jack. They tossed a coin for him, the Liberals won and Jack made the first of 245 centuries in all cricket, with a polished 102. Immediately after, for Ainsworth, he scored 70 not out against the Cambridge University Press XI, an innings that catapulted young Jack into the Cambridge XI against Tom Hayward's professional side in a charity match. Against first-class opposition, Jack scored 26 not out (26*) coming in down the order.

To cut a long story short, Hayward's head was turned by the resilience and impregnable defence of young Jack and recommended him for trials at Surrey. Lord Harris insisted on cricketers from outside a county having to undertake a two-year qualification period, in order to represent that county in first-class cricket; so, Jack had to wait until 1905, aged 22, before making his first-class debut. Obviously pouting with pedigree, the season before, the 21-year-old had struck 696 runs at 58 for Surrey Club and Ground. His skills as a batsman accelerated upwards, at a steep learning curve, from the age of 18.

While Herbert spent his first year as an orphan in Pudsey, Jack made his first-class debut for Surrey against the Gentlemen of England on a cold April day in 1905. The Gentlemen were captained by the legendary W.G. Grace, now in the very late Autumn of a peerless and magnificent career, yet the 58-year-old Victorian was still a marauding and colossal presence on the field. In the absence of any Gentlemen, Hayward captained Surrey and opened with himself and Jack. Facing Walter Brearley, at the top of his bent as an England opening bowler, and leg-spinner Charlie Townsend, Hobbs reached 18 before edging a medium paced outswinger from George Beldam. Surrey capitulated to 86 all out but the Gentlemen could only muster 125 in response. In the last hour of that gelid April day, sunny but chilled from a brisk northerly wind, Tom and Jack survived intact; indeed, Jack had played an uplifting hand in reaching 44*.

Hobbs in 1905

There's a humble dignity masked behind those steely eyes. Hobbs spent the first hour of the next day moving his score upwards without any apparent alarm. Facing the slow round arm of W.G., Hobbs dropped one onto the off-side but before he could snatch a saucy single, the authoritative yet high-pitched voice of the Champion called out: "That's right youngster, just tap it back here". A request the timid Jack was only too quick to oblige. At any rate a draw ensued and Jack had arrived in the first-class game. To those who witnessed his 88, caught pulling a short ball to square leg, there was the realisation of a future star.

Jack scored over 5,000 first-class runs with 10 centuries and an average in the high thirties by the end of his third season for Surrey. This proved sufficient for Henry Leveson-Gower to pick him on the England tour to Australia for the 1907/08 Ashes series. Opening the innings, Jack broke into the England team for the last four Tests in a losing cause but returned home pocketing 302 Test runs at 43.14. From then on, when fit, Hobbs became an automatic selection for England.

When Jack rushed England to victory over Australia at Edgbaston in 1909, with a spirited and blazing 62*, Herbert, the 14-year-old, was now a member of the Pudsey St Lawrence Club on account of his father – now deceased – having been a long-standing member. Pudsey St Lawrence were down to play Stanningley and Farsley Britannia Club, away at Farsley, when they discovered they were one short so along came Herbert, in his white shorts, every inch a boy. Batting second, Pudsey St Lawrence seemed to be sliding towards defeat then Herbert came in, borrowed bat in hand, at number six. He held out for 45 minutes, playing with a dead straight bat and getting in behind the ball like his life depended on it. His 1* saved the game; it was then Herbert realised he wanted to play for Yorkshire and England.

Little is known of Herbert's early cricketing performances. Even in his autobiography: *For Yorkshire and England*, published in 1935, Herbert starts his life, aged 14, playing for Pudsey St Lawrence. Even then he looked dapper, his short-back-and-sides raven-coloured hair, neatly side-parted and combed into place, became Herbert's defining feature until afflicted with baldness in late-middle-age. In the time it took for Herbert to rise through the ranks in the Yorkshire 2nd XI, Jack had cemented his title as the world's greatest batsman. Losing the series in South Africa 2 – 3 during the winter of 1909/10, Jack Hobbs scored 539 runs at over 67.37. He went further with 662 runs in the 1911/12 Ashes at 82.75. Nor did any other Englishman score more than his 387 runs at 48.37 in the rain-ruined Triangular Tournament of 1912 and on the 1913/14 England tour of South Africa, Jack helped himself to 443 runs at 63.28. In every series

Hobbs scored more and at a higher average than any of his contemporaries.

Herbert joined the Army in the Great War, rising to the title of Second Lieutenant in the Green Howards. His was a long journey starting in 1915 when he got the call to join the Royal Army Ordnance Corps in York. From there he joined the Sherwood Foresters and then received his commission to join the Green Howards as a second lieutenant where he could expect, for all his hard work, a life expectancy of three weeks. If Herbert was not going to be killed outright inside his first three weeks on the front line, he could at least expect injury somewhere on the continuum between temporarily inconvenienced but scarred nonetheless, all the way towards permanent disfigurement. Sent to the Western Front he had the good fortune to arrive in Etaples the day after the Armistice was signed and when he returned to Pudsey, he had acquired the clipped and polished accent of a London stock broker.

In contrast Jack was married with four children and had a widowed mother to care for; so, he fed his family on Surrey's professional cricketing allowance and the meagre proceeds from his first benefit game which, owing to the outbreak of war, could not be played at the Oval (commissioned by the Army as a training ground) but at Lord's where he picked up around £600 instead of the average at the time of around £2,000. Crowds poured away from cricket games as news of the growing casualty list filtered through. Jack bided his time before giving his services to the war munitions effort in 1915, helping out at Nine Elms factory near Battersea. It seems from records, there was an office clerk under the name of J. Hobbs. Jack felt the public disapproval at not throwing himself onto the front line like a hero. He received more disapproval for seeking employment as a professional cricketer in the Bradford League during the summer of 1915, sparking off a surge of indignation across the land.

By the Summer of 1916, Jack sheltered under the umbrella of cricket coach at Westminster School. At the time Major Booth fell on the first day of the Somme, Jack would have been in the nets coaching public school boys. If this seems harsh. They are facts. Three in ten of the United Kingdom's male population between the ages of 20 and 24 in 1914, perished. Over 70% of all county cricketers enrolled in the Armed Forces. Some, like the 45-year-old George Hirst, were simply too old. Bachelors with no ties received the call up first. Hobbs at 32 years of age in 1914, a national treasure for his gift as a batter, perhaps deserved a higher level of protection. The value of the world's greatest batter remaining alive through the conflict, is that he alone may one day provide so much inner contentment in peace time, to so many, that the uplift in morale would be incalculable. Just like Jack, Frank Woolley, Wilfred Rhodes and Sydney Barnes were all cushioned by fatherhood, as well as by their status as cricketing rock stars.

Chapter Two: The post-war landscape of English cricket

"Golden long-ago summers which left their warmth in the pavilion timbers of the land'",

John Arlott

1919 was a cool summer; one that chilly has not been witnessed in Central England since 1956. The first season back after the Great War spawned a county championship based on two-day games. The smell of freshly cut grass and the reopening of pavilion doors came as a welcome return to normality. The trouble was: the days were too long. Since all games had to finish inside two days, play extended long into the evening so crowds noticeably dwindled around supper time. The experiment of reducing a two-innings-a-side match to two days failed, unsurprisingly, as too few games ever reached a conclusion. Nonetheless, at the start of the season Herbert Sutcliffe, fast approaching his 25th birthday, was a first-class virgin although he had long been identified as a batting talent worth a second glance. Back in 1914, Sutcliffe had averaged 35 for Yorkshire 2nd XI. He had been waiting on the cusp of his first-class debut all that time.

Jack Hobbs by contrast had already climbed to the summit of English cricket. His name had an assured place in cricket history as, uncontestably, the greatest batsman of all-time. His Test record, suspended since 1914, set the Surrey opening right-hander apart from all other contenders. Hobbs had played 28 Tests, starting in 1908, and in that span had 2,465 Test runs (next most for England was Hayward: 1,999). His overall average of 57.33 towered over his nearest rivals (F.S. Jackson 48.79, Ranjitsinhji 44.95, George Gunn 42.20).

Victor Trumper and Clem Hill, the most prolific Australians until then, each had played 48 and 49 Tests respectively and scored over 3,000 Test runs though neither had an average of even 40. Hobbs stood alone. He was the first to conquer the famous quartet of South African googly bowlers and had vanquished all that Australia could muster against him, including neutering the pace of Tibby Cotter and unlocking the deception of Hordern. Hobbs had a wristy flourish, all manner of strokes at his disposal and batted with Trumperesque brilliance. That, at least, was the memory that served so many. Those fresh recruits who saw Hobbs take a double hundred from the much-fancied Yorkshire pace attack of Booth and Drake, just days before the curtain came down in 1914, had it etched on their minds as a pleasant contrast to the horrors on the Frontline.

To usher in the second half of his career after almost five years, the great opener bagged a century in each innings in a trial match for Mr Badcock's XI against Mr Hayes's XI at the Oval in mid-May. All seemed in order but Hobbs ran into a relatively barren patch and seemed to be a little reckless with glamourous shots at the start of his innings, especially playing around his front pad to turn straight balls to leg. Hobbs emerged from his minor slump to complete the 1919 season with 2,594 runs at 60.32, stacking his tally with three centuries for the Players against the Gentlemen and no one scored more than his eight centuries in the season. He came fourth in the first-class batting averages, behind the veteran Notts opener George

Gunn, the Middlesex middle-order right hander Patsy Hendren and the Sussex amateur, Mr J.N. Crawford. For Hobbs, it was 'business as usual' in terms of churning out runs. Keenly sensing the cravings from his legion of followers, he eschewed the risky repertoire of shots that involved lofting the ball over fielder's heads. Instead, he played straighter and kept the ball along the ground.

Meanwhile 1919 saw Herbert Sutcliffe, fresh from his wedding with ex-Pudsey Grammar School girl Emmie, begin his Yorkshire career in the middle-order. The Yorkshire changing-room looked a little different after almost a five-year interval. Major Booth perished at the Somme; Alonzo Drake died of Spanish flu. Both had been at the peak of their careers as opening bowlers when the war came. A further four were either not reinstated or had retired. George Hirst and Wilfred Rhodes, legends both, returned, so did 45-year-old Denton. Of the new intake, and there were six to replace the six gone, Sutcliffe's elevation to the first team had been a long time coming. He was next cab off the rank when war broke out. His first innings was 11 against Gloucestershire. Sutcliffe would later reckon the step up from club to county level a bigger transition than county to international. Nestled as he was in the middle-order, the 38 he struck in the first innings against the MCC at Lord's was a noted contribution out of a team total of 120. He scored his first fifty (67*) against Cambridge at Fenners, coming in as low as number eight.

At Old Trafford, in his debut Roses match, Yorkshire lost that encounter though Sutcliffe made 26 and top-scored with 53 in the second innings. He fell to the enigmatic Cecil Parkin in both innings. Parkin, a 33-year-old medium paced off-break bowler, was enjoying a barnstorming return to cricket. Over six foot tall, Parkin was once dropped by Lancashire for being too thin. It was thought nine stone too light for the demands of a county season. Now he had returned fatter and was actually on route to becoming 17 stone, and considerably more skilled. Parkin had as many variations as the great Sydney Barnes, whom he admired and watched from close quarters during their encounters in the Staffordshire league; he even copied Barnes's insubordinate demeanour towards authority. His outspoken nature ruffled feathers in high places.

Sutcliffe harvested five centuries in that debut season and finish 15th in the national averages with 1,839 runs at 44.85. Aside from Hobbs, only his fellow Yorkshire opener Percy Holmes scored more runs (1,887) though at 43.88. Holmes, seven years older than Sutcliffe to the very day, played expansively much in the manner of Hampshire's James Vince, a century later.

Before the war, Hobbs and Wilfred Rhodes opened the innings for England, and did so to record breaking effect. Hobbs and Rhodes set the first wicket England opening record partnership of 323 at Melbourne in 1912. Now over 40, Rhodes shifted position with Sutcliffe in the Yorkshire batting order and allowed the junior man to accompany Percy Holmes.

There were no Tests in 1919 though the Australian Imperial Forces played a full program of first-class fixtures against the counties. They lost only four from 28 fixtures. Hobbs splashed out with 205 not out against them and seemed unperturbed facing the fastest bowler in the kingdom that year, the young powerful stallion: Jack Gregory. Built the size of a second-row rugger player, Gregory made short shrift of Sutcliffe, bowling him for 13 in the Yorkshire game. The county freshman played on off his unprotected left thigh, the ball's trajectory veering towards his protected groin to enact the sound of a rifle shot as the firm box structure fractured. The indignity of curling up on the ground clutching his groin forbade Sutcliffe from displaying such weaknesses, other than for a few seconds. As he stood up to prepare to face the next ball, Collins had to politely inform the Yorkshireman that he was bowled. Sutcliffe departed the scene in agony, defeat and, with the fielders – all from Australia – failing to suppress their amusement. Finally, after sitting down in the sanctuary of the dressing-room, pads still on, he held his head in his hands, and started to process what had just happened to him.

'You'll come good against 'em one day Herbert'' said Rhodes, ''you'll see''.

By the end of the first season of cricket since the war, Sutcliffe had won many admirers while Hobbs remained the supreme talent.

Both Jack and Herbert were, according to all available knowledge, loyal husbands all through their lives. Of the two, Herbert enjoyed a good flirt with any smiling lady who met his specific requirements. He would gravitate to the most attractive ladies in the room and spark up a conversation with them. So long as they caught his eye, he would smother them with charm and be a good listener. Herbert enjoyed the company of pretty women though he kept his hands to himself and his marital vows intact. Pre-internet and even pre-boys' magazines, he simply enjoyed gaining images for his w*** bank. As Herbert once explained in his clipped officer vowels that all but concealed his Yorkshire accent: ''one can get an appetite out and about but one should always eat at home''. Jack neither strayed nor flirted.

Sutcliffe, persistently immaculate in appearance, added a professional dimension to the social standings of professional cricketers of the day. He bucked the trend. Back in the 1890s, professional 'Players' were considered little more than net bowlers and outfielders. Many lacked the finer qualities of batting technique. Some were illiterate. Most spoke with colloquial clutter, localised accents derived from native soil and adorned with a rich assortment of Anglo-Saxon sexual swear words. Consequently, the England top-order was comprised predominantly of amateur Gentlemen such as W.G Grace, A.E. Stoddart, A.C. MacLaren, C.B. Fry, K. Ranjitsinhji, F.S. Jackson and so forth.

Right up to the end of this distinction in 1962, Players were expected to dress in a separate and more cramped dressing-room than the dressing-room the ex-public-school amateur 'Gentlemen' shared. They often ate at different tables, slept in different hotels, and travelled by separate means. The Gentlemen collected their expenses and enjoyed the superior, privileged facilities.

All through their careers, both Hobbs and Sutcliffe were consummate professionals, fully aware of their standing in society, comfortable with their place in the lower-caste echelon of the paid professional, personable and polite to authority. Sutcliffe sported a short back and sides haircut, with a side parting that rakishly moved towards the centre on occasions, as was the fashion in society at the time. Never a hair was out of place. When batting occasionally Sutcliffe wore a cap, only under the hottest of suns. Five ten, medium build with broad shoulders and wiry forearms, shaped like a strong and fast swimmer, handsome with dark hair and brown eyes, Herbert Sutcliffe had been pushing for an England opening slot since his breakout season of 1919, jostling for attention with the likes of Andrew Sandham of Surrey (Hobbs's Surrey opening partner), fellow Yorkshire opening partner, Percy Holmes, and Mr C.A.G. Russell, a mysterious fellow from Essex, not pretty to watch, but a worthy run accumulator nevertheless.

Hobbs, slightly taller, always wore a peaked cap hung over his slightly long, pointed nose and sleepy brown eyes; those eyes were centrally positioned among the crinkled laugh lines of a jolly prankster.

By September 11th 1922, at the Scarborough Festival, that long established popular curtain-call on the domestic season, Sutcliffe narrowly failed to gain selection for the South African tour. He was unlucky but Russell got the nod instead.

Use the most powerful tool at your disposal: your imagination. Picture the scene. It is a blustery day in September 1922; herring gulls squawk overhead; the scent of the North Sea blends with the clouds of tobacco smoke and you are sitting on the terraces at Scarborough in readiness for the start of play between Mr C.I. Thornton's XI and the MCC South African touring party. It is the final act of 1922, the chilliest summer since 1816, and no summer has suffered such persistently cold temperatures since, either. For the record, no month reached an average temperature of 14°C in Central England. The chill had continued through into September.

Thousands are gathered. Young women are gathered together in a group of hens, openly smoking like men, sporting short bob haircuts, dressed in trousers, apparently mimicking male dresswear. Bizarre, but this is a direct consequence of the Great War. Speaking of which, a roped off area in front of the pavilion is reserved for crippled ex-servicemen, too many to count. They go rows back. This is far from a stadium, more an out-ground, with almost all seats open to the elements. At full carrying capacity, there are around 7,500 spectators. Many children on blankets just beyond the boundary ropes, deckchairs erected haphazardly on the green banks, some mundane rows of terraced housing beyond the ground close enough for C.I. Thornton to have smote one or two over back in the '70s, and the ambience is snug, if urbane.

A gentleman in front, sporting a white jacket and a Panama style hat, smokes a pipe that gives off rich, pungent fumes with wafts of cherries. He reads a paper, one of the broad sheets. To find out the main news items of the day would involve looking over his shoulder which might spark a sudden, negative reaction. What might he be reading, as he mulls over possible headlines? After all it is still half an hour before the start of play.

The United Kingdom of Great Britain and Ireland was in a transitional period, fracturing into the United Kingdom of Great Britain and Northern Ireland, governed from Westminster, and the Catholic dominated Republic of Ireland. David Lloyd George's Coalition Government, a legacy since the Great War, was only weeks away from disintegration as was completion of the UK Divorce Bill. With unemployment high- and working-class wages static to a level still below their pre-war peak, the disparity in wealth between the elite and the ordinary working class had never been so marked.

A time of great recent human sacrifice left Britain nursing the wounds from the Great War, almost all of the spectators present at the ground would have known one or more of the 887,000 British servicemen killed with almost double that number afflicted with permanent disabilities. Not only that, the Spanish Influenza Pandemic killed a further 228,000, a figure even in excess of the

Covid-19 UK death toll a century later, but on a much less crowded island. Yet, despite the shimmering poverty at the other end of the scale, a quarter of a million now owned cars with the Austen 7, the first mass produced vehicle manufactured in Britain, within the financial parameters of the professional classes for the first time.

Whereas today in the UK less than three per cent of the population are regular church goers, back in 1922, over ninety percent attended every Sunday. In fact, Jack Hobbs refused to play on a Sunday so strict a Christian was he. George V was the monarch, Centre Court opened in Wimbledon, the British Empire was at its largest extent and the BBC were weeks away from setting up operation. Of great significance although no one knew it at the time, the 11th September 1922 was the date when the 39-year-old veteran Jack Hobbs, of Surrey and England fame, opened the innings for the first time with 27-year-old Yorkshireman Herbert Sutcliffe. The intertwining of two entities has never flowed more reverently from the tongue nor with greater gravity than the pairing of Hobbs and Sutcliffe.

No other opening partnership in Test history has reached the standards set by this pair. No-one comes close to their record of achievement. Both right-handers, of similar height at around five feet nine, always walked onto the ground with Hobbs the senior peer to the right of Sutcliffe, always sporting a peaked cap to shade his eyes while his junior partner, more often than not bare-headed walked shoulder to shoulder with his accomplice. Their record has stood the test of time.

Thornton's XI attracted the game's leading lights, especially during the end-of-season Scarborough Festival. On this occasion, he set the England touring party to South Africa that winter, up against the best eleven England cricketers not chosen for one reason or another. Sutcliffe had yet to reach international standard, so it was thought. Hobbs had pulled out of the South African tour; turning 40 in December, Hobbs had more interest in setting up his Sports Outfitters shop in London than caning South Africa's toothless attack on their matting wickets, a task he had accomplished with relish against better bowlers on two previous pre-war tours in his younger days. For Hobbs, the forthcoming winter would provide a break from the game; for Sutcliffe, the Yorkshireman had another winter at home having narrowly missed out on the tour.

Mr C.I. Thornton, the big-hitting old Etonian and Cambridge Blue, had displayed his youthful cricketing skills alongside contemporaries such as Alfred Shaw and W.G. Grace. Famed for gigantic hitting, the sloping shouldered six-footer once struck a cricket ball 169 yards, to the point of first bounce. The noted cricket historian, Rev. James Pycroft, just happened to be entering the ground and saw the ball land. He marked the exact spot. This occurred during some power-hitting practise, not in a game, but Thornton struck the ball over both the old Lord's and Oval pavilions and, at the St Lawrence Ground in Canterbury, he once struck the ball on to the road close to the Bat and Ball Pub, a carry of 152 yards. A man of independent means, Thornton seemed to thrive on hunting and hitting a cricket ball with the most powerful lofted straight drive-in history, front foot launched down the track and a mighty pendulum swing with the airs of a man who played cricket purely for fun, and happened to be rather good at entertaining ordinary folk with his magnificent feats. An alpha male Thornton undoubtedly was, but now a septuagenarian and out of touch with the game, the reins for selecting his team had passed over to the affable gentleman of high regard and impeccable manners: Major Henry Leveson-Gower, who was mentioned in despatches during the war, had been running the festival since 1899, and was known by his friends as 'Shrimp' because of his small and slight physique. He had captained England away from home in the three Test South African series of 1910, performing moderately with the bat and spoke eloquently in a tone that suggested Eton but was actually Winchester.

Hobbs had just enjoyed a second and better benefit that yielded around £1,600, enough to set up his shop. He decided to invest in his business and as a result threw the doors open for his contenders to scrap over the temporary vacancy at the top of the England batting line-up.

Thornton's XI won the toss under the screech of sea gulls in front of an expectant crowd chatting excitedly from the terraces, the Scarborough ground choc-a-block with cricket enthusiasts. Overlooking the ground, a street lined with three storey Victorian terraces provided plenty of good views from upstairs windows. Johnny Douglas won the toss for Thornton's XI and elected to bat first.

Douglas was a pre-war veteran who stumbled into the England captaincy back in 1911/12 and led England to a 4 – 1 victory after losing the first Test. With Jack Hobbs, Wilfred Rhodes, Sydney Barnes, Frank Foster, Frank Woolley, George Gunn and Tiger Smith in that side, some reckon it was England's strongest Test team of all time. The Great War ruined all that, preventing some of England's greatest talents from exercising their skills in first-class cricket and killing others who, like Major Booth, may have become household names.

Rushed into combat against the Australians before England had replenished her stocks, the mother country had suffered the ignominy of the first 5-0 whitewash on the 1920/21 Australian tour, against Warwick Armstrong's mighty post-war team, adorned as it was with MacDonald and Gregory, two right-arm opening bowlers of genuine pace, that operated as a pair of warheads.

Johnny Douglas captained that England team as well. The vicissitudes of captaincy swung with large amplitude for J.W.H.T. Douglas. He oversaw the crest of the 4 – 1 Ashes win in 1911/12, parachuted in last moment owing to Pelham Warner's mystery illness, and was at the helm all through the trauma of a five-nil whitewash in 1920/21. One of the top allrounders of his time, Douglas's statistics fall short of true greatness but he bowled right arm brisk medium accurately, with decent seam movement and he could bat as resolutely as any stalwart since. By 1922, Douglas's long cricket career was approaching its dotage and the veteran Essex and England player watched on from the quaint pavilion, short-dark hair centre-parted and combed down flat. He once won a boxing Gold at the 1908 Olympics, defeating the Australian, Snowy White. Anyway, as Douglas sat down at Scarborough and lit his pipe, he watched as Jack Hobbs, eyes shaded under his England cap, trotted out on to the turf, another pre-war veteran, the champion opening bat from his 1911/12 team. Heck, even among the wreckage of the 1920/21 Ashes slaughter, the Surrey maestro still stroked more than 500 runs at over 50.

Alongside Hobbs a slightly slenderer man, bare-headed, dark shiny hair greased down into a side-parting. The loud clapping may just have been as much for Yorkshire's fine opener, Herbert Sutcliffe, as for England's indisputably best batsman of his generation.

That day in Scarborough, Hobbs and Sutcliffe gave their team a platform, wearing down the prolific Hampshire swing bowler Alec Kennedy, and the brisk off-break bowler, Yorkshireman George Macaulay. Both were in prime form. Neither batsman looked remotely bothered. In fact, the only time Sutcliffe looked startled was in between the overs when Valance Jupp - exceptionally vulgar for an amateur and a gentleman - crept up behind him and suddenly enquired whether it was true: had Sutcliffe been caught on the outskirts of Pudsey, by a packed passing train at that, when in the throes of intercourse with a pig?

Before Sutcliffe could answer back, Jupp explained not to worry and that he would get the details off George. (George Macaulay played for Yorkshire alongside Sutcliffe)

Hobbs thought it was funny, chuckling like a good mid-week sinner. Sutcliffe did not know quite what to think but pushed thoughts of legal action to the back of his mind, vowing to concentrate on another century. Next over Jupp came on and Hobbs (45) missed a straight one right in front.

After Jack Hobbs, came 'young' Jack Hearne - 'young' on account of being the youngest England Ashes century-maker in history. J.W. Hearne burst onto the Test scene at the start of the 1911/12 Ashes series when, as a brilliant new starlet of England cricket the 20-year-old from Middlesex scored 76 and 43 on debut, in defeat, then followed with 114 and 12* as England levelled the series. Since then, 14 Test appearances later, roughly spread either side of the war, Hearne had a top score of 57, his solitary fifty, and a single five wicket haul. In first-class cricket for Middlesex, season after season, he provided almost as much batting ballast as the short, cheerful cockney from Irish ancestry, Patsy Hendren, and collected decent hauls of wickets delivering leg-breaks. England selectors kept picking Hearne when there was no other option. The persistent underachievement in Test cricket made Hearne a melancholy fellow, decent enough as a cricketer but the failure to convert that bright start into a great Test career cut deeply.

''Hi J.W., nothing to worry about here Jack just missed a straight one that's all'' said Herbert in mid-pitch.

J.W. looked at Sutcliffe and strained a smile. Before he could reply, Jupp intervened in mid-pitch and told Sutcliffe that George Macaulay (Yorkshire team-mate representing the MCC Tour Party) had told him it was oral sex with a ram and apologised for earlier getting his facts wrong. Jupp displayed sincerity with a pseudo-concerned expression on his face, with open-hand gesticulations completing the appeasement picture.

Not in on the joke and barely knowing the Northerner, straight-faced J.W. turned and walked back to his crease. As ever, Hearne made a start, hinted at more, then edged Fender behind to Dolphin for 21. Kilner fell for nought then Hendren joined Sutcliffe and the pair took a royal command of the England tour party bowlers.

Sutcliffe had only just got to know Hendren properly the evening before. Their hotel rooms made them neighbours and they smoked and drank at the bar. Jack Gregory's name kept cropping up. Sutcliffe searching for advice on how to deal with him. Polar opposites in terms of character: Sutcliffe formal, serious, stoical; Hendren chirpy, cheerful, chatty. Aside from the career of a professional cricketer, they also shared strong faith as Christians. Both were devoted husbands.

Hendren could not have done more to win back his England place but the scars from 17 runs in four Ashes innings the year before had not yet healed, so the selectors handed him more time to heal. Macdonald, Gregory and Mailey had more about them than Kennedy, Macaulay, Jupp and Woolley. After Sutcliffe's (111) dismissal, Hendren (105) and Mr Hubert Ashton (93) combined in a magnificent 174 run partnership, overshadowing Hobbs and Sutcliffe earlier in the day. On the second morning, Douglas declared at 407/7.

Ashton had a destiny to serve for 15 years in the Conservative Party and would remain the most talented batsman in England, between the wars, never to have played Test cricket. Where Hendren had shrivelled in the face of Macdonald, Gregory and Mailey the year before, losing his place after Lord's, Hubert Ashton had scored 107 against them for Cambridge University before a blow to the hand put him of the game. Nobody had played Macdonald better that year. Ashton faced Gregory in the Essex versus Australia fixture a few weeks later and, though Essex lost by an innings and 87 runs, the dashing Cambridge graduate hit 7 and 90, stroking eight boundaries in all. Archie MacLaren's famous win over Armstrong's mighty team, at Eastbourne, after his England XI had been bowled out for 43, owed at least something to Ashton's carefully constructed 75 in the teeth of Armstrong's full strength bowling attack. It was strange that Ashton never received an England cap. In 1922 he was the highest ranked Amateur in the first-class averages for those with over 500 runs. Ashton had 1,128 at 51.27.

Thornton's XI took a sizeable first-innings lead, forcing the MCC touring party to follow on. The MCC touring party to South Africa recorded the one fifty: Arthur Carr's 73. Kilner, Rhodes, Douglas and Hearne shared the wickets and Carr's ultra-aggressive innings - under the circumstances of trying to avoid the follow-on – attracted criticism.

Rain ruined the last day in a game which would forever be associated in the warm glow of a winter's fire with the birth of the Hobbs and Sutcliffe opening partnership. Since the dawn of Test cricket only five England batsmen have completed their careers with a batting average in excess of 50 for both Test and first-class cricket. Indeed, the first two cricketers on the planet ever to complete their careers with averages north of the 50 mark, in both formats, were Hobbs and Sutcliffe. What is more, unlike Bradman, both played Test cricket beyond their fortieth birthdays. This is their story, pieced together from eye-witnessed accounts, lifted from biographies, glamorised with quotes from contemporary journalists, and told through the lens of history. All accounts of the famous cricket matches are as accurate as possible; most of the rest is true or embellished based upon seeds of information regarding the characters in question.

Chapter Three: Establishing their kingdom

No international team visited in 1922 but Hobbs, who would turn forty by the end of the year, scored 2,552 at 62.24 for the season, second in the averages only to the temporarily shunned Elias 'Patsy' Hendren.

1923 though saw a moderate season for Hobbs. He managed 2,087 runs but at an average of only 37.94. No one dared whisper the significance of age as yet because at times the batting of Hobbs appeared as composed and inspiring as ever. Sutcliffe had stalled after his promising first season of 1919 but had regained more consistent form by 1922, with 2,020 at 46.97. This included his first double century (232 versus Surrey at the Oval). Herbert's 1923 season (2,220 at 41.11) looked marginally better than Jack's.

The big games in the domestic calendar were reserved for the Gentlemen versus Players fixtures. With no international team arriving in 1923 either, the MCC organised a couple of Test Trials: The North versus South, then England versus the Rest. For the ambitious professional, 1923 held plenty of carrots.

Hobbs (44 and 31) opposed Sutcliffe (53 and 0) in the North versus South Test Trial at Old Trafford in late June. As a building block for the future of England cricket, it proved a genuinely exciting game with the South winning by 38 runs in a low scoring contest. The burly coal miner turned right-arm fast bowler, Fred Barratt, dismissed Hobbs in both innings and returned 7/132 in the match. Cecil Parker, Lancashire's brisk leg-break expert, kept his England credentials alive with 7/133. Arthur Carr, Barratt's Nottinghamshire captain, earned plaudits for his 27 and 77. However the contributions from two all-rounders in the South of England proved decisive. Maurice Tate (9, 25* + 9/103) and Percy Fender (19, 49 + 7/80) went their separate ways chuffed with their rewards.

No question surrounded Sutcliffe's inclusion in the Players team for the first fixture, at the Oval in the first week of July. Yorkshire had him and Lord Hawke said so. The second such fixture at Lord's all counties unanimously released their best players, even those involved in the other four first-class fixtures operating at the time. Both teams were filled with mouth-watering prospects. In the end the Players fielded dreadfully, dropping at least 10 chances. The wicket-keeper, H. Smith, probably due to nerves, simply could not do himself justice.

The Gentlemen, powered along by a fortuitous 122 from G.T.S. Stevens (dropped four times) and a magnificent 120 by M.D. Lyon, reached 451 by lunch on the second day. Face forlorn as a funeral, J.W. Hearne's 11 overs sailed away for 58 with only England skipper F.T. Mann's wicket. Woolley (3/63), Kilner (3/66) and Tate (2/76) achieved some success. When Hobbs (6) and Sutcliffe (3) both failed in the first innings the Players had to follow-on. Young upstart, Greville Stevens, had the audacity to remove Hobbs (20) cheaply but Sutcliffe (78*) and Hearne (69 and 79*) batted out time.

With forensic desire to eventually arrive at England's finest, Leveson-Gower, Perrin and Warner settled on the second Test Trial displaying the full England team, strongest available at the time, up against the Rest, effectively the England 2nd XI. The selectors picked the strongest possible batting line-up with an eye to countering Gregory and Mailey late next year. They rested upon an England batting order beginning with Hobbs and Sutcliffe for the first time. Following them came a mountain of first-class runs made in county cricket from Hampshire's Phil Mead, Kent's Frank Woolley and

Middlesex's Patsy Hendren. With Sussex allrounder, Arthur Gilligan batting at eleven, the England team looked to be full of runs.

In at six, the enigmatic Percy Fender, Surrey's Captain, acted the complete wildcard cricketer and true maverick. Fender happened to be one of the many casualties from Armstrong's offensives yet on his curriculum vitae included: striker of the fastest first-class century of all-time: 35 minutes. He bowled a bundle of liquorice all-sorts honing around brisk leg-breaks. Fender's profile belonged to a cartoon caricature for he became one of the most instantly recognisable cricketers in the land. Fender possessed distinguishing features: dark, frizzy hair; exceedingly small chin, slender figure often hidden under a woolly jumper a size too big and prematurely receding hairline. Great personality, popular, frequently seen in the West End living it up and loved by his Surrey fans, Fender wanted to be England Captain; moreover ... Fender felt he *deserved* to be England Captain.

Roy Kilner, Yorkshire's second-best slow left-arm bowling allrounder, Captain F.T. Mann, Maurice Tate, Wicket-keeper George Wood and Arthur Gilligan completed the team.

The Rest provided worthy challengers: Lancashire's Ernest Tyldesley harvested runs almost at the Hobbs/Hendren rate; Middlesex amateur all-rounder Greville Stevens provided flair; Nottinghamshire Captain Arthur Carr enjoyed counter-attacking; another amateur plying his skills for Berkshire, left-hander Percy Chapman enjoyed counter-attacking even more while Lancashire's Richard Tyldesley (no relation to Ernest), Leicestershire's allrounder George Geary, Yorkshire seamer George Macaulay and the tall, slender George Louden - whose bowling action many assessed as perfect – combined to provide an inform bowling unit that would make runs hard to come by. From a relatively short run-up, Essex amateur Louden moved it either way at pace and could generate excessive bounce from a length.

The Rest made first use of the pitch after a washout prevented play for all but the last hour. The Rest slept on 59/1, batted resiliently to reach 200/4 then Tate (6/62) blasted out five wickets without a run to his account to leave them all out for 205. According to Wisden:

The wicket was in a nasty state when England went in, the ball popping up in most disconcerting fashion, but Hobbs and Sutcliffe played superbly and overcame all difficulties. The greatness of what they did was hardly realised till other batsmen were seen against the same bowling.

Hobbs (43) dominated the stand for the first forty minutes, casually pinching the strike, but fell at 57/1. Sutcliffe (65) batted far longer but the rest were swept away to give England a lead of only one.

The Rest had Greville Stevens to thank for making a game of it. This 22-year-old had played for the Gentlemen while still a schoolboy and plied his trade for Oxford University and Middlesex. He played sexy cricket, could hit a long ball and had the knack of defeating good batsmen with bad balls. Tall, slim and handsome, G.T.S. Stevens had the look of a young officer. He took out Hobbs twice, Sutcliffe, Woolley and Mead at a cost of 58. He top-scored in the Rest's second innings with 46. Had George Louden not broken down half way through the game, having taken 4/45 in the first innings, the five wicket win for England might have been far closer. Though Hobbs (18) and Sutcliffe (7) failed in the second innings, it was the memory of their first-innings exploits that lingered.

Back to Scarborough and that sea air in the early Autumn and the traditional curtain to the first-class season. The top match of 1923, in the absence of touring teams, had to be the Gentlemen versus Players fixture from September 6th-8th because both teams enjoyed all the cricketers in the entire Kingdom to pick from. Satisfying local needs and wants, Shrimp Leveson-Gower ensured a strong Yorkshire contingency with Sutcliffe earning the right to open with Jack Hobbs again, with fellow Yorkshire opener Percy Holmes slotting in at three. Both Yorkshire slow left-armers: Wilfred Rhodes and Roy Kilner squeezed into the eleven as well as wicket-keeper, Arthur Dolphin.

Hobbs, Sutcliffe, Holmes, Tyldesley and Hendren looked a formidable unit, packed full of runs but pitted against them the Gentlemen would unleash Sussex express bowler, Arthur Gilligan, and 21-year-old George 'Gubby' Allen, together with cunning veteran swinger Johnny Douglas. Fender's package of questions that hovered around medium paced leg-breaks and good old steady-eddy Nigel Haig, who delivered military-medium, completed the package afforded to F.T. Mann's Gentlemen attack.

Not ideal conditions in which to bat - dampness in the wicket - the Players batted first and Hobbs (39) and Sutcliffe (34) put on 70 but though Rhodes (34), Kilner (31) and Tate (29) chipped in, 220 all out looked par for the course. Tate (6/51) and Kilner (3/34) blasted out the Gentlemen for 128 then the Players maintained their dominance by hoisting up 297/7 declared. Hobbs (105) was seen at his best and Hendren (100*) enjoyed a life on 64; Sutcliffe (24) fell to Gubby Allen but time ran out before the Players could bowl the Gentlemen out. Allen (23 and 53 + 4/105) alerted the selectors of his future England credentials.

1924 saw the South Africans visiting. It rained in large measure through the summer, a bit like 2007 and 2012 in recent years, and it rained on the night before the first Test at Edgbaston. Selected to partner the 41-year-old Surrey veteran, Herbert Sutcliffe, the 29-year-old Yorkshireman, could consider himself rather fortunate. The temptation to partner Hobbs with his Surrey opener, Andrew Sandham, must have been tangible; in 1924, Sandham finished top of the first-class batting averages. Yet Sandham had been tried and tested in six Tests already. He was one of the 30 selected in 1921 against Armstrong's Australian Juggernaut and played in all five Tests against South Africa in 1922/23. In 10 innings, he made one fifty and averaged 21.3.

Charles Russell from Essex was another possible selection and his England credentials were worthy in anybody's estimation. Russell had 910 Test runs at 56.87, an average comparable with Jack Hobbs, but his form in 1924 was patchy. Representing the MCC, Russell scored four and 45 against the touring South Africans but, never aesthetic in his harvesting of runs, Russell was still recovering from ill health after returning from South Africa the year before. Moreover, his first century of the season came during the first Test, too late for the selectors to appreciate. Just about everyone found his style 'industrial' and pragmatic rather than a spectacle of genuine interest for the paying public. Meanwhile Sutcliffe, younger than Russell by some seven years, had endured a poor run of scores leading up to the first Test but did manage 67* for Yorkshire against the South Africans. The Yorkshireman's time had arrived.

South Africa started their campaign ignominiously, not helped by the wettest Spring in living memory. Most games against the counties were drawn as a consequence but when the clouds lifted sufficiently for a result, Nottinghamshire defeated them by three wickets and Lancashire crushed them by an innings and 78 runs. Gangly off-spinner Cecil Parkin, a bolshy eccentric, and the rotund leg-spinner Richard Tyldesley, captured all 20 South African wickets. Though South Africa defeated Scotland by an innings prior to the first Test of the summer, their form caused little anxiety.

England versus South Africa 1st Test Edgbaston 1924

It rained hard over Birmingham so when Herbie Taylor, the South African captain, ventured out from the warm Victorian-timbered pavilion onto the lush green outfield and won the toss, he had no qualms about inviting England to bat first. The sun shone and the drying wicket should prove treacherous, especially given his two proven Test performers: James Blanckenberg and Sidney Pegler. Up to this point Blanckenberg's right-arm medium-quick seamers had hauled in 56 Test scalps at 25.05 while Pegler's brisk leg-breaks had yielded 38 at 28.21. The pair complimented each other: Blanckenberg spinning in from the off at some pace; Pegler performing likewise from the leg. George Parker, a right-arm fast bowler drafted in from the Bradford league to spearhead the attack, had played just one previous first-class game. All in all, Herbert Sutcliffe could not have parachuted into Test cricket on a more comfortable bed of feathers.

More than 10,000 spectators witnessed the first day and Edgbaston in 1924 was so far from the bullring stadium of today that the modern viewer could be forgiven into thinking he or she had arrived at some county out-ground in need of tender loving care. Save for the sightscreens, spectators sat ten deep on rows of exposed seats right round the ground. A ring of great oaks, elms and ash trees lent a rural air to the fledgling Edgbaston ground, soon to be engulfed by the rapidly expanding Birmingham.

Herbie Taylor, South Africa's venerable opening batsman and captain, won the toss and elected to bowl first on a drying wicket. Out stepped Hobbs and Sutcliffe for the first time in Tests: Hobbs in his first Test since turning forty, Sutcliffe on his debut; Hobbs in familiar peaked cap walking on the right side, Sutcliffe bare-headed on the left - neat side parting to his shiny well-coiffed hair, not a single strand out of place, immaculate in fact. ''Play your natural game'', advised Hobbs.

Anxious to open his account, Hobbs played a ball from George Parker towards mid-on and started on a run, only to call Sutcliffe back when he had got half-way. The throw missed the stumps at Sutcliffe's end by inches and he survived. After that, sharply run singles kept the scoreboard ticking over nicely. Sutcliffe had received a brief from Wilfred Rhodes. Before the war, Hobbs and Rhodes ran singles at the top of the order, like burglars. All Hobbs did was look up and run. By defending the ball slowly out towards cover and scampering for a single, Hobbs drew Taylor's fielders in until it became easy to pierce them for four. In that first session both batsmen survived until lunch and looked utterly unruffled.

Hobbs batted with the ease that earned him the sobriquet: the 'Master'. There was no single shot that defined the Surrey opener. He had the full, orthodox range at his disposal, allowing him to gather runs like blackberries. He smiled a lot, it was all just a game to Hobbs, or so the veneer suggests. Those deep crinkles to the side of both eyes emblazoned him with a perpetual smile. His bronzed face sported a long beak of a nose, shaded under his cap.

Sutcliffe, shiny hair combed into place, appeared serene. No one could tell what he was thinking, he hid his thoughts behind the most poker of faces. Dark eyes radiated a powerful calmness. His stance epitomised conventional expectations in technique. As the bowler approached, there were no mechanisms of preparation, no trigger movements, other than a minor raise of the bat to acknowledge the oncoming bowler and back down again, bat touching the little toe of his right foot just at the point the bowler released the ball. When Parker pitched outside the off-stump at the start of the innings, Sutcliffe withdrew his bat from the activity, resting it on his right shoulder, as his nose followed the path of the ball. Blanckenberg fretted at the lack of spin. Waiting for the ball to arrive on his pads, Sutcliffe collected runs on the leg-side with a calm, felicitous air. In the 130 minutes before lunch, the pair added 136. Unhurried, time to spare, a rock-like reliability, the age of Hobbs and Sutcliffe had arrived.

Sutcliffe yorked himself after lunch for 64 and Hobbs (74) followed soon after. Their first opening partnership paved the way for Woolley (64) and Hendren (74) to ram home the advantage. Woolley's innings flowed fluently from start to finish, whilst Hendren's bore a more dogged appearance, keen as he was to rectify the terrible beating he received at the hands of Gregory and MacDonald back in '21. England's 438 lasted until an hour into the second day and then the record books became outdated within 45 minutes as South Africa crumbled to 30 all out, with the Sussex opening bowlers: captain Arthur Gilligan (6 for 7) and debutant Maurice Tate (4 for 12) bowling unchanged. It took 12.3 overs to wreck the summer's main feature.

Veteran of the Boer War and now cricket correspondent for the Daily Telegraph, Colonel Philip Trevor C.B.E., had followed the game since a seven-year-old boy in 1870 during the early years of over-arm bowling, when a 22-year-old cricketing colossus, William Gilbert Grace, first bestrode the game and, through his efforts, helped to pull the game up from its boot straps all the way to the international stage. Trevor described South Africa's batting in the first innings as 'sheer rank bad'.

From this abyss, the South Africans improved their batting with a decent fist of it in the second innings ('some splendid hitting') to record 274/4 by the close of an enthralling second day with the contrast in South Africa's two innings either side of lunch provoking Colonel Philip Trevor C.B.E. to write about the 'glorious uncertainty' of cricket but the bowling unit failed miserably as the summer wore on. Used to the matting wickets back home, J.M. Blanckenberg – upon whose 'sting' hinged South Africa's hopes - could capture but four wickets in the five Test series at over 100. England won at Edgbaston by an innings and 18 runs. Nonetheless, the England selectors dropped Cecil Parkin who was angry at being given only sixteen overs in the South African second innings. Parkin made a clear error of judgement: he complained about Gilligan's captaincy in a national newspaper and went on to recommend that Jack Hobbs – a 'Player' – would make a better captain. At least that is what his ghost writer had printed in a national newspaper. Parkin hadn't actually seen the copy to sign it off. Regarded as one of

Bolshevik tendencies, Parkin never appeared for England again. Pity. Parkin became popular during the last Ashes in Australia. An entertaining cove with a rich humour, he made folk laugh, a priceless commodity on tour. Set in the context of Parkin's 200 first-class wickets at 13.67 for the season: third highest wicket-taker at the third lowest average, and the fact Parkin took most Australian wickets during the 1921 series, his omission would only weaken England's attack for the Ashes winter ahead.

England versus South Africa 2nd Test Lord's 1924

Only the great Pavilion remains today from the Lord's landscape. The surrounding stands were at least partially covered but none had of the grandeur of today. The exact site of the Warner Stand had a squalid eight-foot-high spectator enclosure with no more than eight rows of seating. Taylor won the toss for South Africa and his team batted through most of the day for 273, watched for a while by King George V. 20,000 spectators attended. Robert Catterall scored 120, having scored exactly that in the second innings of the first Test. To bulk up the bowling, Herbie Taylor recalled the once great all-rounder 42-year-old Aubrey Faulkner.

In the final twenty minutes before stumps on the first day, Hobbs and Sutcliffe took the score to 25. On day two England pulverised the South African bowling. Hobbs and Sutcliffe began stealing singles at will and every over, it seemed, one or two bad balls would emerge to make the experience of batting for England as comfortable as at any time in history. Dropped at deep square leg by Deane when on 31, Sutcliffe continued as though nothing had happened. In two and a half hours of the morning session, Hobbs and Sutcliffe caned the bowling to the tune of 200 runs. Their great stand of 268 was ended only when Sutcliffe pulled Parker on to his stumps for 122.

Woolley entered with the specific wish from his captain, Mr A.E.R. Gilligan, to entertain the crowd. The tall Kent left-hander used his long levers to clear any boundary and it is safe to say that he exceeded the aesthetics of Sutcliffe and the only other batsman in the land to command so much respect, was there at the other end, his old pre-war England teammate Jack who had, with their band of brothers, conquered the globe of cricket before the war.

Woolley drove magnificently and the pair plundered 142 runs in eighty minutes, during which Hobbs passed the two hundred mark.

Feasting had become fun but Hobbs soon fell, lifting an easy catch to cover, for 211. He failed to realise that one more run would have given him the Test record score in England. As it was, he had to tie with the Australian, Billy Murdoch, Oval, 1884.

When Hendren joined Woolley, the pair flogged the wilting impotence offered by the South Africans and scorched 121 more in 55 minutes, a chapter of cricket that reduced MCC members to hoots of approval. Gilligan declared with the score on 531 for two. Many felt he should have allowed the slaughter to continue but so one-sided was the contest, Gilligan felt a moral duty to terminate the mismatch. South Africa lost by the exact same margin as in the first Test: an innings and 18 runs. Aubrey Faulkner had not played a Test for 12 years. In this latest hammering, Faulkner bowled 17 wicketless overs for 87, scored 25 and 12 run out and declined to represent his country again.

England versus South Africa 3rd Test Headingley 1924

The third Test at Leeds brought another England win by nine wickets; Hobbs (31 and 7) had a quiet Test. The openers put on 72 in an hour but Hobbs would have been run out earlier had Deane not hurled the ball hard at the bowler's stumps instead of lobbing it gently back. After Hobbs fell, edging a left-arm away-swinger from old Dave Nourse, the South Africans persisted with a leg-stump line to slow down the scoring rate and though this was achieved to a certain extent, Sutcliffe gave no chance until the team total had passed the 200 mark, whereupon he fell to Blanckenberg for 83.

Walking off he received a rapturous reception from his home crowd, thousands standing to applause. Hendren powered on to his first Test century, thrilling the crowd with 20 boundaries in a sparkling 132. England were bowled out for 396. Two South African wickets fell for 15 by the close.

The humiliation continued on Day Two, with South Africa forced to follow-on after the burly Maurice Tate snared six for 42. As in the First Test, South Africa fared significantly better second time around with fifties from Taylor and Catterall but England required only 60 to win and did so, comfortably; Hobbs, the only wicket to fall, played on for seven to provide Blanckenberg with one of his only four wickets in the series.

Gilligan brought in several crates of ale and his successful team swigged heartily from the bottles. Big Tate finished his first, almost in one go. Jack lit a cigar and a mood of conviviality rent the air as Hendren belched. After the laughter subsided Gilligan gave a speech along the lines of:

''Congratulations guys, well played, a series win in straight games, Australia here we come, still two Tests to go … enjoy the beers and thank you … oh and don't go without confirming your availability, or not, for Old Trafford and the Oval. Cheers''.

Gilligan sat back down. A rousing applause came from all around. Only George Wood, the Kent wicket-keeper, and Arthur Gilligan were Gentlemen; the team comprised nine professionals, representing a huge imbalance. One such, local Yorkshireman George Macaulay, had bowled 38.3 overs in the game, toiled economically to 2/83 and ran out Herbie Taylor, on 56, with a direct throw to the stumps from third slip. What is more, Macaulay headed the first-class bowling averages yet failed to win a place in either of the last two Tests.

''Good run-out George'' offered Gilligan as he walked over to Macaulay, the proud 27-year-old Yorkshireman. Gilligan walked over and looked quizzically at Macaulay.

''Tell me, was the ball not swinging for you out there?'' enquired Gilligan.

Macaulay, growing red with anger, answered back in an insubordinate tone that may have included both the f-word and c-word. The fact was George Macaulay had hoovered up 6/66 for Yorkshire against the South Africans the week before, hence the call-up. He went on to rip through county attacks for the rest of the season to claim 190 wickets, at a little over 13, and finish top. Gilligan didn't warm to him.

A word on new England skipper Arthur Edward Robert Gilligan: representing the Gentlemen against the Players at the Oval the week before the final Test, he received a blow to the heart from Frederick Pearson. Now, Pearson was known to be a right-arm slow bowler. His bowling average of 28, for the time, was a satisfactory return. Although not a world-beater, Pearson had a faster ball that came like a rocket with no discernible change in run-up or action. One such failed to land, came right out of the blue, and struck the 29-year-old ex-Dulwich College boy, from South East London, flush above the heart at a tad over 70 mph. Gilligan seemed to have recovered and thrashed a thrilling century in response, the blow had a delayed impact such that the fires in his bowling appeared to dim. His doctor warned him that attempting to bowl at hurricane force would prove detrimental, possibly disastrous, to his health. Gilligan ignored the advice but everyone could see his speed had declined.

Forever more and although no one knew it at the time, Mr A.E.R. Gilligan became a spent force as a fast bowler. Up until the point where Pearson bowled a chest high full-toss at the England Captain, Gilligan had taken 68 wickets at 15.59 across 16 first-class games that season. In the two Tests thus far that summer, he had 16 wickets at 13.37. After the impact, England's great hope to rival the thunderbolts delivered by Australia's Jack Gregory, Arthur Gilligan, picked up a further 41 wickets at 22.80. The decline against the counties was not so marked as in the remaining two Tests against South Africa where he took one more Test scalp at a cost of 108 runs.

Gilligan was an influential member of the British Fascists. This information only became mainstream courtesy of an article written by Cricket Historian, Arunabha Senguptal, in July 2015. Arthur Gilligan liked to spout his fascist principles to his team, only the minor, mainstream values – the kind that sucks you in – such as: 'The good of the side should be put ahead of personal glory'.

Gilligan, appointed England Captain for the 1924 series against South Africa, had a respectable, if small, role in the 2-2 drawn series in 1922/23. Yet he returned to enjoy a prime season as perhaps the brightest fast bowling talent in the land in 1923. Because of his obvious fascist beliefs, he along with the several thousand members of the British Fascists, were identified as extremists by the British Special Squad and monitored. More on Gilligan later.

The selectors decided to experiment for the fourth Test at Old Trafford, trying out a few new faces for the Ashes series that winter. Hobbs took a rest. The Surrey veteran had already stipulated that he would remain in England with his wife and child instead of spending four months away on the other side of the world. He disliked long sea voyages anyway. However, a Mr S.B. Joel offered Hobbs and his wife a place on another tour to South Africa that winter, captained by Lord Tennyson. The voyage to South Africa was significantly shorter and the chance to take his wife proved a game-changer. Lord Harris heard of the business and negotiated with Hobbs: an extra place was available for him on the Ashes tour and he could take his wife. This unprecedented cushion of a move towards a professional swayed Hobbs back into the England fold again.

At any rate the fourth Test at Old Trafford, missed by Hobbs, Hearne and Gilligan (now suffering the delayed impact from the blow above the heart), was utterly spoiled by rain such that less than three hours play on the first day was the limit of the action. South Africa were four down for 116; from 4.00 pm on the first day no further play took place at all.

England versus South Africa 5th Test Oval 1924

At the Oval rain also ensured a draw. Hobbs returned in front of his home crowd. The South Africans elected to bat first in front of 12,000 which, given the one-sided nature of the series to date, was an impressive audience. Jack ran out G. Hearne from cover after a Frank Woolley fielding error at point. Tate bowled Commaille to leave the South Africans seven for two. A stand of 79 ensued between Nourse and Susskind until Nourse gave a dolly catch to Sutcliffe at short leg. Catterall again batted enterprisingly to record 95 in only two hours and the South Africans batted out the day for 342 all out.

Rain came overnight and runs on the second day proved difficult. Sutcliffe (5) fell early edging Nourse behind to the excellent Ward but Hobbs (30) spent 75 minutes occupying the crease, during which the wicket dried out, then edged behind a brisk leg-break from the persevering Pegler. Hendren (142) scored his second successive hundred to rescue England further but was charmed with two lives early on. On the third day the Test closed with England on 421 for eight. Woolley (51) thrashed his runs out of 65; Tate rattled along a quick fire 50, Andrew Sandham (Jack's county opening partner but in at five here) put down his marker for the winter tour with 46 and Gilligan, wicketless in 16 overs none for 44, plundered a spirited 36.

A comprehensive 3-0 series win for England gave them much needed confidence for the winter. Hendren's 398 runs at 132.66 placed him top of the averages; Woolley's 249 runs at 83 placed the

Kent left-hander second but Sutcliffe with 303 runs at 75.75 and Hobbs, 355 at 71, both enjoyed the honeymoon of their partnership. Even if the South African bowling fell short of international standard throughout the whole summer, the top four of England's batting line-up: Hobbs, Sutcliffe, Woolley and Hendren, looked a match for Australia come the winter.

Chapter 4: The story behind the 1924/25 Ashes

Newly elected Chairman of Selectors, Henry Dudley Gresham Leveson-Gower, of Marlborough College and Oxford, also had no qualms about England's batting. 'Shrimp' as he was known since schooldays, was a 51-year-old who served as Major in the Royal Army Service Corps during the Great War and was mentioned in despatches. A very 'good egg' indeed would sum up H.D.G. Leveson-Gower in a nutshell. In appearance he had a long nose, relatively narrow facial features, eyes slightly slanted upwards towards the bridge of his nose, adding character. Hair balding and prematurely white, 'Shrimp' possessed about the finest manners in the land. Much more than that though: Leveson-Gower had cricketing nous by the bucketload. He paired Hobbs and Sutcliffe back at the Scarborough Festival of 1922 for a reason. The Stockbroker picked on numbers, literally. Shrimp knew cricket was a game where numbers absolutely mattered. In choosing his batsmen for the Ashes series in Australia in 1924/25, Shrimp glanced at the first-class batting averages and selected the eventual top six on the list.

He picked Andrew Sandham, who had made only one fifty (58), in seven Test matches across three series, because he continued to score heavily in first-class cricket. The Surrey opener, Jack's fine Surrey partner, topped the batting averages with 2,082 runs at 59.48. Hobbs (2,094 at 58.16) came second followed by Patsy Hendren, Frank Woolley, Herbert Sutcliffe, and William Whysall. He took J.W. Hearne, who came 11th, because of his experience in Australia and useful leg-spin. There was a place for 24-year-old A.P.F. Chapman, a gregarious and hearty soul, product of Uppingham and Pembroke College Cambridge, a Gentleman who gave the ball a delightful, free-spirited thump and batted with the jolly impetus of an ale enthusiast. Chapman stood tall, sported blond locks and wore a perpetual smile

Regarding the bowlers, Leveson-Gower's squad ignored first place George Macaulay of Yorkshire, a determined firebrand type of bowler who gave it everything. Roy Kilner in second place, was picked but Cecil Parkin was black-balled from the process due to beliefs that he was a Bolshevist. Specifically, Parkin had stated in a national newspaper that Arthur Gilligan should not be captain of England when players the calibre of Jack Hobbs were available. Parkin paid a hefty price for his anti-establishment remark. So did Macaulay.

Yet Shrimp also selected Richard Tyldesley; the rotund Lancastrian was on his journey towards 204 scalps at 13.98. He looked as large as Colin Milburn in the 1960s yet his slowness of foot was partially compensated by Tyldesley's quick reactions and surprising agility, especially fielding off his own bowling.

Maurice Tate in fourth place demanded inclusion as the best of his type in the land. Tich Freeman bowled leg-spin with greater reward than all his kin for the last few seasons but Henry Howell, the

Warwickshire seamer was an odd choice, given his 34 years, the knowledge that he had not especially showered himself with glory on the previous visit and delivering 20 wicketless overs for 69 at Headingley. Also, Johnny Douglas, now 44, was still expected to perform as a seam bowler. Apparently, he went past the outer edge of Jack's bat five times in one over during a recent Gentlemen versus Players fixture.

J.L. Bryan, the Kent batsman, was fortunate to be chosen while Herbert Strudwick was universally recognised as the number one wicket-keeper in the land, despite also being 44.

Essentially, Leveson-Gower picked his players for he possessed the riding vote over both the others on the Selection Committee of three. Of the two other selectors, Pelham Warner would become Chairman in time and the third selector was the stylish Edwardian batsman Reggie Spooner, both Golden Age England players. Leveson-Gower listened to the sage advice of two significant cricket analysts, holding his hands as in prayer to exude the air of open-mindedness to the persuasions of his colleagues. At least they all agreed on the Manager.

Longstanding Yorkshire Secretary, Frederick Toone, had performed so well as MCC Manager on the last (disastrous 1920/21 whitewash) Ashes tour, he was asked again. Toone was another member of the British Fascists and Wilfred Rhodes disliked his pettiness over minor financial matters. For instance, Yorkshire players complained to Toone about having reduced payments on away fixtures to the Universities, compared to county fixtures. Penny pinching Toone, stood firm. Toone was not a universally liked fellow but he had popularity nonetheless. He was interested in figures so ran the finances and organised the transport and accommodation, good at the details. Gilligan provided the front-of-the-house media opportunities, speeches at functions and played the ambassador well. He possessed sufficiently low basal ganglia to be slick and gregarious.

Here they are, overleaf. Notice no moustaches except Toone, must be a generational thing.

THE 1924 ENGLISH CRICKET TEAM IN THEIR JAEGER SWEATERS

J.L.BRYAN   R.TYLDESLEY   M.W.TATE   F.C.TOONE   W.W.WHYSALL   A.P.F.CHAPMAN   F.HENDREN
J.W.HEARNE   H.STRUDWICK   A.E.R.GILLIGAN   J.B.HOBBS   F.E.WOOLLEY
R.KILNER   A.SANDHAM   J.W.H.T.DOUGLAS   H.SUTCLIFFE   H.HOWELL
                             A.P.FREEMAN

MCC. Australia 1924/25

Sailing in the seven-year-old two funnelled Orient liner *Ormonde*, the team departed Tilbury Docks in mid-September, Jack Hobbs on his fourth Ashes tour, Herbert Sutcliffe, his first. The voyage lasted five weeks, with one stop for several days in Sri Lanka (then Ceylon) for a game against Ceylon. The result was a narrow win for the MCC, but the details have faded from history; owing to the considerable mismatch in ability, batsmen retired or got themselves out to give team mates a chance. A stretch of the legs, a bit of fun, the team sailed on for a fortnight more before landing to a great reception at Fremantle in the second week of October.

So gentle was the start, Gilligan's men wafted their way through fixtures against Western Australia, drawing the first encounter, winning the next by an innings and 190, and with Gilligan striking 138 in two hours, the stars of English cricket had their egos polished in readiness for greater tussles. Strudwick reports of near fatal collisions while he and teammates sat in a car driven by a prominent politician, who drove 15 foot off the road by accident at one point, then missed a swerving van by inches on account of being distracted at the moment his hat flew off. Said politician hosted the MCC and made an eloquent speech about the importance of cricket in Empire building, and urged the MCC to extol the virtues of Australia as a place to live.

Every MCC member had to say something, a short speech, with many, including Jack, a little tongue tied and quiet. Andrew Sandham couldn't hear him at any rate. From Perth, the squad moved to Kalgoorlie against the Goldfields Association. Jack, his wife, Bert Strudwick, and Percy Chapman had the game off and had a first-class carriage to themselves, heading to Adelaide. Chapman, the hearty fellow, had arranged to meet a young lady and had imagined thoughts of romance. Anyway, the train got held up and was four hours late. Chapman was beside himself with anger, unable to conceal his annoyance, red with stress at the thought of his date having to wait all that time. He imagined the inevitable reduction, by every hour, of his allure.

Sutcliffe meanwhile reached 38, then got himself out LBW, against a chap called Ditchburn, playing for 15 of Goldsmiths. This was still warm-up cricket against fringe players, of no real consequence, but it gave Sutcliffe the chance to visit the chief mining plants on the goldfields and buy souvenirs such as mineral specimens, boomerangs and Aborigine carvings. The team received a great send-off after four and a half days in Kalgoorlie then trained it to Adelaide for the first serious game of the tour, against South Australia.

South Australia had a varied and potentially potent bowling attack, including the highly successful pre-War left-arm seamer, Whitty. Clarrie Grimmett, the short, skinny New Zealander, who would become the leading Test wicket taker of all time with 216 Test wickets, bowled leg breaks and googlies. Tim Wall provided pace and would go on to spearhead the Australian bowling attack in the Bodyline Series of 1932/33.

Adelaide had increased its attractiveness with thousands of new seats for spectators. The iconic scoreboard, with each cricketer's name painted on a plank, giving the intimate details of a genuine scorecard, was operated manually with up to four hired hands at any one time. The spectator experience was exquisite.

South Australia won the toss, batted on a perfect strip of turf and posted 346 for four but, rather than go on to a mammoth total, they declared early on day two when Arthur Richardson had reached his double hundred. Tate had collected a couple of early wickets while Gilligan bowled the one fast ball, first up, then reduced himself to the level of a medium pacer. Douglas looked short of a gallop and a shadow of his former self, while Richard Tyldesley, the heavy-set Lancastrian spinner, got spanked for three Arthur Richardson sixes. The bowling it seemed, Tate apart, was worse, even, than in 1920/21. What a pity thought some, including Strudwick the veteran keeper, that the selectors left behind Cecil Parkin and George Macaulay.

Victor Richardson, no relation to Arthur but grandfather to the Chappell brothers, scored 87 and went off in a huff, hit wicket, having played a backfoot drive through point. The leg bail fell off though many, including Victor Richardson, reckoned it was a gust of wind – especially when the bail blew off four times in the next half an hour.

Rain drenched the wicket overnight and once the sun came up, drying the pitch into a 'sticky', the South Australians set to work on the England batting. Hobbs and Sutcliffe laid down their marker on Australian soil, with a stand of 89; not a giant stand by any means but under the circumstances of a sticky wicket, in the teeth of a new bowling sensation in Clarrie Grimmett, their tenacity impressed onlookers. One such was ex-Australian Cricket Captain and Edwardian legend: Monty Noble. Following the MCC touring squad from start to finish, Noble wrote:

Hobbs proved himself once more to be a master of tactics, and showed that he had lost none of the consummate skill that endeared him to Australian sportsmen years ago. He gave a perfect exhibition of wet wicket batsmanship, again and again receiving the plaudits of the crowd on his skilful defensive play as well as his beautiful timing, his forceful punishment of anything over-tossed and his clever pulling of short-length ones. Sutcliffe was somewhat more stolid than his partner, but showed a wonderful degree of confidence in both his offensive and defensive strokes. Most of his runs were made on the leg side where he placed the over-tossed ball with the utmost freedom of action, whilst anything short he just as effectively forced to square-leg. His footwork was particularly fine, and the running of the pair between the wickets was an education in itself.

Following Hobbs (50) and Sutcliffe (75) came a laboured 78 from Hearne, Woolley with a barnstorming 90, then a run out 42 from Hendren. So that the Englishmen, benefitting from a generous declaration – only four wickets down early on the second day for 346, found themselves with 406, a handy lead of 60. Then, by golly, if the South Australians laid down and died at the feet of Jack Hearne's leg-breaks. The Middlesex all-rounder, now on his third Ashes tour and in his mid-thirties, proceeded to snare five for 17 from 5.6 overs. The overs were eight ballers and it took England less than 28 overs to dismiss them for 103. Among Hearne's victims were three lbws, representing the overspin ball that skids on straight as a bullet.

On the still good wicket, the MCC set 44 to win, achieved their target for the loss of Sutcliffe (24), stumped off a short-pitched one from Clarrie Grimmett, the impressive looking leg-break and googly bowler. Grimmett, from New Zealand and forced to move to

Australia in pursuit of first-class cricket, was a short wiry fellow, approaching his 33rd birthday.

Sutcliffe was rested for the Victoria game but travelled, by train, with the rest of the squad, in the two days between fixtures. Tate was also rested, so too, first choice keeper Strudwick. In the absence of these three certainties for the first Test, the MCC lost. The Melbourne Stadium is a colosseum, even in the 1920s its sheer size could intimidate. Although the game was not a Test, the intensity of the struggle attracted 25,000 spectators on the first day.

Hobbs scored a brace of thirties, Johnny Douglas played a hard-hitting rearguard 59 not out in the first innings, Sandham compiled a sound 66 in the second. Woolley and Hendren played over-extravagant drives and paid the price in the first innings. Both made some runs in highly entertaining manner, just not enough.

Without Tate the bowling looked flat. Gilligan bowled innocuous drivel in the first innings, without bite. The wicket looked more like an English green seamer because it had rained a lot in the previous month. Even so and allowing for the low, slow nature of the pitch, Gilligan had no pace and any spin turned only lazily for leg-spinners

Freeman and Hearne, barely at all for the slow left-armers Woolley and Kilner.

Setting Victoria 253 to win, only Gilligan – bowling with more pace – took wickets, four in all. Gilligan went down a storm in Melbourne, the crowd giving him three cheers as he went out to bat, and in response Gilligan ensured the MCC bowled their overs with haste.

Bill Woodfull gave a passing audition for future captaincy of Australia during the fourth innings run-chase. In the young Victorian's second wicket partnership of 120 with E.R. Mayne, a straight drive rocketed into the shin of Tich Freeman, who hobbled about in discomfort but nonetheless got on with the rest of his over without a passing thought. Gilligan may have been a noted fascist but here he was, facing probable defeat, chivvying his bowlers and fielders along without an unscrupulous whiff of delay – all in the name of good sportsmanship. Woodfull played the next ball for an easy single into the covers, but declined to run, believing it to be in poor taste after inflicting such pain on his adversary.

Gilligan shrugged off the defeat under the notion that the recent game, lost as it was, happened to be played in the right spirit, provided genuine entertainment and went down well with the locals. With Sutcliffe, Tate and Strudwick back in for the New South Wales game, Gilligan rested Hearne and Woolley. Both of these pre-War veterans carried minor knee injuries.

New South Wales enjoyed the strongest top six in the Sheffield Shield and in Jack Gregory and Arthur Mailey, two of Armstrong's most potent weapons unleashed on the '21 tour. Gregory stood an imposing six foot three and charged in like a galloping stallion before launching into a giant delivery stride, with a whirl of arms bolted onto his powerful shoulders, plenty of firepower, rib ticklers and menacing snort. The most intimidating bowler of his time had film star looks, caught astoundingly well in the slips and batted, without gloves, in a thrilling manner of do-and-dare, and had already recorded the fastest Test match century, albeit against South Africa. Gregory acquired the status of team talisman. He encompassed all that was bona fide about Australian masculinity and the crowds adored him. Arthur Mailey, 10 for 66 and all that, had been

Armstrong's teasing assassin, a leg-break bowler on a par with Hordern from before the war; the perfect foil, Mailey looped his best efforts slowly down onto a length from below average height. For those shell-shocked from Gregory's bombardment at one end, Mailey's tantalising floaters often drew indiscretions at the other. This would be Herbert Sutcliffe's biggest game yet on Australian soil.

Herbie Collins, a sun-wrinkled lean and hungry chap, had taken over the Australian captaincy after Armstrong. He opened the batting with one of Australia's greatest: left-hander Warren Bardsley. To follow came Charlie Macartney, Australia's most explosive batsman, T.J. Andrews and J.M. Taylor – both established international players and then, on the cusp of international honours, Alan Kippax. After bowling through that lot, the tired bowlers then had to keep Jack Gregory quiet.

Maurice Tate made a couple of rapid incisions and pegged NSW back to a total of 271, which would have been considerably less had it not been for the meticulous concentration and plain, uncluttered, technique of veteran Warren Bardsley, who scored 160. Tate, the standout bowler for the MCC, took seven for 74. Richard Tyldesley captured the remaining three, also for 74.

In response. Hobbs and Sutcliffe fluffed their lines. Facing Gregory and Scott, brisk bowlers both, the total rose to 17 when Hobbs (8) snicked a rising one on off stump over the keeper's head. Instead of racing away for a fortuitous boundary, Gregory at first slip, leapt in the air, finger-tipped the ball with his left-hand, then caught it mid-air on the second attempt. Sutcliffe survived a leading edge that bobbed up high above him as a dolly, only to land at his feet, each slip believing it to be the other's responsibility. Gregory soon bowled the Yorkshireman for 17. Only Hendren enjoyed prolonged success with 75 not out, although Tyldesley (36) hit Mailey over the infield a few times but nonetheless MCC could muster only 193.

Tate (3 for 59) and Tyldesley (6 for 83) bowled NSW out a second time for 221, with T.J. Andrews 86 not out. That left the MCC with 300 to win. Hobbs and Sutcliffe gradually hushed the crowd with their high level of professionalism. They ran between the wickets with total understanding, stealing singles at will, then when Sutcliffe (45) fell to Gregory for the second time in the match, Sandham soon followed for his second failure, then Kilner hung around like a bad smell, resting on his bat at the non-striker's end oblivious to the singles Hobbs patted on to the off-side. Hobbs fell (81) possibly in frustration but the total was overhauled by a thrilling 72 by Chapman, who fell trying to finish the game with a six.

This was undoubtedly a strong all-round performance from the MCC and with Woolley and Hearne back for selection before the first Test, Gilligan had reason to be cheerful. If nothing else, his MCC team had eradicated complacency from the Australian camp.

As November turned into December the first Test loomed ahead on the 19th. The MCC travelled from Sydney to Queensland. In the serious match against Queensland, the MCC struck up 522. Hobbs (51) and Sutcliffe (24) began well enough but Hendren (168) played a stupendous hand while Chapman (80) stamped his outrageously good form on the game. In response Queensland followed on after being dismissed for 275 (Tate 4/54, Freeman 3/79) and reached 131/3 at the end of the game.

With Tate and Hobbs resting once again an Australian XI, near to Test standard, amassed 526. Relatively unheard-of C. Thompson scored 114, Ponsford 81, Taafe 86 not out, Hendry 61, Oxenham 54 and keeper O'Connor 50. Tich Freeman cemented a place in the Test side with 6/160, out-bowling both Tyldesley (2/105) and Henry Howell (2/123). In response the MCC managed 421, with Hendren (100) and Chapman (92) in sparkling form yet again. Sutcliffe missed out: LBW to Arthur Richardson for 19. The Australian XI batted again and reached 257 for five in the drawn game, with everyone getting a bowl. Strudwick snared his very first bowling victim while Sutcliffe delivered three wicketless overs of steady military medium for 13.

Both Hobbs and Sutcliffe liked an occasional bowl, though as a veteran the enthusiasm to run in no longer excited Hobbs. Sutcliffe took his part rather seriously, never mind the context of a farcical draw petering out. His unwavering professionalism brought dry humour among the chaps.

Against 13 of Toowoomba, a distinctly non-first-class game, Hobbs treated the small crowd to a steady 24 before falling lbw but J.W. Hearne hit 174 not out, Sutcliffe a run out 90, Tate a belligerent 94 and the MCC reached 394 for three. The bowling was honest club quality but it gave the ordinary amateur cricketer the chance to pitch their skills with the very best, to hell with the mismatch. David and Goliath matches rarely come off. Freeman picked up six for 48 in the first innings, Kilner seven for 36 in the second.

Monty Noble then put his journalistic pen down and captained the Australian Colts XI against the MCC in Sydney, the final fixture before the first Test. Hobbs (114), Sutcliffe (68) and Hendren (54) all gave flawless batting displays against modest bowling, an education for the boys. The boys held out for a draw; Noble's undefeated 41 reminding old folk of his prowess.

Australia versus England 1st Test 1924/25 Sydney

Gilligan announced his team for the Sydney Test: Hobbs, Sutcliffe, Hearne, Woolley, Hendren, Sandham, Chapman, Tate, Gilligan, Freeman, Strudwick. Top heavy in specialist batsmen, three specialist bowlers only with Jack Hearne and Frank Woolley semi-fit at best, to bolster the bowling when required. This England team was undoubtedly short of a seam bowler, someone capable of drying up an end, a George Macauley for instance. In the end, a timeless Test could last a week, Richard Tyldesley might struggle that long, in the heat, given questions over the Lancastrian's fitness level. The lean, fast running outfielder Andy Sandham got the nod as an extra batsman.

In the days leading up to the first Test, the newspapers and placards all round Sydney were abuzz with anticipation at the Ashes curtain-raiser. Interest in the Ashes had never, to this point, achieved such fever pitch obsession among the population. Hotels and Inns swelled with the intake from outback towns, trains arrived bursting with cricket folk. Men wore Panama style hats and sports jackets, astonishing, given the near solstice-high sun.

Record crowds attended, right from the start 33,000 piled into the SCG, most of the crowd bathed in direct sunshine. Two-shilling entrance fees brought the spectator out under the glare of the sun. Four shillings brought the comfort of shade. Like all Test matches in Australia, it was a fight to the finish whether the contest lasted two days or ten. Collins won the toss and batted first. Frankly, until the last 30 years, winning the toss was a colossal advantage; so significant in fact, if the teams were similar in ability on paper, whoever won the toss would usually win or draw the game.

Tate aside, England's bowlers offered few issues and Australia piled on 450 in the best part of two days. Poor Hendren dropped Bardsley and Collins, both off Tate, and Sutcliffe put down Taylor off Woolley. "Same old England" muttered a few. When Hendren chased a drive from Bardsley all the way to the boundary, as fast as he could, and still failed to prevent a boundary, he got mocked to raucous guffaws:

"Oi 'endren, where's yer bloody tail?"

Tate, with a Herculean spell of 4/9, pulled the game back for England, largely unassisted as the scorecard evolved from 364/4 to 388/9. Then tailenders Oldfield and Mailey added 62 climbing Australia up to an imposing 450. Tate soaked in the applause after delivering 55 overs (roughly 73 six-ball overs), 11 maidens, six for 130. No doubt he was the great oak in the England forest.

With an hour or so to go before the close of play, Hobbs and Sutcliffe walked out for the first time together in an Ashes battle amidst a crescendo of vocal support. They all knew Hobbs, who first toured 18 years earlier, but Sutcliffe most had only read about. Apparently, he had more than a little of the Wilfred Rhodes about his technique; the Yorkshireman liked to scamper singles, defend for all his might but always had the wherewithal to punish the loose ball.

Despite Gregory racing in like a large ocean wave crashing against the shoreline, both batsmen looked relatively comfortable. Kelleway's medium pace from the other end merely played both openers nicely in for the hour and they ran plenty of cheeky singles to rattle the score along. By the close they walked off undefeated on 72, an opening partnership of more substance already, than any previous England partnership in Australia on the previous 0-5 whitewash. Sutcliffe had somehow acquired 28 to his name, yet apart from one cover drive to the boundary no one could remember a single other shot. He placed impeccably on the leg side, finding the gaps with nudges here and there that barely scratched in the memory bank. Hobbs looked his assured self, hogging the bowling somewhat, quite a few times stealing a single from the last ball of the over. He slept on a comfortable 42.

On Day Three Hobbs continued this habit of taking the strike and reached his fifty out of 89. The dominance continued through the morning session until lunch, both openers undefeated, 151 to the good, Hobbs 93*, Sutcliffe 55*. Next door in the Australian dressing-room, Collins received devastating news of his sister's sudden death and retired for the rest of the day. Warren Bardsley took charge.

After lunch Bardsley posted a silly point, a silly mid-off and a square leg to Mailey and Sutcliffe struggled to time the ball. Eventually a leg-break of half-volley length on off-stump was struck in the air to point, where Richardson took the catch. Sutcliffe had played the opening bowlers with a broad defensive bat, but Mailey's teasing spinners troubled him. No one spun it more than Mailey and in that last Ashes series in 1921, in England, he had taken 36 wickets.

Sutcliffe thought he heard some taunts from less polite locals, referring to him as Rudolf Valentino, when he walked off. Certainly, Sutcliffe so obviously took pride in his appearance. The Yorkshireman with a clipped accent perfected during the war that reeked of Home Counties opulence, received a generous clap from tens of thousands anyway.

Not long after Hearne (7) hit a slow full toss from Mailey right down square leg's throat. Woolley played on to a Gregory yorker for a duck. Then out strode happy-hitter Percy Chapman, the high-wide and handsome cavalier, aged 24, the youngest in the group. Chapman abused himself for fun. He was that type of character. When he let his hair down, he behaved like an undergraduate over-indulging. For instance, a few days earlier, in Brisbane, he won a raw oyster-eating contest by devouring no less than 210. He drank a lot and had, for a few days after, the worst flatulence imaginable.

Hobbs executed a late cut from Gregory and reached his seventh Test match century, a record eclipsed from Australia's most revered batsman of all time, Victor Trumper. The crowd erupted. Hobbs was, of course, used to applause but from home fans. Back in the 1911/12 Ashes, when Hobbs, in his shot-throbbing prime, plundered 662 runs in nine innings at 82.75, the crowd applauded his shots graciously but did not necessarily warm to him because the Australian cricket supporter was in the process of adjusting to Victor Trumper's reign (as the best batsman in the world) coming to an end. The Australians applauded his efforts on the ill-fated 1920/21 tour, when Hobbs alone could handle Gregory and Mailey (505 at 50.5). Hobbs turned 42 in the week before the first Test. The Australian supporters had grown to love Hobbs; he was a direct link back to the Trumper era, a golden age of cricket when everybody was still alive.

Their applause, prolonged and heart-felt, drew a lump in the Surrey and England opener's throat. At any rate, after raising his bat, Hobbs scratched around still choked in the moment, touch gone, looking like an inferior version of himself and fell (115), edging a lifter from Gregory into the safe hands of Kelleway. Jack Hobbs walked off the most prolific scorer of Test centuries in the 48-year history of the game.

The rest fell like ninepins, all except Hendren, left high and dry on 74. Chapman belted a few in his amateur manner, playing to the crowd, oozing in that popularity and succumbing to a ridiculous run-out, for 13. The total of 298 handed Australia a 152-run advantage on first innings. Gregory swept through the tail and struck several Englishmen on the chest and arms, though not Hobbs. Australia finished the third day on 61 for one, and the fourth day had a truncated end, due to a severe dust storm that blew thousands of newspapers around the outfield. Australia had taken their second innings to 258 for five, a lead of 410. Everyone rushed off. Pages of newspaper were caught in the stumps or blown against the pavilion rails. At any rate, before long England were back on the ground and play resumed, though only for six balls when several fieldsmen complained of grit flying into their faces causing sharp, intense pain.

Day Five saw a brief tumble of wickets to 325 for nine; from where Australia's last wicket in the form of Taylor (108) and Mailey (46*) added 127, and each run felt like the prick of a dentist's needle. The memory angered Hobbs well into old age. He felt certain Taylor had edged one to the keeper early on in the stand and had started to walk off when, incredulously to Hobbs, the umpire gave Taylor not out. It was after the let-off Taylor started to slog, burying the game for England once and for all.

With an hour of day five to unravel, Hobbs and Sutcliffe began England's second innings with 605 required for victory. Earlier in the year two British mountaineers, Mallory and Irvin, may have conquered Everest and been the first in human history to do so. They succumbed, either on the ascent or the descent. The news item of their disappearance and gallant effort resonated far and wide. England had their own Everest, completely unaided, do or die, no chance of a draw in these timeless Tests. In the face of such a daunting task, Hobbs and Sutcliffe strode out in the lengthening shadows. All the England batsmen could do, was bat for pride and tough it out for as long as possible.

The last hour was a struggle for both openers, tired from all that fielding in the sun, but Hobbs (13*) and Sutcliffe (27*) lived to fight another day.

A two-day game upcountry just before Christmas had to be cancelled owing to the Test going into a sixth day. Hobbs and Sutcliffe took their stand to 110 in 105 minutes on the next morning with Hobbs reaching his fifty-two balls before Sutcliffe. In defiance of the ultimate result and handing England fans back home some crumbs of comfort, Hobbs and Sutcliffe became the first pair of openers to achieve century stands in both innings of a Test match.

Then that short fella, the comical conjurer, Arthur Mailey, delivered a looping floater that lured Hobbs out of his crease but landed shorter than presumed. Hobbs adjusted to a forward prod at the ball but sent it calmly into short-point's hands (57). Mailey could spin the ball an almighty amount. No two deliveries were the same, if so, it was by accident and not design. Mailey could bowl the unbowlable just as easily as a wide long-hop or full-toss.

Hearne looked all at sea and fell for a painstaking duck, bringing in happy-slapper Percy Chapman who spanked the leg-spinner twice over the sight-screen for six before edging Hendry behind the wicket (44). Hendren seemed in form but with rain clouds approaching and Sutcliffe stranded on 99, Hendren reached out at a ball to pat it into the covers to give Sutcliffe the strike but edged behind (9). Rain fell and they all trooped off for forty minutes but Sutcliffe managed to take his score to 115 in four hours seven minutes upon resumption but he top-edged a pull off Mailey that lobbed over Oldfield's left shoulder but stayed air-born long enough for Gregory to race around from first slip. Sutcliffe had shown a true fighting spirit. His defence was a revelation. Serene at the crease and utterly unruffled, Sutcliffe's almost black hair shone in the sun, still neatly parted as he walked up the steps of the pavilion for a much-needed shower. He took England not quite half-way to their total but nobody could have expected more from him.

A flutter of wickets reduced England from 263 for four to 276 for eight. Indeed, play was extended to give the Australians time to take the last couple of wickets but received an unexpected assault from the all Kent pairing of Frank Woolley and Tich Freeman, both of whom drove and pulled tired bowling to rack up an unfinished 95 run partnership and take the game into a record seventh day. Woolley (123) and Freeman (50*) brought fresh respect to the England team. Gilligan's side lost by 193 runs yet 411 in the fourth innings brought plenty of praise nonetheless. If England had won the toss, perhaps it would have been closer still. 166,000 watched the game and £16,300 was taken in gate receipts – both Ashes records.

If Hobbs (172 runs in the first Test) and Sutcliffe (174 runs) were seen to fine effect – Hobbs eclipsing Trumper and the pair of them being the first openers in history to have century opening stands in both innings – the man of the match for England would still have gone to Maurice Tate, with match analyses of 89 eight ball overs (equivalent to 118.4 six ball overs), 19 maidens, 11 wickets for 228. The rest netted nine 9/524 in comparison.

Once the match finished on 27th December, the MCC squad trained it south to Melbourne to see the New Year in and start 1925 with the second Test on New Year's Day.

Australia versus England 2nd Test 1924/25 Melbourne

Collins made one change to the Australian side, replacing Hunter 'Stork' Hendry with a big hitting right-hander who bowled slow, accurate leg-spin answering to the name of Albert Hartkopf. Both were Victorians but the decision still seems harsh on Hendry, who took match figures of four for 73 in the Victoria victory back in November. Hendry had match figures of three for 41 in the Test, but Hartkopf, though wicketless for 93 in the state game, had, after failing in the first innings, struck a match winning 56 not out, guiding Victoria to their five-wicket win.

Gilligan dropped Tich Freeman. The Kent spinner had toiled away the equivalent of over 100 six ball overs during the Test and recorded match figures of five for 258. Despite Freeman's unexpected not out 50, Gilligan removed him from the attack, and replaced his mystique with a different set of teasers from Richard Tyldesley, Lancashire's favourite leg-spinner released the ball a good six inches higher than Freeman and earned recognition on the back of 184 wickets in the 1924 season at 13.98. Jack Hearne somehow survived the cull but not Andrew Sandham, his double failure tempting Gilligan into recalling 42-year-old seam-bowling Essex all-rounder Johnny Douglas.

In front of a capacity crowd, awash with excitement, men in stands on their own, uncovered and in the direct pathway of the sub-tropical sun, shaded under Panama hats, busily smoked their fags and their pipes while the ladies flocked to the shelter of the ladies stand. Collins and Gilligan walked out to a cheer and saw a wicket of great beauty, perfect for batting first despite a tinge of green suggesting seam movement in the first session or so. Both would have batted first, knowing that to bat last on a crumbling wicket would, as like as not, lead inevitably to defeat. Collins won and elected for his batsmen to make hay under the sun with almost 50,000 supporters willing their heroes on.

Tate started where he left off at Melbourne and drew first blood for England by forcing Collins to fence at one and hand Strudwick an easy catch behind. Arthur Richardson and Warren Bardsley steadied the ship for a while before Bardsley played one into the covers, Richardson ran too far down the track, Bardsley turned his back and Hobbs threw in straight as an arrow to Gilligan who executed the run-out. Bardsley fell soon after, Australia 47/3.

From here on the home team recovered and England wilted. Ponsford and Taylor took Australia into lunch (60 for three) and all the way to tea (193 for three). The pair took the score to 208 when Ponsford hit the ball hard to Hobbs in the covers and Hobbs, alert as ever, threw down the stomps with Taylor (72) gone. There was no further success for England as Australia reached 300 for four at the close.

Ponsford (128) fell early on day two, bowled Tate, then Victor Richardson, grandfather to the Chappell brothers, was run out for 138. Hartkopf batted with conspicuous care for his 88 and Gregory flogged the tiring attack for 44, batting without gloves to highlight his alpha male qualities. 600 the Australians racked up, a new Test record, eclipsing England's 589 at Melbourne in 1912, the innings where Hobbs (178) and Rhodes (179) put on the record England opening partnership in Ashes cricket of 323, which to this day still doth stand.

Closure of the second day came when Douglas removed Mailey LBW for a single. England would have to respond to a mountain the altitude of 600 runs, with no place to hide, at the start of day three.

48,000 attended that third day's play. Sutcliffe once more received barracking near the boundary line concerning his apparent metrosexual similarities to film star Rudolph Valentino, especially in appearance. Sutcliffe looked immaculate as ever; shiny hair freshly combed; chin free from the stubble of ruffians. Gregory to Hobbs, Kelleway to Sutcliffe, the score ticked over from the start.

The pitch was hard and true, the sun hot, a day for batting. Singles were stolen and when Mailey came on, Hobbs felt so unconquerable he danced down the wicket and belted him for three boundaries in one over. By lunch the pair had reached 70 for no wicket, Hobbs 39*, Sutcliffe 28*.

In the afternoon a late cut off Hartkopf gave Hobbs his fifty in 101 minutes. Sutcliffe reached his 21 minutes later. In just under three hours the partnership realised 150, the third successive century opening partnership in their first three Ashes innings, and still they were going strong, playing flawless cricket. No chance was given, neither batsman appeared in any discomfort no matter what combination of bowlers Collins launched. It was a masterful performance. At tea they reached 187, Hobbs on 94 and Sutcliffe 82. They drank water by the pint and dunked their heads in basins of cold water. After towelling down, they wolfed down a couple of sandwiches, quick cup of tea, visited the latrine then back out into the sun to break some records.

Gregory was no longer the dangerous bowler known in England. Mailey appeared the only threat but he was watched carefully and both batsmen had now decoded Mailey's leg-break from his googly and the rest of Collin's bowling arsenal looked patchy. Nonetheless every run had to be earned because the fielding was sharp throughout the day. When Hobbs ran his hundredth run, increasing his Test record to eight Test centuries, Sutcliffe and he actually stopped mid-pitch for a handshake. By the close Hobbs (154*) and Sutcliffe (123*) remained not only undefeated but also in each case utterly unblemished. What is more, with a rest day to come both heroes could nurse their aches and pains and return refreshed and ready to start again. The fast-becoming famous pair had taken England almost halfway to Australia's total.

Herbert Sutcliffe (*For Yorkshire and England*) takes up the story:

We batted through the day for 283, and on the way back to the pavilion an Englishman I had not seen before patted me on the back and said: "That will make a wintry day look brighter for a lot of folk in England." .... When the long day ended my happiness was complete. The runs counted for a lot, as we all knew, but the important thing to me was that, after my century in the first Test at Sydney, I had satisfied myself again that I could open the innings for England. ... The joy of our colleagues was sincere, and the enthusiasm there was in their congratulations when we got back into the dressing-room was even greater than that displayed by the crowd outside.

Sutcliffe had his eyes on the Hobbs/Rhodes 323-run partnership record from 1912, as a target to knock off, on the fourth day of the Test, Monday 5th January 1925. Just before play, Hobbs seemed relaxed in a deckchair amicably chatting away to bystanders, pads on but in no hurry for a net, enjoying a cigarette. Allow Sutcliffe to voice his disapproval in his own, tight-lipped manner.

We got those runs on the Saturday; on the Monday about half-past eleven I went out for a knock, more

to get my eyes accustomed to the light than anything else. On the way from the dressing-room I said

to Jack: "Are you coming with me?"

He replied: "No, I shall be all right."

The first ball to him was a full-toss. He played over it. The second ball was a full-toss or a "Yorker."

He missed it and was bowled by Arthur Mailey. Often, since then, I have wished that he had gone out

with me just for five minutes' work before the day's play started.

Strudwick, England's veteran wicket-keeper, also expressed disappointment with his Surrey colleague. In his autobiography: *Twenty-five Years Behind the Stumps* he reckoned that especially under the glare of a hot sun: 'it would be wise to have a few balls in the nets before going in to bat'.

Back in the dressing-room Hobbs sensed the disappointment of his team-mates. It had seemed arrogant not to have practised beforehand. Hobbs had 154 to his name. Woolley got cleaned out by Gregory for a duck; soon after Hearne played on to Mailey. Hendren kept Sutcliffe company while 68 were added but edged Kelleway to Oldfield for 32. Chapman came out and started hitting the bowling for fun. The score went beyond 400 but, moments later, Sutcliffe's seven-hour marathon, pock-marked with 18 boundaries, came to an end. On 176, with the England score at 404, Kelleway bowled a straight one that kept low and bowled Sutcliffe, neck and crop. The extra pace from the wicket of the new ball defeated him.

Chapman perished for a swashbuckling 28; Tate played some seriously good off-drives and square cuts, reached 34, before one of Arthur Richardson's claustrophobic off-spinners bowled him. After losing all 10 wickets for 196 runs, England surrendered a first innings deficit of 121.

Fortified from a Gilligan team-talk, England strode purposefully out onto the ground. Tate rocked his broad beam into every delivery and soon accounted for Bardsley, leg-before, then Arthur Richardson and

Ponsford were clean bowled as the ball gathered pace on the rock-hard surface and Australia were soon 27 for three. Collins and Taylor survived to the close. Day five epitomised the gargantuan arm-wrestle as first England fought back gallantly, despite Taylor's gutsy 90, to reduce Australia to 168/8 but ended the day still long odds from safety. Oldfield (39) and Gregory (36) fought back angrily to record a 71-run partnership at greater than a run a minute. When Tate (6/99) bowled Mailey, England required 372 to win.

With an hour to go to the close of day five, Hobbs and Sutcliffe set about the task with apparent ease and picked off 36 of them when, inexplicably, Hobbs (22) missed a straight one from Mailey. Strudwick (15*) performed a fine role as nightwatchman, actually outscoring Sutcliffe (12*), to take England to 54 for one at the close.

The ball looked as though great grooves had been cut into it on the flint hard pitch. According to one source the cuts looked to have been made by a carpenter's plane. Before adding to his overnight score, Sutcliffe was dropped in the slips off Mailey. He casually continued on as though nothing had happened, dead-pan, with a calm, collected expression of dreamy indifference. Sutcliffe picked off the bad balls and prodded decent ones into gaps for easy singles and appeared in no hurry. He lost nightwatchman Strudwick (22), who had performed his role with merit, but Hearne looked solid, still there on 23 at lunch, Sutcliffe on 46.

No run had been added in the afternoon when Hearne fell lbw to Gregory, but that brought in Frank Woolley and the Kent left-hander found his touch. Together Woolley and Sutcliffe wore down the attack and by tea, Woolley had 40 to his name and some memorably hard-hit boundaries. He walked off having just split his bat down the middle. With Sutcliffe (78*) still there, fighting tooth and nail, the total stood at exactly 200 for three, just 172 more.

With the incredulity of a win at last, within grasp, one more good session should do it. Unfortunately, Woolley's sunshine touch that had illuminated the afternoon session now, at this crucial juncture, deserted him and he laboured for his last ten runs (50). Collins packed the off-side with three covers and a mid-off, all of whom crept nearer and nearer, daring Woolley to hoist Mailey beyond the ring of fielders to the unprotected boundaries; neither Sutcliffe, playing as a sheet-anchor, nor Woolley risked upping the tempo. It took Woolley an hour to chisel out those last runs then he fell lbw to Arthur Richardson. Shortly after, an all run four off Gregory took Sutcliffe to his second century in the game. Hendren added 43 with Sutcliffe, looked good, then Gregory bowled him for 18. Before troubling the scorers Ernest Tyldesley gave Mailey the charge and spanked an aerial drive straight to deep mid-off where Ponsford took the catch cleanly, in front of his face. Douglas survived to the close, as did Sutcliffe (114*). For two whole days in the Test, Sutcliffe had batted throughout. This extraordinary achievement meant that, despite losing the toss, England had taken the game into the seventh day. They needed 113 with four wickets left.

On the seventh day, Sutcliffe and Douglas looked comfortable against Gregory and Mailey but the fielding was sharp and every run had to be chiselled out. The score reached 280 for five when Sutcliffe jumped out to Mailey but failed to get to the pitch of the ball and edged an easy slip catch to Gregory who made no mistake. Sutcliffe's great Test ended with a fourth innings century (127) to go with 176 in the first innings. The potency of the attack ensured the last three wickets fell like confetti for the addition of only 10 more runs. England lost by 81 runs.

Though England lost significantly, again, Herbert Sutcliffe had, through achieving the rare feat of a century in each innings of a Test match, created his own kingdom. Let, Monty Noble give the Australian viewpoint:

Sutcliffe had played a wonderful innings.... During his innings he was as safe and impressive as a rock,

and it was no fault of his own that the team was eventually beaten. He was given a wonderful ovation

as he walked to the pavilion.

Australia versus England 3rd Test Adelaide 1924/25

The MCC squad had the best part of eight days off with only an overnight train to Adelaide on the agenda. It was a time to rest up and recharge the batteries. Even if Maurice Tate and Herbert Sutcliffe had shown themselves to be world-class and even if Jack Hobbs still throbbed at the wicket like a willowy genius the simple fact was that England were two-nil down in a five Test series. Fate had not been kind and was about to get downright unfortunate.

Even Monty Noble reckoned winning the toss gave the successful captain a hundred run advantage. Even in timeless Tests it stood to reason: the wicket would become more unpredictable as the game unravelled. Batting first had a genuine advantage. Collins won the toss for the third time in a row and, of course, elected to bat. The first session wicket always throws up a few surprises for the batsmen, particularly the extravagant seam movement and the Adelaide track, sweating under tarpaulins through a recent state game, had sufficient moisture for quite a fruity wicket. Tate and company took full advantage and knocked the stuffing out of the Australian top-order, leaving the hosts reeling at 22 for three. A partial recovery took the score to 119 for six, England well on top.

Then, blow me down with a feather, Tate hobbled off with a sore big toe, the nail of which was in the processes of coming off. The constant pounding into the wicket kept knocking an unsightly big toe against the end of the boot. Gilligan strained a thigh and walked off, handing Chapman the captaincy. To make matters less favourable still, Freeman put down a catch at mid-on and had to walk off with a badly bruised wrist. Three front-line bowlers removed from the attack, all injured.

The Australians, faced with England's support cast, recovered from 119 for six to 253 for seven, to 308 for eight, to 416 for nine and 489 all out. Woolley's slow-left arm – pre-war quite tasty - bowled 43 overs with a dodgy knee, barely able to jog. The Pride of Kent had once taken 10 for 49 in a Test at the Oval against Australia, but that was a long time ago (1912); this time he had to contend himself with one for 135. Roy Kilner bowled 56 overs, also a left-armer, four for 127. Jack Ryder profited to the tune of 201 not out. One had to feel for all that extra chasing. Over the best part of two days only two chances were missed. Monty Noble was full of praise for the English fielding. Hobbs was his usual excellent self at cover. Hendren covered his share of the outfield with scampering feline swiftness. Hendren played football for Manchester City and so was exceptionally fit for a 36-year-old. Chapman fielded brilliantly anywhere and Strudwick, of course, remained superb behind the stumps.

By now there was only an hour to go before the close. Gilligan changed the order to reserve his two world-class batsmen for the brighter light of the morrow. Tate and Whysall, playing on debut, opened but Gregory bowled Whysall (9) soon enough and nightwatchman Strudwick fell for only a single so Percy Chapman elevated himself in the order to number four to see out the day on 39 for two.

On the third day, the temperatures soared under a huge sun. You could see the ground shimmering. Panama hats by the tens of thousands, ladies with cute bob-hats showing thighs in the ladies stand, pipes wafting rich tobacco fumes in an atmosphere of vocal un-coordination. Out they came, umpires R.W. Crockett and D. Elder, broad rimmed sunhats, followed by the angular form of Collins and his entourage of Gregory and co.

Soon Mailey suckered Tate (26) into indiscretion and Gregory yorked Chapman with a beauty, beaten for pace. At 69/4, the firm, once more reunited, began to battle England out of trouble. By lunch Hobbs (19*) and Sutcliffe (17*) had advanced the score to 103/4. The afternoon session brought 71 runs for the loss of Sutcliffe (33), who unexpectedly in their cautious, almost stodgy, stand, touched one from Ryder to Oldfield behind (159/5). Woolley (16) survived until tea but fell soon after, lobbing one to Andrews off Mailey. He was, of course, hobbling with his gammy knee.

Hendren came in at 180/6 and played pugnaciously, feasting on loose deliveries yet batting as though his life depended on it. Hobbs displayed a backs-to-the-wall style, minimising risk. He never once hunted the slow bowlers down the track, yet by the close of the third day, Hobbs (99*) walked off tantalisingly close to his ninth Test century, extending his record further into the stratosphere. Hendren slept on 47*, England 270/6.

Two minutes into the fourth day, Hobbs tucked that coveted single, raised his bat to the generous applause as the Australian crowd marvelled at his capacity in suppressing his natural desire to attack. The first chance offered by Hobbs (119), a sharp slip catch off the persevering Mailey, Gregory pouched low down to his right. Hendren shepherded the tail to fine effect. Though Kilner and Gilligan fell all too quickly, Freeman once more held tight as Hendren displayed jollity in his strokeplay, throwing caution to the wind and ended up falling for 92. England, all out 365, had to concede a first innings deficit of 124.

By the close of day four, Australia had thrashed their way to 211/3. Tate managed 10 economical overs without reward; Freeman's wrist still gave him lingering discomfort but he nonetheless bowled two of the finest batsmen in the world in Herbie Collins and Taylor.

Then it rained overnight delaying play by 45 minutes. England, especially in the form of Kilner (4/51) and Woolley (4/77), ran amok on the drying surface to sweep away the last seven Australian wickets for 39. With Australia dismissed for 250, England required 374 to win the Test and keep the Ashes alive.

Hobbs and Sutcliffe gave a masterly performance on how to bat in such awkward conditions. When the track was still spiteful, the two England openers saw off the first 50 runs by tea time, their scores neatly symmetrical on 25 apiece. At 63, Hobbs pulled Arthur Richardson's medium paced off-break low and hard to square leg where Collins took a horridly difficult catch. The England veteran trudged off in conspicuous despondency at what he thought was the key moment. Wrote Hobbs: 'How bitterly disappointed I was! I feared the effect on the rest of the side.'

By the close England had lost Woolley (21) and Hendren (4) but Sutcliffe and the regular Notts opener 'Dodger' Whysall remained to leave England on 133/3. On the next day a further 22 runs were added before Sutcliffe (59) fell caught by Ponsford off Mailey. Adding ginger to the England batting, Chapman (52) and debutant Whysall (75) motored along in an 89-run partnership, taking England to 244/4 in sight of victory. At 279/7, it appeared all over but Tate (21) and Kilner (24) chipped in and by the close Gilligan and Freeman had added 45 for the ninth wicket, adding some telling blows against a weary attack. Australia looked a touch bedraggled out there, almost on the ropes. Then the Antipodean Weather God brought drizzle and play came to a premature end. Strudwick seemed less than impressed:

This is where we lost the match. We had *fielded* for an hour at Melbourne while it rained much harder

than this and the ball was like a piece of soap. I certainly think we could have gone on in this match

for a few more overs. It was most unfortunate *for us* as we only required 27 runs for victory. Our two batsmen had got their eye in, and the bowlers were tired. Half an hour would have finished the match

in our favour – probably less, with a damp ball.

Refreshed after a good night's rest, Gregory soon removed Gilligan (31) and Mailey induced an edge from Freeman (24) to Oldfield, leaving the Ashes with Australia, the scoreline 3-0 after three Tests. England had come within 11 runs of a famous victory. All three tosses had been won by Collins; all three tosses shaped the outcome.

Since December 16th, when Hobbs captured 4/15 against Monty Noble's juniors, the great Surrey and England batsman now only turned out for the Test matches. In the return match with Victoria, Sutcliffe scored 88; he revealed once more an outstanding defence while taking every opportunity to punish slack bowling when it arose. During the course of this innings, he reached 1,000 runs for the tour. England reached 500 thanks to Jack Hearne's 193 and further bolstered by Whysall's 89 and J.L. Bryan's 59. In the one-sided contest Victoria crumbled to 179 and 50. Kilner enjoyed a match return of 10/66, Hearne 8/69 in a glorious all-round performance.

Australia versus England 4th Test Melbourne 1924/25

Three weeks passed between the third and fourth Tests. Hearne took the place of Freeman but there were no further changes to the England line-up for Melbourne's second Test of the series. The sun beat down with a hot radiance and Gilligan at last called correctly and without hesitation elected to bat first.

The first session at Melbourne is notoriously difficult to negotiate as the pitch behaves with two distinct paces. Sutcliffe reached 9 in 40 minutes then hooked one high and straight to Ponsford, holder of the world record individual score in first-class cricket (429 Victoria versus Tasmania two years earlier), who was fielding at deep fine leg and … blow me he put down the chance. Hobbs edged one that clipped Kelleway's fingertips at gully and may also on a different day have been held. At lunch, both openers were still together, 70/0, Hobbs 41*, Sutcliffe 27*. The most difficult period had been conquered, albeit fortuitously on occasion.

There followed a terrific burst after lunch from Gregory who struck Hobbs painfully on the hip. Hobbs continued and reached his fifty in 95 minutes then drove a ball firmly back at catchable height to

Gregory, only for the fast bowler to grass the chance. He then square cut Mailey for four to bring up England's 100 – their fourth century partnership of the series - and Sutcliffe brought up his fifty 10 minutes later. All seemed set for another gigantic score when, out of the blue, Ryder moved one away from Hobbs (66) and Oldfield completed a stumping of rare brilliance, 126/1.

Hearne (32*) remained until tea by which time he and Sutcliffe (83*) had added 62, 188/1. After the interval Sutcliffe benefitted from another life when Oldfield of all people missed a chance to catch him off Jack Ryder. The good fortune engendered within Sutcliffe a breaking of the shackles and he drove Gregory powerfully through the covers for four and two balls later smashed him for four through point to reach his fourth century of the series. The crowd twice gave Sutcliffe three cheers of support. His purple patch yielded 31 of the first 32 runs scored after tea and though Hearne (44) fell at 232/2, Woolley held firm to the close with Sutcliffe having batted out an entire day's play for the third time in the series, sleeping contentedly on 141* and England in a strong position for once, 282/2.

Though Sutcliffe (143) soon became victim to Mailey's top spinner, the middle-order batted for much of the day with Woolley (40), Hendren (65), Whysall (76) and Kilner (74) taking the total to 548.

On the Monday morning Tate smashed through with the early scalps of Collins and Ryder. Hobbs looked off colour in the covers, his 42-year-old legs betraying him at last. Or so this seemed to fellow old-timer, Warren Bardsley, who should have known better. For Hobbs, executor of so many run-outs in the past, was laying his trap. Left-hander Bardsley pushed into the covers and started on a quick single only to witness Hobbs dash in, pick up one handed and throw the stumps down before Bardsley could get back, 64/3.

The rest of the Test unfolded into an England victory by an innings and 29 runs – England's first post-war Ashes Test victory, on the fourteenth occasion. The last England Ashes Test victory, the Oval in 1912, had contained only three of the team that won at Melbourne in 1925: Hobbs, Hearne and Woolley. For Australia, only Warren Bardsley played in both. For English cricket, the victory was not just a badly needed boost, it provided the vaccine to ensure its survival. The England players were relieved that, at last, their skipper Arthur

Gilligan, could reside over victory. Yet again, the team who won the toss, won the Test.

England took succour from Melbourne. Suddenly Kilner (match figures of 5/70) backed up Tate (7/145) and the England middle-order held firm in the face of Gregory and Mailey. The victory provided euphoria in the England camp but they were soon to come down to earth with a bump.

Australia versus England 5th Test Sydney 1924/25

Collins won the toss at Sydney, the second Test at the venue in the series, and Australia duly won the match by 307 runs. Hobbs and Sutcliffe both failed, twice, so did the rest of the England team as see in totals of 167 and 146. The main reason lay in the unleashing of Australia's new bowling sensation, the New Zealander Clarrie Grimmett. New Zealand were still five years from Test status. Grimmett migrated to Australia to earn his living through cricket. Although a leg-spin and googly bowler like Mailey, unlike the skilled cartoonist, Grimmett bowled with far greater accuracy though the spin he imparted was a fraction of Mailey's. Grimmett, of average height, angular features, wiry and with a forehead protruding a bit, had plenty of experience and delivered the ball from a higher point than the Mailey. In essence, Collins gambled on including both bowlers and it paid off handsomely.

Some 40,000 watched as Hobbs and Sutcliffe walked out to bat. Hobbs glanced Gregory off the middle of the bat at the start of the first innings yet somehow Oldfield anticipated the shot and dived across to hold a breath-taking catch several yards to his left. Hobbs had to walk off for a duck. Sutcliffe looked distinctly unsteady for him, edging two boundaries through the slip cordon in one explosive Gregory over and, wafting with an end of term feel to it, edged Kelleway to Mailey in the slips for 22, with the score 27/3. Woolley (47) top-scored in the first innings before being baffled by Grimmett's wrong 'un that dismantled his stumps.

Grimmett mesmerised the England batting: bowling top-spinners to win lbw appeals against Hearne and Whysall, then floating up tempters that accounted for Kilner and Gilligan, both of whom danced down the track only for the loop to pitch shorter than presumed and Bertie Oldfield, behind the stumps, did not miss his lines.

Following on, Sutcliffe fell for a duck, bowled by a vicious breakback from Gregory. Hobbs (13) fell on the forward defence, lunging too far forward he missed the leg-break, overbalanced and Oldfield, who astonishingly for one so revered for his craft, had dropped two earlier chances, stumped Hobbs with no mistake.

The defeat left a hollow feel in the England camp. Australia's new bowling sensation, Clarrie Grimmett, captured 11/82 in the match. The 4-1 Australian victory in the 1924/25 Ashes, relied on good fortune in winning the toss. Certainly, the narrow defeat by 11 runs at Adelaide owed so much to the toss. According to Strudwick, the Australians used no fewer than five new balls in one England innings alone; but then Strudwick liked to moan, but in the politest manner possible.

Tate could at last put his feet up. 38 wickets in an Ashes series broke the record, actually held by Arthur Mailey (36) from the 1920/21 series. On wickets that lasted into the seventh day on three occasions during the series, and against a long batting line-up, Tate's great haul cost 23.18 apiece. Though Jack Gregory bowled faster through the air, he announced his high velocity with a charging gallop but only took 22 wickets at 37.09. Tate took more wickets than both Gregory and Kelleway combined.

Hobbs (573 runs at 63.66) and Sutcliffe (734 at 81.55) had neutered Gregory and as for Arthur Mailey, 24 wickets at 41.62, the Englishmen certainly coped. The reliance on Tate alone when the Ashes were still live, cost England but then so did the lack of consistency in the middle-order. Both Hendren (average 39.25) and Woolley (36.11) played splendid innings during the course of the series and provided the vast Australian crowds with genuine entertainment but their consistency faltered on the occasions when it mattered most. Both were worth persevering with.

By now it was March but still there were games to honour in the fixture list. Hobbs played no further part as a cricketer in the wind-down 'picnic' games. Sutcliffe missed the Ballarat XV game which ended in a draw, and the two games against Tasmania, but returned having brushed aside his staleness to score 136 not out in an innings victory against the Northern Districts XV. The last fixture against South Australia pitted Clarrie Grimmett against England one final time to ram home the psychological advantage gained from his 11/82 debut.

Neither Hobbs or Sutcliffe played and England capitulated to 179. They seemed devoid of interest except Sandham (59) who was the only one to bat in a representative manner. Arthur Richardson hoovered up with 5/52, Wall (0/31) bowled fast, Palmer (4/50) enhanced his fledgling career but in the second innings Grimmett once more sent England packing with 7/85, backed up by Richardson's 3/36. Losing by 10 wickets to South Australia reminded folk back home that England would need strengthening further in order to defeat Australia in England in 1926.

1925

By the time England's weary cricketers arrived back at Tilbury Docks, where they received an unexpectedly hearty welcome from the public, the 1925 first-class season had but days before bursting forth.

For Jack Hobbs, 1925 would prove the summit of his career. Unquestionably the number one ranked batsman in the world, the

Surrey and England opener had already secured ten centuries by the time he came to captain the Players against the Gentlemen at Lord's. As the fixture list dictated, no Test matches or touring teams that summer, this was the only occasion when the two great openers batted together in 1925.

The Gentlemen had only days before defeated the Players at the Oval through undertaking a thrilling run chase of 200 to win by four wickets. Hobbs (bowled 5 and run out 51) looked in great touch during the second innings. 23-year-old ex-Cambridge and Middlesex all-rounder, Gubby Allen, scored a sensational 130 in response to a Jack Hearne century. Hobbs declared seven down and the Gentlemen, in certainly the last over of the game, got over the line battling against the clock and an attack containing Tate, Howell, Kennedy and Hearne.

Five days later, at Lord's on 15th July 1925, in glorious weather, the Gentlemen won the toss and batted first, cautiously reaching 67/2 by lunch. Another youthful Middlesex all-rounder, 24-year-old Mr G.T.S. Stevens, ex-UCS and Oxford University, became infected with Mr A.W. Carr's forceful bravado at the crease and the two batted with free abandon. Stevens ran himself out for 72 and Richard Tyldesley enticed Carr (82) into lofting a drive into cover's hands.

The Players bowling attack comprised arguably England's finest four available: Tate, Macaulay, Kilner and Tyldesley with Hearne and Woolley as backup. George Macaulay should have gone to Australia. His versatility as a right-arm bowler incorporated classic in-swing after a brief shuffling run-up, all the way through to off-breaks delivered from round-the-wicket. He had a bag of weapons at his disposal, an all-sorts package and a desire to bowl all day if need be. On this day Macaulay (3/62) outbowled Tate (0/57).

The best batting came in the last hour when Hobbs and Sutcliffe opened the Players account. Immediately the 15,000 crowd clapped and cheered in adulation as the two walked on to the turf. Against them, Gubby Allen's brisk right-arm seamers delivered in a well-coached action not dissimilar to Darren Gough's from the 1990s. The pair batted through to the close without error or luck and continued the next day to a partnership of 100. Hobbs dominated but then he faced more of the strike.

According to *Wisden*: *'Anything finer than the batting with which Hobbs and Sutcliffe opened the Players' innings could not be desired. Just at the start they found Allen and Calthorpe required rather careful watching, but once these two bowlers had been mastered, the famous pair scored with delightful ease and skill, even if Sutcliffe was a little overshadowed by his colleague. The partnership might well have reached a huge figure, but it came to an end when it had lasted an hour and three-quarters and had produced 140 runs, Sutcliffe then started for a sharp single and when sent back by Hobbs, narrowly failing to regain his crease.'*

Hobbs (140) duly scored his eleventh century of the season, Sutcliffe (50), Woolley (run out 32) and Kilner (59) helped the Players to a first innings lead of 148 but then G.T.S. Stevens added to his first innings 72 and 4/72 (including Hobbs) by scoring a superb, match-saving 129 in the teeth of the strongest attack in England, for four and a half hours.

By mid-August Hobbs had eclipsed the 126 centuries scored by W.G. Grace in his first-class career, equalling it in the first-innings at Taunton, against Somerset, surpassing it in the second. By the time of the Gentlemen versus Players fixture in early September, Hobbs had 14 centuries to his name for the season. No Sutcliffe in the Players team, or other Yorkshire players for that matter, but perhaps with Macaulay in the attack, the last Gentlemen's second innings wicket might just have fallen before time was called.

The Scarborough game was noted not so much for A.W. Carr's 101 in the Gentlemen's first innings nor the match-saving Hon. L.H. Tennyson's 79 in the second, but for the vast 480/3 declared total posted by the Players. From this 480/3, Jack Hobbs scored 266 flawless runs before declaring, still undefeated. In all he batted five hours and 10 minutes, hit two 6s and twenty-five 4's but accelerated only after grafting for his first hundred. From then on, he played all round the wicket in a spectacular partnership with Patsy Hendren (129) of 298 in 170 minutes.

The final fixture of the season saw Sutcliffe represent the Champion County, Yorkshire, against the Rest of England, a fixture that had remained for the fourth season in a row. Hobbs, fed nothing outside the off-stump from Macaulay, Robinson, Waddington, Kilner and Rhodes, scored his sixteenth and last century of the season. It took his season's tally to 3,024 at 72.32. He headed the list of first-class batting averages and no one came within 400 runs of his total.

Woolley (64), Carr (61) and Fender (56) took the Rest to 430, with Macaulay 7/135. The innings finished before lunch on the second day of four. Blowed to be outshone and facing Tate, Parker, Fender, Jupp, Woolley and a youthful Walter Hammond, Sutcliffe *'played a great innings that made up for the early loss of Holmes. Pulling and driving in his best style Sutcliffe hit eighteen 4's during a stay of two hours and three-quarters. Thanks almost entirely to him 96 runs came for the second wicket and 76 for the third.*

Yorkshire saved the follow-on and when the Rest batted again Hobbs made 30, Woolley 104 and, overshadowing all others, a firework 83 from Carr that helped set up a declaration. Rain and Sutcliffe (50*) saved Yorkshire from the probability of defeat.

Sutcliffe's season was lower key than that of Hobbs. He scored more centuries (7) than any Yorkshireman but had to wait until June before reaching his first 50. Indeed, his partner Percy Holmes – the Yorkshire Hobbs – actually scored more runs and at a higher average than his Ashes record-breaking partner. The time of Hobbs and

Sutcliffe coincided with the time of the great English opener. This may not resonate as prominently in cricket historian minds as say the 1970s and 80s coincided with a plethora of fast West Indians but the simple fact was that England, in 1925, could have called upon Hobbs (3,024 at 72), Percy Holmes (2,453 at 57), Sandham (2,255 at 55), Sutcliffe (2,308 at 54), Charlie Hallows of Lancashire (2,354 at 52) and Charles 'Jack' Russell of Essex (2,081 at 48). These openers occupied the top nine in the averages.

England still needed a fast-opening bowler to counter Jack Gregory. From the coal mines of Nottinghamshire and the same school as 'Dodger' Whysall came forth a short, lean fellow with a broad, rippling back. In 1925 he snared 73 victims at 18.01 and went by the name of Harold Larwood. Larwood stood out from all England contemporaries for his speed though slow left-armer Charlie Parker of Gloucestershire also advanced his England credentials with 222 wickets at 14.91. Tate (228 at 14.97), Tyldesley (144 at 15.31), Macaulay (211 at 15.48), the slow left-arm of J.C. White (121 at 16.53), Fred Root's inswing (219 at 17.21) and George Geary's accurate medium-brisk seamers (108 at 17.78) all gave the England

Selection Committee options to ponder before the 1926 Ashes.

Hobbs warmed up with three centuries: 112 versus Gloucestershire; 108 against Cambridge University and, indulging himself, he pulverised Oxford University for 261.

Sutcliffe meanwhile emerged from his winter free from cricket with a pregnant wife and a slow, stuttering start by his standards. Indeed, the scorer of those 734 runs in the last Ashes series had made 531 runs at 35.4 in all first-class cricket by the time of the first Test of the 1926 summer. What is more he had to retire hurt with a strained side, on 35, when facing the Australians for the North of England. This meant the Yorkshire and England opener missed the England versus the Rest Test Trial Match, at Lord's.

For the record: Fred Root of Worcestershire was not selected because he had already advanced his England credentials with 7/42, bowling leg theory. What is more his scalps, if you please, included the meat and veg of the Australian batting line-up: Woodfull, Bardsley, Taylor, Andrews, Ryder, Gregory and Ponsford.

A.W. Carr, Nottinghamshire's hard-drinking captain gained promotion to the England captaincy on the grounds of being an amateur who had enjoyed a decent 1925 season (2,338 runs at 51.95). The same England versus the Rest fixture had such a positive impact on the South African 1924 series that its arrangement was on the understanding that the England team had been more or less chosen for the first Test and the usefulness came from Carr having the experience of leading the England cricketers before the start of the series.

In the event, 20,000 spectators attended the first two days but only a smattering on the final day, where heavy overnight rain dissuaded many. Nonetheless, that young fast bowler from Nottingham bowled with exceptional skill to remove Percy Holmes (deputising in Sutcliffe's absence), Frank Woolley and his county skipper Arthur Carr in the first innings as well as Jack Hobbs and Arthur Carr again in the second innings. Larwood's match figures of 30 overs 5/79 left no-one in doubt as to his talent. What is more, in the Surrey Nottinghamshire fixture played out in late May, Larwood had bowled Hobbs, his schoolboy idol, twice in the game with lethal break-backs both times, and for just 16 and 6. From then on Hobbs always wanted Larwood in the England team.

Back to the England versus the Rest fixture: Hobbs (85 and 2), Woolley (21, 58 and 2/43), Hendren (run out 20 and 65*) and Maurice Tate (8/105) all displayed reassuring form for England but no one else advanced their credentials significantly. George Macaulay (35 overs 0/112) conspicuously failed.

Meanwhile the Australians ploughed a so far unbeaten run. Indeed, only Root's 7/42 had ensured a first innings deficit against the Australians, who had so far amidst rain ruined draws despatched Hampshire by 10 wickets, gained a first innings lead of 184 against the MCC, conquered Oxford University by an innings, and were in the processes of destroying the South of England. The talismanic Jack Gregory had warmed up with 15 wickets at 27 but his batting had truly raised English eye-brows with 494 runs at 98.8.

Australia's main weapons looked to be assembled in their spin department with Clarrie Grimmett (19 wickets at 22.4) and Arthur Mailey (19 at 21.5) vying in healthy competition for the number one leg-spin title. Their seasons had until the first Test been dwarfed by old-timer Charlie Macartney's seemingly innocuous left-arm demons that had reaped 30 scalps at a mere 13.2. Macartney played the pantomime villain well. Shorter than average with a wiry strength and sharp facial features, he resembled some ageing light-weight bare-knuckle street fighter. What is more, Macartney's primary function was as a forceful, pugnacious top-order batsman.

Arthur Richardson's off-breaks had netted 28 victims at just 11.2. Should Gregory return to 1921 form, England had an almighty task ahead of them. Allied to the fine form of their bowling attack the Australians had almost no tail and could be expected to wag irritatingly throughout the series.

Pelham Warner, Peter Perrin and Arthur Gilligan brought in Wilfred Rhodes and Jack Hobbs to the selection panel. These appointments had been made as early as February. Installed as Chairman of Selectors, Plum Warner undertook his role with the utmost diligence, like a benign Commander-in-Chief but with astute military-like details. Above all, Warner believed that the Committee of venerable cricketers had to pick the team most likely to win the Ashes, regardless of the future.

An army of scouts, mainly retired cricketers, monitored the form of each and every first-class cricketer in the land. They discussed the likely wicket, then who were the best to pick.

Hobbs, Sutcliffe, Woolley and Hendren, fell easily onto the paper, inked in. Arthur Carr as England captain based upon a good previous season with the bat, meant only one more batsman. Mead, Tyldesley, Sandham, Chapman, G.T.S. Stevens (149 for Middlesex versus the Australians), Cambridge allrounder H.J. Enthoven - who enjoyed a fine performance (93 and 0, 3/51 in the match) against the Australians - were all discussed at length. In the end J.T. Hearne won the slot, his respectable leg-break bowling adding depth to the attack. Chapman's sexy 89 for the South of England earned him a place. Then Sandham's fielding nudged him ahead of others as a 12th Man, principally.

Herbert Strudwick, once understudy to Arthur Lilley on Warner's 1903/04 Ashes tour, took the gloves despite being 46 and a half years old. This highly respected and popular Surrey and England Edwardian relic would go on to live until he was 90.

Tate's name fell to the paper with ease, inked in as spearhead. Fred Root (7/42 for the North against the Australians) won him universal approval, narrowly ahead of young Larwood, who had burst on the scene as this little fellow with a strong back who bowled missiles faster than anyone in the country. The wicket would be soft and so Root won the vote. Warner tempted Wilfred Rhodes to volunteer his services as the slow left-armer of the team. Rhodes dismissed the suggestion immediately and demanded that they discuss younger options. Roy Kilner, like Rhodes a Yorkshire slow left-armer, rather fortuitously edged in as a bowling allrounder.

England versus Australia 1st Test Trent Bridge 1926

The summer had been unspectacular as regards the weather and Nottingham had over twice its normal spring rainfall. More rain fell overnight before the first Test at Trent Bridge, but being June 12th, the early sunshine dried the outfield and out walked Herbie Collins and Arthur Carr, blazers on, Collins sporting the baggy-green cap while Carr's early widow's peak glistened on his cap-less scalp. Carr, on his home ground, called correctly and elected to bat.

A shower delayed the start for 45 minutes then out came the Australians to warm applause. Shortly after, a storm of applause erupted as out came Hobbs and Sutcliffe. In the gloomy ambience the batsmen noted no sight screens had yet been put in place. Gregory stood at the end of his mark, high, wide and handsome, the alpha. Hobbs took his normal middle-and-leg stance, surveyed the three slips, a short and a long third man, Bardsley at mid-off, surprisingly agile for his advanced years, a long leg, cover and mid-on. He could expect Gregory to attack his off-stump, put in the surprise bouncer at some stage, and allow every chance for the new ball to swing by pitching it full.

In Gregory came to a deafening silence. First ball Hobbs blocked, still silence. Gregory delayed play for a while, picking up saw dust and spreading it out in his intended footholds. He came again. Hobbs played it on the forward defence. Third ball the Master placed into the leg-side for a single to break the ice and spark a ripple of applause. Sutcliffe tucked one down to the third man region for a single from the fifth with the same effect. Gregory looked pumped.

On came Macartney as a surprise choice at the other end to bowl slow left-arm from round the wicket with a low trajectory. Australia only selected one proper pace bowler. Ed Macdonald had fucked off to play cricket for Lancashire, qualifying through two years in league cricket, and so discarding himself from selection. Australia had Jack Ryder's medium paced out-swingers but Collins chose Macartney's left-arm spin. Macartney once took 11 wickets at Edgbaston but that Ashes Test was back in 1909. Indeed, he had taken no wickets in seven Ashes Tests since the war. Yet, this season, his spin had made an appreciable comeback.

Collins placed three short-legs for Macartney: Woodfull behind square; Collins himself and Mailey in front. Gregory stood as the sole slip, Richardson third man, Andrews at cover, Bardsley mid-off, Taylor long on, Ryder mid-on. A no-ball soon came, Macartney crestfallen at his stupidity, and Hobbs spanked it for four to the long-on boundary, aided by an astonishingly quick call of no-ball by Umpire Chester who, had it not been for his war injury, may well have been playing in the match.

Sutcliffe sent a Gregory full pitch missile straight back along the ground for his first boundary. They stole a single here and the score mounted. Macartney did manage through early spin to beat the bat of both openers and Gregory bowled with fine spirit. The fielding looked razor sharp. The crowd grasped as a Gregory breakback defeated Hobbs but missed the wicket. Macartney delivered a second no-ball, again a Chester call, and Sutcliffe clouted it to the square leg boundary. The score reached 28. Gregory came off, replaced by Arthur Richardson, and Mailey came on in place of Macartney.

Shortly after, at 32 for no wicket (Hobbs 19*, Sutcliffe 13*), the players came off for rain. So much fell in such torrential quantities, there was no more play for the entire Test.

After the wash-out at Trent Bridge, very next day, the Australians played Yorkshire in Sheffield. Again, the weather ruined the contest, the Australians reaching 148/6 on a slow, low wicket. There were two run-outs and the 48-year-old slow left-armer, Wilfred Rhodes bowled 15 overs for 36 and the prized wickets of old foe Charlie Macartney, struck on the pads for 54 and sensible young gun, Bill Woodfull – soon to be known as the 'unbowlable' - bowled for 8.

Over the Summer Solstice the weather cleared enough for the Australians to thrash Lancashire by an innings and 77 runs at Old Trafford. Huge games from Arthur Mailey (match figures 11/165) and Charlie Macartney who, not only scored a wondrous 160, but gained the extraordinary match figures of 46 overs, 28 maidens, 5/35. The baggy green they call the Guv-nor General, just days from his fortieth birthday, showcased his talents to great effect.

Rain, again, curtailed the game against Derbyshire but the Australians had grown accustomed to English conditions by now. And so, to Lord's, high summer, the second Test, another three-day game. The first four Tests had been designated three-day affairs. If the Ashes had not been decided by the time of the fifth Test, then for the first time on English soil, the game would go on to the end with time eradicated as a factor.

England versus Australia 2nd Test lord's 1926

The Lord's pitch looked perfect for runs, flat as a pancake, the outfield lush but fast, the ground filling up with 25,000 spectators. A breeze blew the flags on the Mound Stand and Old Father Time pointed from the South-West. The only clouds were isolated and high, a few strati, a hint of cirrus.

Warner's selection committee made one change: a debut for 21-year-old Harold Larwood, an uncouth and poorly educated miner from Nottinghamshire, at the expense of old Jack Hearne. Carr had a strong crew of pacemen. Maurice Tate's relentless accuracy, Fred Root's superb inswing and the pace of a relatively short bowler who possessed a wiry strength and a broad back.

Using a new shilling with King George's head on it, Carr tossed and Collins called in front of the pavilion and the silence radiated the result in favour of angular jawed Herbie Collins, who chose to bat first. Play commenced on time at 11:30am.

Lord's was still filling up when Root bowled an inswinger that came in so late, Collins simply lifted his bat to watch it go by and to his dismay, the ball cannoned into off-stump and sent it cartwheeling back. Macartney began slowly then thrilled the crowd in a 20-minute exhibition, all shots executed to perfection. The tough fighter loved bragging about the time he faced Sydney Barnes back in the 1912 Triangular Tournament and struck the great bowler for six. In deference to Barnes, Macartney admitted he had to get 60odd first before his eye was sufficiently in. He had the ground in the palm of his hand, all eyes on a wonderful player, then Larwood came on with his extra notch of pace and got one to rise awkwardly towards Macartney's face. The veteran fended it to Sutcliffe at second slip, gone for 39. An immense roar of approval echoed round Lord's. This was Colosseum of Rome stuff, if only for a brief moment in time.

Day One belonged to veteran Warren Bardsley, who reached the end of the day intact. He enjoyed an afternoon break while the teams lined up in front of the pavilion to meet the King, who stayed for a couple of hours. In a day where the struggle between bat and ball had an intriguingly fine poise, Bardsley slept on 173* in a team total of 338/8. Bardsley did not have it all his own way however; Larwood struck him painfully on the hand towards the close.

A rest day on the sabbath meant both teams were suitably refreshed and the weather held fair for Monday. Foolishly, a member of the groundstaff left a hose on most of the night and water poured out drenching a large section of the cover region shaded from the evening sun under the Grandstand and Old Father Time. Thankfully the wicket was unaffected.

In the first hour of play, Bardsley carried his bat for 193* in a total of 383. Strudwick had dropped him twice and Woolley once but none the less, his score was the second highest in an Ashes Test in England, behind only Billy Murdock's 211 back in 1884.

Hobbs and Sutcliffe emerged from the pavilion an hour into the second day. Down the steps they came, four century stands against Australia already etched into the record books. The ground rose and applauded to thunderous effect. Hobbs to the right, cap down shading his eyes, Sutcliffe on the left, hair shining black. Their great deeds from the 1924/25 series had been memorised by a generation. Hobbs and Sutcliffe gave the crowd hope.

At twenty minutes past mid-day Herbie Collins had carefully placed his field, same as at Trent Bridge, testing Hobbs on or just outside his off-stump. If Hobbs possessed a weakness, that minor flaw came from medium paced outswingers. Gregory had paced out his run, turned and faced Hobbs. The crowd silenced itself as one, in complete obedience, and in the deafening hush only the sound of

Gregory's feet pounding the turf could be heard. Full it came, first ball, floating just outside Hobbs' off-stump. Forward the Master played, leaning a forward defensive shot into the extra cover region causing Andrews to chase while the batsmen ran three under an eruption of applause.

Warner commented on the beauty of their batsmanship. The perfect techniques and the astonishing ease with which they stole singles allowed the score to tick along until 40/0, when Collins made the change from Macartney to Mailey, and at 45/0 Arthur Richardson's dart-like off-breaks replaced Gregory's undistinguished first spell. In the entire morning session only once were either batsman beaten by a single delivery, Arthur Mailey ripped a beauty past the outside edge of Hobbs; otherwise, the Master continued on to an undefeated 50 at lunch, with Sutcliffe on a solid and unruffled 27. England 77/0, once again had their peerless openers to thank.

The Australians regrouped at lunch, Collins in animated discussion with his team, all listening intently as though well-behaved students in front of a magnificent teacher. Hobbs and Sutcliffe looked on across the dining-room, in quiet contemplation of the task ahead.

The wicket held no devilry. Gregory seemed to be firing on only two cylinders, Mailey had become a known quantity, Richardson could simply be blocked at will and Ryder bowled medium-paced part-timers. Macartney's slow left-arm had ransacked county cricket already that season, but Macartney also held little fear.

Right from the start of the afternoon session Gregory roared in to sweep away doubts about his fitness, or indeed how far he had declined since 1921. In this second spell, Gregory ran in properly pumped from the Nursery End and Macartney took the Pavilion End. Hobbs and Sutcliffe survived and picked off singles, creeping the score a long for the first twenty minutes then a rare Macartney long-hop was square-cut to the boundary by Sutcliffe to bring up the hundred partnership, their fifth against Australia, Hobbs 64*, Sutcliffe 37*. Cheers rent the air, thousands of men took off their hats and waved at their heroes.

Mailey fell to pieces and delivered a couple of full-tosses to Sutcliffe, despatched without ceremony for fours and, after 135 minutes either side of lunch, the partnership reached 150. Then the scoring rate fell alarmingly as Richardson and Ryder probed away on a good length to a field designed to cut off the singles, heavily set on the leg-side to Richardson.

Nonetheless, the score ticked along but at 182, Richardson bowled Sutcliffe for 82, compiled in 190 minutes and unblemished until his departure.

Hobbs had reached 90 in his most commanding style but then played more for his century than for the crowd. This is the only instance where Hobbs appeared to prioritise personal glory ahead of pushing the game along to try to force a win inside three days. The lure of only his second century against Australia at home slowed Hobbs to a crawl, not helped by a leg-stump line from Australia's bowlers. It took an hour to take his score from 90 to 99 then a howling appeal from Richardson received no signal from umpire Chester and a couple of overs later Hobbs pushed a single for his tenth Ashes century, four more than any batsman in history at the time.

Warner loved Hobbs. Hobbs could do no wrong. The slow scoring towards his century was a consequence of accurate bowling and the responsibility of batting his team to safety. After his minor role during the Great War, Hobbs felt the burden of expectation on his shoulders. He batted in an orthodox, risk-free manner. After this innings Warner wrote:

With the score at 219, Hobbs's great innings came to an end, Richardson catching him at third-man.

He had been batting for three hours and fifty minutes, and had given no chance. Before lunch he

batted magnificently. After lunch he was kept very quiet by the accuracy of the bowling, but there can

be no doubt that, remembering the lessons of past Tests, he fully realized his responsibility, and

moreover it should be recollected that he is no longer a young man. It was a great innings, and his

second hundred against Australia at Lord's.

Hobbs is a most severe critic of his own play, but in my humble opinion he is still the greatest batsman

in England. If not the brilliant player he was some years ago, he has a remarkable temperament for a

big match, and, though less of an attacking batsman than formerly, he is still essentially sound.

With his bowlers drained of inspiration and Gregory panting like a dehydrated hound, Collins's forces were overwhelmed. Woolley (87), Hendren (127 not out) and Chapman (50 not out) did very much as they pleased, showering Lord's in an orgy of hearty hitting to propel the score to 475/2 declared. The game drifted to an inevitable draw, but not before Charlie Macartney had thumped 133 not out on the last afternoon, an innings in terms of eye-catching shot selection no one at the time, not even Woolley, could have emulated. The press speculated that the Australians erred in not selecting Clarrie Grimmett.

From June 29th, the last day at Lord's, until July 10th, the first day of the Headingley Test, the Australians thrashed Northants, Nottinghamshire and Worcestershire and the main force of destruction came from good old Arthur Mailey. Just as England's finest sensed they had the better of Mailey, hunting him down the track in predatory fashion, Mailey rebounded with match figures of 10/87 against Northants and 15/193 against Notts. Bardsley (113) scored his third consecutive century - during the innings and 147 run victory over Northants - but narrowly failed (87) in the innings and 136 run victory against Notts but only because Larwood (3/88) bowled him for pace. The 176-run win over Worcestershire saw Fred Root (4/61) to good effect; his scalps were notable ones: Macartney, Taylor, Andrews and Oldfield. On the bowling front, Collins could see once again where his main weapons lay. Macartney (5/38), Mailey (5/32) and Grimmett (8/33) all excelled.

Sutcliffe meanwhile had a quiet time for Yorkshire. He followed a 23 against Kent at Blackheath with a run out 52 from the Sussex attack. Hobbs stole the headlines with a superlative double century in Alec Kennedy's benefit match, Surrey versus Hampshire. His mode of dismissal very much indicated Hobbs had enjoyed his fill, now was the time to be generous: stumped Livesey bowled Kennedy 200.

After that Hobbs turned out for the Players in the Gents versus Players fixture at the Oval. He batted delightfully for 70, sharing another opening stand with Surrey opener Andrew Sandham (125). The Players, mainly comprising Southerners and skippered by Hobbs, included Charlie Parker, who took 4/29 in the second innings to hasten the Players towards a seven-wicket victory. Hobbs left the Oval after the game, took a taxi and a long train ride north to Leeds, ready to play in the third Test.

England versus Australia 3rd Test Headingley 1926

On this very evening of July 9th, it rained over Leeds. On the morning of the first day England Captain Arthur Carr inspected the wicket with Jack Hobbs and Pelham 'Plum' Warner. Carr pressed his thumb into the pitch, looked up at the sun and reckoned a drying wicket would make batting hazardous during the morning session. Hobbs and Warner had known such tactics to succeed, in Australia during the 1911/12 campaign, so appeared to nod approval. Carr duly won the toss and elected to field first. Not only that, he failed to select the best wet wicket bowler in England, Charlie Parker, omitting the wet-wicket expert from the twelve.

First ball Tate removed Bardsley, caught low down by Sutcliffe at second slip; the vicissitudes of the game never more vast. In came Macartney who tapped a couple nonchalantly onto the leg-side before edging the fifth ball of the over into the hands of second slip - skipper Arthur Carr - and out again, a catch the England Captain reckoned he would have taken 99 times out of 100. Hip height, travelling at a fair pace to his left-hand side, it should have been swallowed. Australia could have been 2/2. Instead, they recovered.

Clouds came in and no sticky wicket made Carr's decision to field first look more mediocre by the minute.

The crowd continued to swell throughout the morning session as Macartney unfurled a classic range of pulls, cuts and drives and raced away after his let-off. Carr's head, hair thinning on top and combed back to reveal a large egg-shaped forehead, blushed red and remained that way all through Macartney's brilliant display. The diminutive dynamo, already forty, reached his century before lunch and off he walked, Woodfull a step back in deep reverence, with the England team applauding him in.

Over lunch Warner and Carr barely spoke a word to each other. Carr could not think what to say while Warner's look of deep disappointment could not be disguised. His look of thunder, face pale as a sheet, eyes down on the table mainly, or upwards at various people, but not at Captain Carr, was the face of someone who would forever distance himself from the decision-making behind inviting the opposition into bat, on a perfect batting wicket. It was simply not the correct option in England.

Macartney's 100 came out of a total of 131 at exactly a run a minute. He continued on in the afternoon toying with all members of the England attack except Tate and fell for 151. Colonel Philip Trevor C.B.E. reckoned 'After due deliberation, I say that this was the most magnificent innings I have ever seen played in any Test match'.

The bowlers had been chosen by Carr, claimed Chairman of Selectors, Plum Warner. ''He got the side he wanted'' Warner was quoted as saying. Larwood had been dropped. The pitch looked too soft for him to have an impact. George Macauley took his place, the Yorkshireman recalled on his home ground of Headingley. Yorkshire's second-best slow left-armer, Roy Kilner, and Leicestershire's all-rounder George Geary (match figures in the Gents versus Players fixture 7/72) completed the frontline unit, with Woolley's slow left-arm reserved in extremis.

By the end of the day's play all except Tate failed and the Australians closed on 336/3. Critics sharpened their knives. C.B. Fry, Warner's England peer from the Edwardian era, claimed the Selection Committee errored in not including Gloucestershire's Charlie Parker as the left-arm spinner, for Parker had captured more first-class wickets than anybody on the circuit and was acknowledged as a wet wicket expert. Parker was left out. Warner continued to fume, especially in light of his gushing letters to Carr in the days before the game.

Australia scaled 494 before all were back in the hutch. Tate's 51 overs cost him 4/99 but Macaulay (1/123), Kilner (1/106) and Geary (2/130) all went around the park, innocuous on such a good batting strip. Hobbs and Sutcliffe went out to bat on the second afternoon requiring 345 to avoid the follow-on. Both started solidly and the pair hit up 59 in 80 minutes, crowd transfixed on the certainty of their techniques and apparent infinity. Then, with a sharp inhalation from the crowd, Sutcliffe (20) played too soon at Grimmett and spooned a catch back to him. Hobbs played some fine shots all-round the wicket and appeared set for yet another century before being caught at point for 49, trying to turn Mailey to leg. England wickets fell with upsetting frequency to end the second day on 203/8, still 291 runs adrift with the prospect of following-on and batting on a worn wicket.

Yet Geary and Macaulay, the overnight batsmen, added 108 for the ninth wicket. Macaulay failed as a bowler, but his Yorkshire grit blocked every decent delivery and he clouted the bad ball with a glowering fury as though trading punches with bully-boys. Cheered on to brave wonderments, the Yorkshire folk heartily applauded their kith and kin as Macaulay smote a dozen boundaries with varying displays of elegance. Cardus described Macaulay, in his heroic hour, as batting with 'a face like an angry rock'. Geary defended resolutely and nudged the score along here and there. Even so finishing on 294, 200 behind, Collins sent England in again just before lunch on the third and final day.

Hobbs and Sutcliffe ''*batted with refreshing confidence as well as success, some worn places on the pitch notwithstanding. For nearly two hours and a half they remained masters of Australia's attack''*. (Wisden)

Unlike his Lord's century, where Hobbs received criticism from the Times correspondent, here he played unshackled, a faultless display that allowed Hobbs to eclipse Clem Hill's record Ashes aggregate (2,660). In the end he played on to Grimmett for 88 in a partnership of 156 with Sutcliffe. Sutcliffe (94), Woolley, a painstaking 20, and Chapman, a boisterous 42 not out, brought the Test to a close – the third successive draw.

Warner adored Jack Hobbs. He had a 'man-crush'. Let Plum, in his own words, tell the story of the sixth century opening partnership from Hobbs and Sutcliffe, against Australia:

Following on 200 behind, England had twenty minutes' batting before lunch, and Hobbs and Sutcliffe scored 15 runs without loss.

After luncheon Gregory, Pavilion end, and Grimmett were the bowlers .... England were not out of the woods yet, and the early dismissal of either batsman would have been fraught with serious consequences. But Hobbs and Sutcliffe are great not only in technique but in temperament, and their cricket was superb. No risk could legitimately be taken, but when a loose ball came along it was hit with certainty.

The great pair raised 156 together, virtually ensuring a draw with a fine and faultless rearguard until such point when Hobbs tried to cut a straight one from Grimmett. Still nil-all after three Tests.

No recuperation period whatsoever, Hobbs and Sutcliffe trained it down to London that evening, arriving soon after midnight, Sutcliffe to his hotel room, Hobbs back home and then next day, both met up at Lord's for another three-day Gents versus Players fixture. Hobbs won the toss and opened with Sutcliffe and the pair faced some good bowlers. J.C. White caused the most concern, his slow left-arm was especially accurate and probing. Percy Fender delivered his usual bag of tricks at a military medium pace. Nigel Haig bowled accurate medium-brisk pace.

In 90 minutes to lunch they had added 105, their eleventh century stand together. In the hour after lunch Hobbs reached his sixth century of the season then accelerated in a blaze of glory, clearly with no regard for his wicket, offering a couple of chances on 108, then moving from 100 to 150 in half an hour.

Sutcliffe batted without any of this high glitter but won all his moral battles in reaching his first century in this famous fixture. He fell for 107, with the score on 263, and Hobbs (163) soon after. Ernest Tyldesley stole the show thereafter, scoring 103 of the next 155 and at the close of the first day the Players had reached 418/4.

The finished on 579 but then the Gentlemen launched a superb response, totally neutralising any remaining potency from the England attack. Poor Tate, fresh from his marathon effort at Leeds, had to put in a shift of 34 overs for his 2/94. Root's 38 overs were pillaged for 139 runs, two wickets. Kilner, wicketless for 118, Woolley 2/113, received rare punishment; however, to expose these tiring bowlers to a perfect wicket - in between Ashes Tests - seems, a century on, to be flogging very tired horses. The only bowler who enjoyed decent figures, George Geary (3/36), twisted his ankle mid-over and incapacitated himself.

Percy Chapman's 108 and Douglas Jardine's run out 85 were highlights from the Gentlemen's 542, also Bob Wyatt's 75. The Players replied with Holmes and Sutcliffe, the Yorkshire pair, Hobbs preferring to rest his feet up. Holmes failed, Tate came in and the game ended on 97 for one as the match petered out into a run-glut draw. Sutcliffe, with 50 not out, reminded everyone of his qualities.

England versus Australia 4th Test Old Trafford 1926

The fourth Test at Old Trafford produced a fourth successive draw and started with rain washing out all but ten deliveries on the first day. Collins had won the toss and elected to bat, Australia 6/0 at the close. A.W. Carr caught tonsillitis on the rest day. That was the formal line at any rate. Sir Home Gordon had dined with Carr that evening and insisted that Carr had eaten something peculiar to his digestive tract. Other reports hinted at fibrositis. What is for certain: Carr woke up on the Monday morning barely able to speak, with a sore throat and a stinging headache. Subsequently it looked as though Carr had spent a late night on the lash.

Warner intervened. Before Monday's play and as the incoming crowd swelled to 34,000 the frail and gentle Warner burst into the England dressing-room and asked Hobbs to take over the leadership reins. Hobbs humbly and aware of social protocols in the rigid class structure of the mid-1920s suggested G.T.S. Stevens, the only amateur standing. Warner insisted. The announcement came loud and clear just as Hobbs gingerly took his team out on to the Old Trafford playing arena.

Centuries once again flowed from the bats of Woodfull (117) and Macartney (109) in a partnership of 192 that might have laid the foundations for a huge total but, with over half the game gone, the

England bowlers bounced back to leave Australia 322/8 at the close. Hobbs never over-bowled his bowlers and although the pitch did not suit Tate, Fred Root provided an immaculate length and gained 4/88, sometimes with seven on the leg-side. G.T.S. Stevens delivered some freakish leg-breaks yet gained a couple of scalps with long-hops to finish with 3/88. Early on the last day the innings closed for 335. Warner reported that Hobbs captained to the satisfaction of all and his players responded positively to his direction.

Replying to Australia's total, Hobbs and Sutcliffe added 58 in 75 minutes before Sutcliffe (20) was held at the wicket off Mailey. Hobbs and Tyldesley added a further 77 before Hobbs fell for 74 lofting Grimmett to mid-off. Tyldesley, buoyed by a rousing reception from his home crowd and enjoying the form of his life for Lancashire, benefitted from several lives in making 81. Woolley (58) and Hendren (32 not out) also ensured England saved face and by the close reached 305/5. The fourth draw in a row meant that, for the very first time on English soil, the final Test would be 'timeless', played to a finish. Never has the mother country been so engrossed in Ashes cricket. Everyone from the Chairman of Selectors to the cockney selling cabbages from a wheel-barrow had opinions on who should get selected.

England versus Australia 5th Test Oval 1926

The gravity leading into the final 1926 Test at the Oval, timeless to ensure a definitive result, magnetised the whole nation. Preparing for the Selectors' Meeting in the Committee Room at Lord's, Warner had his own agenda. He had gone right off Arthur Carr, with all his 'hail-fellow-well-met' shit, especially since the baboon won the toss at Headingley and put the 'old enemy' in on a plumb pitch and dropped Macartney. Tonsilitis? My arse! The bugger had consumed as much beer, wine and port as a docker, and during a Test match at that.

Warner once performed a role in the Royal Navy during the Great War and imagined himself as the Commander-in-Chief of English Cricket. Lose yet another Ashes series, with only one win in 20 Tests since the Great War, would be a catastrophe. Warner dreaded the idea that 'soccer' or 'rugger' should claim bragging rights over cricket in the nation's esteem. Another defeat could represent a slide into eternal oblivion. Above all, Warner wanted the England team most likely to pull off the vital Test victory that would save English Cricket. Warner had already chosen his team over a hot chocolate the evening before, using a biro and the back of an envelope, while Agnes knitted.

Hoooooobbbbs, Sutcliffe, Woolley, Hendren, Tate … Chapman … Rhoooodes. For the rest of the places, Warner would listen to the others and have the casting vote.

Peter Perrin stood over six feet in his socks and, although approaching 50, still played regularly for Essex. He wore green tweeds and sat heavily in his chair, coughing uneasily as Warner read out the leaders in the averages. The best batsman never to play for England at last had his form dip in the County Championship and had an average plummeting below 20. He never even got chosen for the Gentlemen of England, too ponderous in the field. Warner, trembling with passion, spouted some cliches including: 'doing it for England'.

Gilligan wore his old England sleeveless sweater on top of a clean white shirt with MCC tie proudly on display. His season had been better. He sat erect in his chair, exuding health and vitality, in the hope that his fellow selectors would look upon his services again; after all, not much distance to go for his thousand runs for the season, seventy-odd wickets at around 20 and, of course, the 1-4 scoreline under his watch flattered the Australians for they enjoyed the rub of the green.

Hobbs, deep brown eyes and pointed nose, creases of laugh lines etched across a lived-in face, thought Arthur Carr should remain England captain. Rhodes agreed. Perrin and Gilligan reckoned he should go. Warner had the casting vote. His season's average had fallen in recent weeks to below 30 and the 'tonsilitis' had obviously been severe. ''It must be the eleven most likely to win the Test. England expects'', championed Warner.

Hobbs looked at Rhodes. Rhodes looked at Hobbs. Both knew that when informed of the decision, Carr would become volcanic. Warner had created a national outrage already. The team loved Carr, good old beer drinking Arthur Carr and Warner had assured him that he was 'worth 100 runs just for his captaincy'. Warner rubbed his hands excitedly against the thighs of his trousers, as the vote fell his way.

Much discussion ensued about Carr's possible replacement. At the time the very prospect of a professional England captain horrified certain upper-class dignitaries such as Lord Hawke of Yorkshire and Lord Harris of Kent, especially the prowling Lord Hawke. Warner proposed the untried 25-year-old Percy Chapman. Hobbs and Rhodes glanced at each other again, knowing that Carr regarded Chapman irritatingly as some hearty, binge drinking loose cannon. That decision added further salt to Carr's wound.

Hobbs and Rhodes agreed to offer a constant source of advice to Chapman, throughout the day, right down to field placings and bowling changes. Chapman had a look of glamour about him. He had put on weight over the years though remained an outstanding fielder and a highly entertaining batsman, and what is more runs had flowed at a hearty lick from Chapman's blade all summer.

Being a timeless Test Perrin suggested the strongest, longest batting line-up possible and put forward the formidable George Brown of Hampshire as wicket-keeper instead of the ageing 46-year-old Herbert Strudwick, a long-standing great from the Edwardian era. Brown had fought eyeball to eyeball successfully against Gregory and Macdonald back in 1921 with 250 runs at 50.00. Brown only kept wicket occasionally for Hampshire these days, but the times when he did keep, his large, imposing frame had stood up well. At 38, Brown had entered the veteran phase of his career. He would only be a stop-gap. But right now, Perrin stressed, his extra runs could come in handy; and Strudwick had dropped Bardsley twice at Lord's.

How else can England deepen the batting line-up? Warner suggested G.T.S. Stevens, the tall, amateur leg-spinning all-rounder from Middlesex. He had taken 149 from the Australian attack earlier in the year for Middlesex, and against Grimmett, Gregory and Macartney, if not Mailey. Old Trafford proved he could take Australian wickets, even from bad deliveries.

George Geary had shown guts and determination with his 35 at Headingley. Although his wickets had been expensive (2/130) at Headingley, the lion-hearted Leicestershire all-rounder had already captured over 100 wickets in the season, at under 20. These figures were not all that far from Larwood's. Geary could also bowl long spells and keep things tight.

The seam department brought much discussion. Hobbs suggested Harold Larwood and reminded everyone of the Nottinghamshire spearhead's break-back that had defeated him twice in the same game. Warner suggested Larwood might be profligate, a view Gilligan immediately seconded. Warner mentioned Larwood's 3/138 match figures from Lord's. Perrin countered that Tate with 9/336, on the slow, low wickets so far encountered could hardly be said to have done any better.

Silence descended.

''Larwood'' murmured Rhodes in his cold, determined manner that immediately commanded the attention of the rest, ''is the one I least … like … facing''.

Warner loved Rhodes almost as much as he loved Hobbs, possibly more. Think about it. Rhodes helped Warner win the Ashes 3-2 in 1903/04 with 31 wickets at 15.74. Eight years later, again with Warner in charge (though illness prevented an active part), Rhodes scored 463 runs at 57.87 in a 4-1 thrashing. If Larwood could scare Rhodes, that resonated around the table. A recall for the young Notts miner meant Fred Root would have to make way. From the lens of history, this appears harsh. Root had proved problematic with his inswingers and heavily congested leg-side field. He had conquered eight Australians for 194 in the series to date, significantly better than all rivals, Tate included. Yet the perception around the table sensed the Australian behemoths had built a resistance to his negative tactics.

All agreed Hobbs, Sutcliffe, Woolley, Hendren, Chapman, Brown, Stevens, Tate, Geary, Larwood. Ernest Tyldesley failed to hold on to his place, even after 81 at Old Trafford. He did have three lives. What England needed was another spinner, but preferably a slow left-armer, one who could be relied upon.

Though 48, Rhodes still played for Yorkshire and by-God he was a Yorkshireman. He looked an old soldier, short-back-and-sides haircut, sideburns trimmed to stubble length, white from the sands of time, a living, beating cricketer of astonishing longevity.

Rhodes had enjoyed an Indian Summer, a golden Autumn, call it what you will. But he sat at the table, as an England selector, top of the bowling averages with 95 wickets at 14.87 for the season. A casualty of the first couple of Ashes series since the Great War,

Rhodes had not played for England since being rejected as a 44-year-old after the first Test of the 1921 season. A relic from the late Victorian era, Rhodes first played for England in 1899 and by some fantastical link in the chain, this great all-rounder's first taste of Test cricket, coincided with the last game in W.G.'s career.

He started as a slow left-arm bowler of the highest class and a dogged number eleven batsman. Among his impressive set of procurements included: seven for 17 to help dismiss Australia for 36 in the Edgbaston Test of 1902; scoring six* in the last wicket stand of 15 with Hirst at the Oval, also in 1902, to win the game by one wicket; adding 130 for the last wicket with R.E. Foster at Sydney in 1903, an England record for over a century; 15 wickets for 124 at Melbourne on a sticky wicket in 1904; a record Ashes opening partnership of 323 with Jack Hobbs at Melbourne in 1912 and so on.

Rhodes, the stubborn old mule, showed no signs of diminishing powers. If anything, his bowling took on new guile, mesmerising young batsmen up and down the land. His batting evolved an ugly two-eyed stance, rather like Shiv Chanderpaul's in recent years, though Rhodes batted right-handed. Warner hated that stance but

Rhodes claimed it lessened the number of edges to the slip cordon and helped promote on-side shots, which became his forte in later years.

Back around the table, Warner, Perrin, Gilligan and Hobbs surveyed the season's first-class statistics. Wilfred, remember, had already hoovered up 95 wickets at 14.87. He still had runs in him too, as a couple of centuries in the County Championship testified and - though approaching his 49th birthday - Rhodes had no all-round peer in the land who could hold a candle to him. And he knew it but Rhodes stubbornly refused to countenance so bold a move as to project himself forward for such an important, high-intensity showdown as a series-defining Ashes Test. He had refused earlier in the season, telling them in no uncertain terms: ''oh give the youngsters a chance!''

Warner tapped his pen on the table, scrutinising the list in front of him. He glanced at Wilfred and (according to A.A. Thompson in his book Hirst and Rhodes) told him in the manner of a headmaster asking a special favour from a senior teacher:

''Wilfred, we think that you should play. You are still the best left-handed bowler in England, and in a match played to a finish it is likely that we shall have rain at some time or other. You can still spin 'em, you know.'

''And your length,'' added Perrin, ''is as good as ever.''

''Well, I can keep 'em there or thereabouts.''

''And,'' said Arthur Gilligan, ''you're making runs for Yorkshire.''

''I can get a few'', admitted Rhodes.

''And your fielding is all right,'' said Hobbs.

Rhodes permitted himself a wry smile. ''The farther I run, the slower I get.''

To the North's great delight and the South's immense surprise, the old warrior returned to England colours after five long years of growing greyer. No longer the lean athletic fresh-faced cherub who grabbed the headlines at the turn of the century, here was a grizzled remnant from a by-gone era, still plying his trade with no obvious superior, in the teeth of the modern world, playing every season and every game like it might be his last.

Carefully examining his statistics for an inkling of terminal decline, Rhodes continued the fight all along his pathway to eventual retirement, knowing one day the tide of anno domini would be insurmountable even for him. Of course, he would play. All along he had secretly hoped to be asked again. This time he knew he was the right man, for no one younger was ready, yet, to fill his boots.

Warner contacted Carr after the meeting, expressing his deep sadness that Carr, should 'for the sake of England' relinquish his position and place in the team. Carr, especially remembering Warner's effeminate letters, hated the man for the rest of his life.

For the greatest Test match of the century, the first timeless Test in England, the chance to bury the Great War and win back the Ashes, the England selectors had sacked the captain, replaced him with a 25-year-old novice, dropped the leading bowler in England's attack, dispensed with the seasoned wicket-keeper in the hope of more runs, and brought back a veteran, soon to be 49, five years after England had last discarded him.

The day of the Oval Test brought only so much as half of the capacity crowd; some had queued all night desperate for a seat but the majority had been scared away with rumours of mile long queues. Chapman won the toss and England batted in too cavalier a manner on a plumb wicket. Hobbs made 37 bright and breezy runs, suggesting all was good in the world, but missed a drooping full-toss from leg-spinner Mailey that came floating out from the shadows under the pavilion awnings, and rocked his stumps. Woolley, Hendren, Chapman and Stevens all fell having blazed away in the manner of a festival game. Only Sutcliffe remained, chiselling out runs hour after hour in that dour Yorkshire manner, tut-tutting at the fall of his restless colleagues. G.T.S. Stevens, in for his defensive abilities with the bat, caught the hawkish mood and stormed down the wicket to lift Mailey on to the pavilion awning. Then, as though to reproach himself for such vigour, he soberly defended the next delivery into the waiting hands of T.J.E. Andrews at silly point.

A rolling wave of cheers broke around the ground as out trod the veteran Yorkshire campaigner. He walked slowly to the wickets, overwhelmed by the massive crowd support. Twenty-seven years earlier to the very day he had played in an Ashes Test at the Oval, upon the same turf, and locked horns with the likes of Fry,

Ranjitsinhji, Hayward, Jackson, MacLaren, Lilley and Lockwood, against legends such as Trumper, Trumble, Noble, Ernest Jones, McLeod and Howell. A generation had retired or died in the interim and the world had changed for ever.

The cheers continued all of the way to the wicket. Rhodes took his time, perhaps wiping some tears from his eyes. First ball from Mailey took the edge towards short leg but the fielder missed the half chance. The crowd gasped with relief. A single was snatched, just like Rhodes had always done. Sutcliffe had been out there defying the Australian bowlers for three and a half hours and had moved serenely on from 61 to 76 in four scoring strokes before the Stevens dismissal. Then Mailey somehow hit him in the face from one that bounced unexpectedly. Next ball, a beauty, bowled him, 214 for 6, and all advantage in winning the toss had dissipated, Yorkshiremen excluded, in the ego of English extravagance.

Geary joined Rhodes and for a while they dug in grimly, eating up a quarter of an hour, barely breathing, then Geary hit a two, a four and a three to keep the scoreboard operators busy. Rhodes, famous for stealing singles in his youth, called Geary for a quick single which trickled out wide of silly-point, but Geary, guilty of ball-watching, reacted too slowly and failed to make his ground, 231 for 7.

Tate continued the hay-making role, swotting boundaries like confetti including a mighty six over deep mid-wicket. Rhodes plodded away and saw Tate die the death of a cavalier. With Larwood falling for a duck, that left only Strudwick, the number eleven, with a Test average hovering around 8.0, for company. Rhodes moved up a gear, taking a two and a single, grabbing whatever he could. Strudwick raised a cheer from his home supporters when he cut a boundary square on the off-side. Rhodes clubbed a four and then a three from Grimmett and the score climbed to 280. Going for a dab down through the vacant slip region for a single from the fifth ball of Mailey's next over, Rhodes could only edge it finely into Oldfield's hands. None the less, his 28 was a worthy effort.

Though not required to bowl in the evening sunshine, Rhodes could bide his time. Four wickets fell to leave the Australians very much on the backfoot after the first day. Two wickets fell to Larwood's express pace, Macartney fell pulling a Stevens' long-hop onto his wickets plus Ponsford got himself run out. Only Woodfull from the top five survived to fight another day. Chapman received praise for the handling of his attack, keeping good old Wilfred up his sleeve, powder dry for another day.

As the Test started on the Saturday, so Sunday became a rest day but the August Bank Holiday brought in nearly 31,000 through the turnstiles on a warm, humid day. Chapman started with Tate and Larwood. Collins bunkered down for the long haul whilst Woodfull, bat close to the ground, displayed moments of fine timing without appearing to move his bat much, just inches, but the right sort of inches each time. Not for nothing did Woodfull acquire the name 'unbowlable'.

The score mounted slowly, a couple of twos here and a stolen single there. Tate came off first, replaced by Geary, and, when Larwood ran out of puff ten minutes later, Chapman brought on the veteran spinner in his place, score 84 for four, the greatest wicket-taker in cricket history against the unbowlable Woodfull. Slowly Rhodes brought his arm over, perfectly on a good length did it pitch. Ball after ball, subtle variations, no two deliveries the same. The pace changed, the drift in from the off varied and the turn from leg to off ever so slight, just enough to take an edge. Into this remorseless current of seemingly innocuous dribble, Woodfull quietly sized up the fading champion. Fifth ball of Rhodes' third over he put through a quicker one, faster than one believed possible from such ageing limbs, but it honed in cold and straight. Woodfull, rushed into a decision, shaped a cut and chopped it into his wicket, 90 for five. Off the opener trudged, suckered by the sage for 35. Richardson played out the last ball with a defiant and defensive prod.

Then Chapman detached Rhodes from the attack, as though all along the veteran's task was simply to break the stand; like a precious stone he placed Rhodes 'back-in-his-pocket' for later so as not to give too much of the old man's repertoire away too soon.

Tate returned and after a while Larwood replaced Stevens. Tate kept Collins quiet whilst Larwood jostled with Richardson. The score mounted, the hundred received polite applause and Chapman replaced Tate with Rhodes once more and the wise old professional hit his length right from the start and bowled an enticing maiden. Three singles came from his next, then maiden after maiden.

Chapman brought Hendren in from the boundary to silly-point. This irked Richardson and after a while the gung-ho Australian smashed a full-bodied drive back towards Rhodes who dived in a manner that belied his years. Some swear that he touched the missile and lent the trajectory to within mid-off's range. At any rate Geary sprang to his right and pulled off an outstanding catch. 122 for six, Rhodes two for eight from eight, crowd crazy with jubilation.

A recovery led by Jack Gregory (73) and Herbie Collins (61) quickly subdued the partisan onlookers and helped take Australia into a slender lead of 22. Rhodes finished with 25 overs two for 35, a noble performance.

Hobbs and Sutcliffe had to last out exactly an hour before close of play on day two. For the spectators this was a time of unbearable tension. If Hobbs and Sutcliffe could survive till the close of play, England should win. If either or both are conquered, the odds would swing strongly towards that mighty and experienced Australian batting line-up in the fourth innings. Surely Hobbs and Sutcliffe could not possibly succeed again? The law of averages smacked vehemently towards a failure; some form of human frailty must surface at some point.

An oppressive, thunderous atmosphere fell upon the Oval, a humid, sticky time. Collins started with Gregory and Grimmett, yet replaced Grimmett with Mailey after only two overs and Hobbs helped himself to seven runs in his first over, six more in the second. Macartney came on for Gregory with a darting variation of slow left-arm, in turn replaced by Grimmett. Collins used many permutations that evening. The crowd spent the last hour immersed in tension, anxiety relieved with runs and the consummate mastery of both openers. Survival, with loud resounding bells of hearty cheer, the great players managed, 49/0 at the close of day two. The crowd dispersed in utter emotional exhaustion.

Two policemen guarded the Oval wicket overnight and while the players tossed and turned in the heat of an August night, vast thunderclouds built up and around 2.00am an almighty clap of thunder signalled the arrival of a torrential downpour. The two policemen ran for cover with a terrible flash of lightning and by the time they reached the shelter of the Grandstand, puddles splashed under their feet and the ground felt obliterated by sheets of rain. Spectators, sleeping rough outside to ensure a seat later that day, scattered for any available shelter.

Hobbs woke up at his home in Clapham Park, not more than a mile from the Oval with deep concern etched over his face. He took the tram, paid the same familiar three-halfpenny ticket, and arrived at the ground, hoping not to be noticed but a flurry of schoolboys ran for his autograph. He signed a dozen or so then waved the rest away. From the player's room to the east of the pavilion Hobbs looked out at the scores of sparrows feasting on worms forced to the surface from the overnight rain. The uncovered wicket had turned black, the ground still felt humid but the puddles had all drained away.

Signs indicating that rain may curtail play were largely ignored as a large crowd were already in their seats to see Chapman, wearing a raincoat several sizes too small for him, walk out to inspect the wicket with Herbie Collins. 'Bosser' Martin, the chief groundsman, told them the wicket had dried out surprisingly quickly. Chapman raised the issue of fast bowler's footholds but Collins replied he'd be only using his spinners and requested saw dust for the bowlers' footholds. Chapman asked for the heavy roller to bring the moisture to the top and deaden the wicket. Meanwhile Sutcliffe practised his defence technique in the outdoor nets.

Against all odds, play commenced on time in an atmosphere of no wind and full cloud cover. Hobbs (27*) and Sutcliffe (20*) began the day playing themselves in on the slow, low pitch. Grimmett started with a maiden to Sutcliffe from the pavilion end, Macartney a maiden to Hobbs from the other. They met in mid pitch for a quick conference.

''Pity about the rain'', said Hobbs, with a calming smile on his face, ''its's rather spoilt our chances''. Appreciable spin, though slow and low, could be seen from the off. Hobbs ran a single to square leg in Grimmett's second over to get the scoreboard ticking and register the 50 up. Sharp singles were stolen off Macartney and Hobbs belted a Grimmett full-toss over square-leg for four, then cut behind square for two, stole another single and farmed the strike.

All the while, each delivery cut a divot from the pitch that needed patting back into place. Hobbs and Sutcliffe spent many times, especially between overs, patting down the pitch with the back of their bats. Twenty minutes passed until the next run, another Hobbs boundary pulled square off Grimmett and after 40 minutes play, all 26 runs added to the England account found their source from the bat of Hobbs.

Sutcliffe cut a two and a three to move his score along at last and with the total on 80, Collins swopped Macartney for Richardson, sensing that his medium-paced off-breaks darting in on a drying surface might prove lethal now the sun had come out and sure enough, as the sun dried the surface, the ball gripped and spat unnervingly. Richardson started over the wicket but Hobbs soon pulled him over the heads of the short-legs for four and took nine in all from his first over. Collins instructed Richardson to bowl round the wicket on a leg-stump line and posted a close ring of fielders, from leg slip to forward short leg, ready for the bat-pad catches.

For over after over, eight in all from Richardson, Sutcliffe played out maidens before working a single on the onside to get off strike. Richardson bowled with exceptional accuracy. Runs came at a trickle from the other end yet had almost ground to a standstill against Richardson.

Sutcliffe wrote: I found myself longing to have a go at him (Richardson), but I knew I could not afford the risk. My business was to stay there until the wicket became easier. Eventually, I scored the run that took Hobbs to Richardson's end, and there was tied down, just as I had been, by Richardson's leg-theory attack.

Hobbs played out maiden after maiden against Richardson, bunkering down as best he could as the demons in the pitch awoke. Collins brought Grimmett in from mid-on to silly mid-on to extend the line of close-in leg-side fielders with Ponsford, Macartney and Mailey as three forward short-legs, Collins himself at leg-slip, Gregory slip, Andrews out at cover, Woodfull mid-off.

Legend has it Hobbs deliberately made Richardson look more difficult than the bowler warranted, manipulating Collins into keeping him on during that treacherous hour before lunch, when the wicket dried. Hobbs disputed this allegation for the rest of his life but perhaps because to admit such a ruse would tarnish his otherwise virtuous reputation. Seeing the arc from silly mid-on to leg slip, he batted a foot outside his leg-stump so anything on his pads became a free hit. Fielders ran round quickly between overs to ensure maximum use of the malignant glue-pot whilst it dried wickedly in the mid-day sun. The number of England wickets tumbling in the hour before lunch would determine the fate of the Ashes. At the end of each Richardson over, a great sigh of relief came from the 28,000 strong crowd and cheers erupted, all for surviving another over. For the first time anybody could remember, the crowd cheered the batsman for playing out a maiden. Umpire Chester reckoned this the most spiteful pitch he had ever seen.

Collins, with a hint of mischief about him, several times ran out of position into a new one just as Richardson delivered the ball. All the while, Hobbs dead-batted the ball to the ground, safely out of reach. At the other end, the wiles of Grimmett, Mailey and Macartney against Sutcliffe did not quite captivate the crowd to the same extent, in the crowd's eyes, the real duel was Richardson's explosive off-break darts that kicked and span alarmingly into Hobbs, as he moved into position from a foot outside the leg-stump.

Especially that last hour before lunch, each time the ball landed a divot cut out from the wicket and both batsmen prodded the offending article back into place with the bottom of their bats. Then, to announce the end of the siege, a beautiful on driven four from Hobbs off Richardson prompted an intense roar of relief from the crowd, who themselves and for the first time unleashed primeval roars with clenched fists pumping and glowering, reddened faces scowling with joy, eruptions of human euphoria, broad smiles, fervent clapping, excited chatter and, as quickly as it came, the noise died to a low dim and Richardson started again. Onwards these two great openers crept, like suspicious bodyguards, inching their side away towards the broad sunlight uplands of a placid, dried out afternoon pitch, one from which England's middle-order might take the game away from the tourists.

Eye-witness John Arlott, there as a 12-year-old boy, soaked up the ambience and magnitude of the occasion. Much later on in his life, the cricket journalist and commentator had this to say in his famous Hampshire burr:

"Hobbs and Sutcliffe, what a magnificent pair. Millions who never entered a cricket ground recognised them as symbols not only of English Cricket but of something English Cricket had often lacked up until then: a rocklike reliability."

The long two-and-a-half-hour morning session came to a close at last. As the Australians and umpires walked off, there still at the wicket, both openers spent time prodding the pitch like honest gardeners striving for perfection. Hobbs dominated that glorious morning with 97*, Sutcliffe 53*.

Early in the afternoon Hobbs first struck a two, then he snatched a single to bring up the most valuable hundred in all his long, glittering career, eliciting as he did so an explosion of approval from the crowd. As a piece of classical music is not judged purely on length so the same rings true of innings and their quantity. Many observers believed this century, the eleventh that Hobbs managed in Ashes contests, crafted from such a treacherous track, was his signature innings - evidence for the Hobbs mastery under all conditions. At the end of that impertinent run, Hobbs waved his bat at the crowd; then he removed his cap and waved that at the crowd, then waved at them once more with both cap and bat. Three cheers roared around the ground in rare adulation at the sporting prowess of a single individual. Across at Aldwych, outside the Morning Post offices, a vast up-to-date scoreboard attracted a large crowd who roared a further loud blast almost to the scale at the Oval. Like a delayed echo.

More than a few men wept openly, unable to control their emotions. Hobbs had been in their thoughts for twenty years, a direct living breathing link to the halcyon days of Edwardian England, a time of innocent fun and simple pleasures.

Gregory bowled him for exactly 100, a peach of a breakback that dislodged only the off-stump bail. The score at the time, nicely placed, job done, 172 for one. Off the Master walked, inciting a further prolonged acclamation of approval.

Sutcliffe went on and on through the day's play, making a right nuisance of himself to all of Collins's bowlers, defying each in turn with his broad bat and iron-will determination. Sutcliffe batted in his own bubble of unflappable concentration, adding 48 with Woolley (27), 57 with Hendren (15), 39 with Chapman (19) and 57 with G.T.S. Stevens. Within five minutes of the close and while resting on his bat at the non-striker's end, Sutcliffe (161*) confessed to Mailey about how knackered he felt. Mailey empathised, telling Sutcliffe that he could 'barely get his arm over'. All day Mailey had bowled either top-spinners or 'wrong 'uns' (googlies). According to Mailey:

As it happened Sutcliffe had to play the last over out and I kept thinking of Herbie's self-confessed

mental exhaustion. As I casually lumbered up to the bowling crease, I don't suppose anybody on the

ground (including Herbie) knew that I was hatching a diabolical plot to liquidate the Yorkshire menace.

I decided to bowl a fast leg-break with all the spin I could possibly command. I put the whole Mailey family for generations into this effort and when the ball left me, I was conscious that so far everything was going to plan.

Herbert Sutcliffe lunged languidly forward but never quite realised what had happened till he heard the 'death rattle'. I had bowled hundreds of overs at my old enemy but this was the first time I had really beaten him in the way I wanted to.

Sutcliffe regarded this as his finest century in England, 'for it was made on a vile, sticky wicket'. Up until that freak Mailey leg-break, Sutcliffe had played a flawless innings; his most fluent strokes were the off drives and square cuts, his defence perfect until dismissal.

Warner reckoned what 'Hobbs and Sutcliffe accomplished will be talked of as long as cricket is played'. In all Hobbs (100) struck ten 4's in three hours forty-five minutes, Sutcliffe (161) lasted seven and a quarter hours and hit fifteen 4's. England closed the third day of the timeless Test on 375/6, a lead of 353. Even so, many column writers believed this lead still insufficient, every run on the fourth day of priceless value.

On the fourth morning, Geary fell quickly but Rhodes (14), who cut a four from Gregory then drove Gregory sweetly back along the ground to the pavilion rails, added 43 with Tate (33*) and the score climbed to 436. Showers curtailed the day so it started late, then a more extensive shower consumed another couple of hours. The bottom line, England had been dismissed at ten past three on the fourth day of the match, 18th August 1926, and Australia's long, strong line-up was invited to get 415 to retain the Ashes. Collins demanded the heavy roller for as long as the laws allowed.

Larwood took off his sweater. Chapman wanted to start with his fastest option and the young man from the Nottinghamshire mines began his shift with an over of extreme pace to generate a buzz of excitement. Bardsley had put himself at number four in this innings, giving the young Bills - Woodfull and Ponsford - their chance to open. Silence, always silence when the bowler turned round and started his run, especially in the case of this young spearhead. A wonderful spectacle, acceleration up to the wicket, perfect sideways action and then the path of the ball, all but invisible. Larwood's full-throttles came so wickedly from the pitch that Ponsford could only edge a rising lifter through a gap in the slips third ball to get off strike. Woodfull somehow managed to survive the three remaining deliveries.

Tate bowled a fine maiden to Ponsford then, for Larwood's second over, Chapman brought Rhodes up from long leg to gully and strengthened the slip cordon by moving Geary into fourth slip.

On his third delivery Larwood induced an edge from Woodfull and it flew to Geary. Eye witnesses remember the shouts, yells and roars from members at the top of the pavilion. Australia 1/1. Rational folk flushed red with wild cheers, veins swelling up their necks. Then the cheers as the Gov'nor General walked on to the ground for the last time. Like some pantomime villain, Macartney always packed a neat punch when it came to facing England's finest. He once hooked Sidney Barnes for six, but that was before the war and Macartney was 40 now. Even so Macartney had scores so far in this series of 133 not out at Lord's, 151 at Leeds – including a century before lunch – and 109 at Old Trafford. No one could counterattack like Macartney, no one in the world.

Rhodes came on and Macartney cover drove him for two in the first over, then took a two and a single from the next. Larwood now raced in and Macartney deftly late cut him for a couple then, imperiously and with magnificent theatre, hooked him for four that crackled with the sound of a rifle shot and set off a spontaneous gasp of admiration from the humbled crowd.

This angered Larwood and the young man soon fired in a thunderbolt and all the indomitable fighter could do was edge to Geary just as Woodfull had done. John Marchant, an eye witness, conveys the atmosphere at the top of the pavilion:

''We began to shout in earnest then. Macartney the Magnificent was gone, finished, dead, done with!... Two wickets down for thirty-one, and the sun shine hotter and hotter for England – do you wonder that we shouted? And we were to be shouting very, very soon.''

Macartney's demise brought out another pantomime villain, one who had tormented England with centuries stretching back to 1909, and

Warren Bardsley, the stout left-hander, wanted to finish on a high. His plan was to defend his wicket at all cost and then move through the gears and repeat his Lord's performance (where he carried his bat for 193*).

Ponsford now received a masterclass from Rhodes. The old stager walked in from gully, handed Umpire Chester his cap and juggled his field around, each to within an inch of his liking, so it resembled a pear, with the thin part behind the batsman's wickets. Wherever Ponsford drove, there was a fielder and he became bogged down. Rhodes had no drift, just perfect length and some prodigious spin from the weather-battered fourth day track. In his third over Ponsford prodded at a slow spinner he thought might hit his off-stump and looked forlornly as the ball lobbed up towards gully where Larwood flung himself forwards to take a 'one in a hundred' catch, for only the swiftest mind could have run in from gully, dived and scooped the ball in front of the wicket. The youngest member of the team received genuine praise from the oldest. Collins played out the rest of the over as a maiden, then Geary replaced Larwood and sent down a maiden to Bardsley.

Collins struck Rhodes for a three, then took a single off Geary to face Rhodes once more. Another ball just like the Ponsford one broke back sharply from the leg, forcing a defensive shot from Collins, who could only watch in horror as an edge flew to Woolley at short slip. The Australian captain muttered some words to Chapman as he walked off, not sure what.

Bardsley and Andrews set about a rearguard. Bardsley took the attack to Rhodes and swiped him square for four, while Andrews jumped out to him and belted him for another couple of fours, taking the total past the fifty mark. When Larwood returned, third ball he unleashed a rapid bumper that Andrews hooked with the very sweet-spot of his blade. Tate, standing at short-square, snatched the ball from the sky with his right-hand, superseding any of the stellar catches already grabbed in the game.

Tate's snatch proved the catalyst for old men to grow hoarse in the stands, voices fading into crackling silence, puce faces of drunken joy, spilt beer, cigar and pipe fumes, today's papers all sodden and crinkled on the ground. Some old fellow with a grey moustache, sporting a tweed jacket and tie, executed a jig, dancing up and down for all he was worth in a rare, raw demonstrative state, 63/5. Soon it would be all over and the Ashes would be England's for the first time since 1912. Oh, for the glory of a bursting spring after the long-haul of winter.

Drinks on the last afternoon. From left to right: Strudwick, Geary, Chapman, Tate, Stevens, Hendren, Sutcliffe, Waiter, Hobbs, Larwood, Rhodes and Woolley. Notice the pile of saw dust.

Bardsley and Gregory, two robust left-handers, had no intentions of surrendering meekly and both came out like cornered gunmen firing great towering catches into the sky for anyone who dared. Woolley moved from short slip to short leg and hung on to Bardsley's offering. Then Gregory sent a Tate ball whirling into the atmosphere over mid-off's head where Sutcliffe held on. Richardson hit Rhodes for a boundary, so next ball the wily old bugger bowled him with a swifter one that kept straight. After this he bowled four more overs, two of them maidens and then bowed out having performed the miracle Warner so coveted. His final spell for England had been 20 overs, nine maidens, four wickets for 44, six for 79 in the match, and 42 runs. The seamers grabbed the tail-enders with Geary finishing the job by spreadeagling Mailey's stumps, who promptly grabbed the ball before Strudwick's dive for the same souvenir.

According to Colonel Philip Trevor, writing in the Daily Telegraph, the final wicket was *'the signal for a frantic outburst of delight and triumph from all over the enclosure. In the stands, erstwhile parsons sacrificed their hats, men hugged each other and danced madly, and women grew hysterical. Retired (and usually retiring) military men leapt the barriers and scampered gamely for the pavilion. The players were 'mobbed, friends and foes alike. And the result was received in the streets with an enthusiasm that became infectious. A forest of hats and handkerchiefs shot up in the air and waved for*

several minutes, accompanied by roar after roar of deafening

cheers, which re-echoed along the Strand and over the bridges.'

The joyous scene at the Oval on 18th August 1926 made many of those who were present happier and more relieved than at any time since Armistice Day. At last, almost eight years after the Great War and in the fourth Ashes series since those guns fell silent, England had regained the Ashes.

First on to the balcony stood Percy Chapman, amidst a rousing cheer. Collins followed and waved a hand at the multitude, then on came Hobbs and Sutcliffe, a titanic applause echoed round London, then Larwood and Rhodes, another crescendo, followed by the whole England eleven. Singing broke out, spontaneous lyrics, as the crowd called out their heroes to the sound of Bow Bells:

We want Chapman, Hobbs and Sutcliffe,

We want Geary, Rhodes and Larwood.

Some quotes at the time.

Warner: This victory means everything to English cricket. Had we been beaten, despondency would have crept over the land.

Macartney: Hobbs played the best innings he has played in cricket. That innings was responsible for winning the rubber for England. He had some very nasty bowling to take and he undoubtedly sacrificed himself in many cases to keep Sutcliffe away from the bowling.

Noble: (on Hobbs) It was an innings worthy of the great batsman he is and it put England in a winning position.

Hobbs, still at the height of his powers, came top of the 1926 first-class averages and scored more runs than any of his younger peers: 2,949 at 77.60. In second place, was a Yorkshireman by the name of Herbert Sutcliffe, with 2,528 runs at 66.52.

Each child would go on to remember that final day, 18th August 1926 until their hair grew white from the glow of time. The relief, and joy, spread like a warm blanket over English cricket. 1926 proved the last Ashes Test for Strudwick and Rhodes and many felt it would be old Jack's last one as well. Signing off with 11 Ashes centuries – when no one in history had more than Trumper's six – would be an appropriate ending to a peerless career.

Herbert and Emmie Sutcliffe became parents on the 10th October: a son named William Herbert Hobbs Sutcliffe, who would within 30 years captain Yorkshire.

Chapter Five Thrashing Australia in their backyard
1927

The following year there was a tangible decline in Jack's statistics,

the years at last appearing to erode some of the old mastery but even

so Hobbs still managed six centuries for Surrey and one for the

Players; he came 12th in the national averages with 1,641 runs at

52.93. There were no Tests to report in 1927 as the visiting New

Zealanders had not yet quite attained Test status. Sutcliffe, in ninth

place, had 2,414 runs at 56.13. One of Sutcliffe's highlights, an

undeniable stamp of class, came versus Nottinghamshire against

Larwood, Barrett and Voce. He made 169 in a draw, lasting out for

over seven hours.

If Hobbs, at 43, deserved to be put out to rich pastureland, then Charlie Hallows, the left-handed Lancastrian had a magnificent season (2,343 at 75.58) and Andrew Sandham and Percy Holmes also came higher than Hobbs. Sutcliffe would have plenty of aspiring England partners. Elsewhere, two emerging talents hinted at a bright future. Douglas Jardine, a tall Surrey amateur with a distinctly long nose and air of superiority, turned out for Surrey and Gentlemen versus Players fixtures whenever business allowed and topped the averages with 1,002 runs at 91.69. Walter Hammond, the Gloucestershire all-rounder, weighed in with most runs (2,960 at 69.04), Patsy Hendren (13) scored most centuries.

A summer without Test matches against foreign opposition notwithstanding, the 1927 season showcased eight representative fixtures, where the best cricketers in the land were pitted against each other. Above normal county standard, fresh emerging talent could be spotted and the form of elder legends vindicated or shattered. Warner always wanted an evolving, living England Eleven, rather than one shut down at the end of a tour. To this effect, on top of the four Gentlemen versus Players fixtures, and the

Champion County versus the Rest of England, there were three Test Trial matches, two of which were billed as England versus the Rest, the other – to kick-start the season of proper representative cricket was North versus South at Sheffield at the end of June.

Bramall Lane provided a grim, rain ruined affair, barely an hour allowed on the first day, barely an hour on the last. Jack Hobbs had stood down owing to a skin complaint and convalesced for five weeks. The South reached 235 with Chapman (70) and Jardine (57) the mainstays while the North countered with 269/0, Holmes 127*, Sutcliffe 131*. The Yorkshire openers conquered 23 overs from Tate and 13 from Freeman, though in the latter stages of their innings the bowling became lukewarm.

Hobbs (43) batted once in the first Gentlemen versus Players fixtures at the Oval in early July, in an innings for the Players where Patsy Hendren scored 150. Alec Kennedy recorded 12 wickets in the match including 10/37 in the first innings. The Gentlemen clung on, eight wickets down. When Hobbs failed to gain a place in the next game the following week, he felt snubbed.

However, Sutcliffe played in the Lord's fixture, scoring 64 before being bowled by off-spinner Vallance William Crisp Jupp. According to Christopher Martin-Jenkins (The Complete Who's Who of Test Cricketers) 'Juppy' was a 'short, prematurely bald man, … had broad shoulders, long arms, great strength, and a rough humour.' Earlier in the game Douglas Jardine's 123 for the Gentlemen proved the highlight in another draw. Here the tall, lean and long-nosed pseudo-duke showcased an excellent defence and an array of skilfully executed on-side shots. In the Test Trial at Bristol, Hobbs (12) played on off his pads against Clark but Sutcliffe, opening with his famous partner for the first time that season, went on to 227, collaring the bowling in a flawless display lasting over five hours. The left-handed Charlie Hallows (135) put on 317 with Sutcliffe.

A curious incident took place in the dressing-room belonging to the Rest. The Bristol pavilion was on the small side with dressing-room doors opposing themselves. Jupp had just returned from Italy where he had been able to purchase a copy of Lady Chatterley's Lover, a book from novelist D.H. Lawrence that was banned in Britain because of the pornographic literature. With the Rest in the field wilting under Sutcliffe and Hallows, Jupp crept in with his well-thumbed copy of the book, found Patsy Hendren's cricket trunk and slid the book into it. Rain prevented a conclusion to the game.

The last Test Trial at Lord's saw Hobbs and Sutcliffe opening once more for England against the Rest. They looked in control on a slippery surface but Hobbs had to retire hurt for 38, after slipping and tearing a thigh muscle. Sutcliffe (65) edged Clark to young Kent wicket-keeper batsman, Leslie Ames. For the Rest, Maurice Leyland of Yorkshire struck 102 off Nichols, Tate, Freeman and Jupp.

Warner's brainwave, to keep an England eleven alive via true representative fixtures, was not the only one he conducted that summer. He also invented a Ladies Night where cricketers could bring their wives to social events such as 'Pimm's nights'. Nobody told Vallance Jupp. Fortified already with a few glasses of Pimm's inside him, Jupp was holding court in front of Hammond and Leyland, telling them the most appallingly misogynistic joke.

Pelham Warner brought his wife, Agnes, a delightful lady of charm, good grace, elegance and class. She stood, so legend goes, not further than three feet from Jupp's broad back when off he spouted.

Two men walking back from the pub spot a couple of dogs copulating in true doggy style.

Bill says to Bert: '' Cor. Wish my wife would allow me to do that!''

''Just go and fill her up with Pimm's and she'll agree, you'll see'' suggested Bert.

Week later they bump into each other again and Bert asked whether his Pimm's suggestion had been taken up and, if so, whether the Pimm's technique had worked.

''Yes'' said Bill, ''mind you it only took a couple to get Mildred to agree to go doggy but.'' Jupp paused for effect ready to deliver the punch line:

''It took a further eight to get her to do it on the same lawn''.

Jupp howled with laughter at his joke; his face crinkled with glee with sweat beads conglomerating on his forehead as a consequence of his own joy. Yet Jupp received no hearty approval from his select audience. Moreover, their faces betrayed awkwardness, as though wishing to giggle but unable to. He caught Leyland's eyes and he glanced down at the floor, face red but silent.

Towards the season's finale, Hobbs (35) played in the Gentlemen versus Players fixture at Folkestone where Hendren (103) and Hammond (138) scored heavily to ensure an innings and 18 run victory for the Players. That night many of the Players travelled by train all the way up to Scarborough for the last Gentlemen versus Players matches that season.

Hobbs opened with Sutcliffe for the third and last time in 1927 but Sutcliffe (13) fell lbw to Vallance Jupp (Leveson-Gower's pick) and although the Northants off-spinner removed Hobbs, one suspects that Hobbs (119) had enjoyed his fill from festival cricket so got stumped and allowed Holmes (127) and Tyldesley (116) to feast. The Gentlemen looked to be sliding ignominiously towards a second heavy defeat in a week but vulgar Jupp (5/158, 42 and 101*) ensured otherwise.

As was the case in this era, the final fixture of the season was the Champion County against the Rest of England. Eventually this fixture had to be scrapped because, almost the whole time, the Rest were far too powerful a side for one county to compete against. In 1927, Lancashire took on the Rest of England and in a highly honourable draw, Charlie Hallows once again puffed his left-hander's chest out and gathered in 120 against Nichols, Tate, Parker, Jupp and Hammond. He may have started fortuitously, and there were a couple of close lbw shouts turned down, but Hallows proved especially strong on the onside. Lancashire reached 290 with Ernest Tyldesley lending support with 63. Tate (4/27) and Jupp (4/92) took the honours.

The wretchedly wet 1927 summer ensured a further rain-ruined draw, not before the Rest reached 181/2. Though Sutcliffe (5) failed, Holmes (61), Sandham (53*) and the emerging Wally Hammond (53*) batted attractively, with the blessed weather preventing Hammond from securing the last 31 runs, for his 3,000 in the year. The Gloucestershire batsman had to contend himself with 2,969.

Hobbs took the winter off from cricket. He had his sports shop to run and family to bring up. England played a Test series in South Africa over the winter followed by new Test kids on the block: West Indies, in England for the 1928 season, courtesy of Warner's great administrative skills and his strong family links with the region. Woolley missed the South African tour, so did Hendren, Larwood and Tate. The largely experimental side consisted of Holmes and Sutcliffe, the Yorkshire openers, Ernest Tyldesley at three and new prospect Walter Hammond at number four.

The series saw England surrender a 2-0 lead after the first two Tests, to finish the series in a 2-2 draw. Tyldesley (520 at 65.00) came top, Sutcliffe (418 at 46.44) second and Hammond third with 321 at 40.13. Hammond also snatched six catches, mostly at slip, and took 15 wickets at 26.60. The composition of the England batting line-up for the start of the summer made for yards of bar talk around the land.

Has Hobbs retired from Tests? If not Hobbs then who? Holmes (302 at 33.55) played some stoic innings for England in South Africa, but had finished on a pair. Sandham and Hallows were both being touted. Would Tyldesley and Hammond come in for Hendren and Woolley? Is it too late for Hampshire's prolific left-hander, Phil Mead? Could Jardine be squeezed in as well as Chapman? There was an extraordinary reservoir of England batting talent building up in the middle order, shielded by Hobbs and Sutcliffe, or Hobbs's successor. This, at least, was the summary of the known England batting talent at the dawn of the 1928 season. Time for a long, hot and dry one, like 1895, the year when the unusually warm Spring sun enabled the Champion, Dr W.G. Grace, to stroke his way to 1,000 runs before the end of May. 1911, another hot, dry summer, helped launch the Test careers of Frank Foster, Jack Hearne, Phil Mead and Johnny Douglas, and enhance the Test careers of Hobbs, Rhodes, Woolley, Gunn and Barnes. An England team fares better after a heatwave summer. With the Ashes in Australia looming at the end of the year, the yearning for fewer curtailed games during the English season, was strong and marked among followers.

1928

1928 became that longed for warm summer, sunshine aplenty to loosen ageing limbs. Hobbs quickly found form and rattled off five centuries for Surrey including 123* against the West Indies, when they possessed an arsenal of dangerous fast bowlers, and 117 versus Northants when he captained an all-professional outfit.

Anecdote time, the scene is Arundel Castle, August 2022, and the fixture unfolding before me involved the Sussex Martinets and Kent's famous Band of Brothers, the modern equivalent of the Gentlemen of Sussex versus the Gentlemen of Kent. The ground itself is a wonderful semi-amphitheatre carved out through the blood, sweat and tears of hundreds of local workers, hired by the then Duke of Norfolk back in Victorian England. Soon I found myself in conversation with local octogenarian Frank O'Gorman about England Cricket history, specifically the fact that it was almost hundred years ago since Hobbs and Sutcliffe first opened together in a first-class fixture. He expressed interest then mentioned in a hushed tone whether I would mind hearing a politically incorrect story involving Jack Hobbs. I told him to proceed. The anecdote is despicable in terms of its obvious undertones to racism yet compelling due to its context in terms of social history. After a long deliberation the anecdote is included under the proviso that it is the author's sincere wishes not to cause offence, but the anecdote adds authenticity to the times. So here goes.

It is the Surrey versus West Indies fixture of 1928. Hobbs (13) failed in the first innings but got off the mark with a deft dab onto the off-side and a stolen single with partner Andrew Sandham. Suddenly the ripple of applause is replaced from a bellowing cockney, complete with tweed cap, dirty scarf and a woodbine stuck to the side of his mouth.

''You'll never ge' 'im 'ow' now!'' bellowed the cockney. Frank O'Gorman's father, a teenager, looked up at the cockney stood not three feet away from him.

Hobbs moved through the gears like a purring Rolls Royce engine and after a little over an hour had posted his half-century.

''You'll never ge' 'im 'ow' now!'' bellowed the cockney, woodbine dangling from his mouth.

Sure enough, Hobbs square cut, cover drove, on-drove, late-cut and glanced his way to a century.

''You'll never ge' 'im 'ow' now!'' bellowed the cockney once again, striking a match to his fag end.

On came Constantine, at the time the fastest in the world or at least the very equal of Larwood. He walked back almost to the sightscreen, turned and ran in with extraordinary gusto before unleashing a terrifying missile that flew past Hobbs's ducking head like a cannon-ball.

Bellowed the very same cockney: ''Now… now… Sambo!''

Meanwhile Sutcliffe's start to the 1928 season had been respectably fruitful for someone with so bloated a Test average. Those with a penchant for cricket statistics were all too aware of Sutcliffe's colossal status in the cricketing world. While Hobbs, the Master, still adorned the game with his grace, Sutcliffe looked more mechanical at the crease, almost robotically effective and the Yorkshireman had scored 1,922 Test runs at the giddy average of 71.18. Of all the other batsmen in history to have scored more Test runs than Sutcliffe, the player with the next highest average, Hobbs of course, had 4,384 Test runs at this stage, at an average of 60.05. The highest average from an Australian, with more Test runs than Sutcliffe, came from Macartney with 2,131 runs at 41.78.

The 1928 season had so far been satisfactory for someone who placed such a high price on his wicket. Among the highlights, Sutcliffe had feasted on the Essex attack with 129 in a partnership of 268 with Percy Holmes (136), enjoyed 81* against Cambridge, scored 140 in the Roses match, 81 against Warwickshire, 73 against Middlesex and 24 against the West Indies. Only once, when Jupp bowled him with an off-break that pitched like an explosive grenade, had Sutcliffe failed to reach double figures as the season approached high summer.

In a three-day fixture starting on June 16th, Lord's became the venue for another Warner representative match between England and the Rest. Hobbs and Sutcliffe duly turned out for England but, fielding first, Hobbs's thigh tear re-surfaced and, following medical opinion, the old timer sat out the rest of the game after tea on the first day. After the Rest had made 307 (Larwood 6/59), Sutcliffe opened with Charlie Hallows and, in the face of Nichols, Macaulay, Staples and Worthington, put on a century partnership.

Sutcliffe (101) and Hallows (55) managed 125 together but Hallows, who many felt would replace Hobbs when the time came, gave away three chances in a timid affair that failed to entertain. Sutcliffe's was a mono-paced and unspectacular occupation that lasted three and a half hours and brought forth but three boundaries in all that time. Tyldesley's carefully constructed 160* received the plaudits, along with Maurice Tate's 58* that took England to 423/6 before Chapman declared. Rain prevented a conclusion although the Rest also relied on Jardine's contribution (48 and 74*); his second innings defied Larwood, Tate, Jupp and Freeman and was duly noted.

Lord's, the obvious venue for welcoming new Test playing nations, saw Chapman win the toss in the first designated Test Match against the West Indies. Chapman elected to bat on a peach of a sunny day in front of a not-quite-capacity crowd of 22,000. Charlie Hallows took the place of Hobbs, the tall, wiry Lancashire opener had played only one previous Test for England, seven years earlier against Armstrong's gang.

When umpire ex- England allrounder Leonard Braund signalled for play to begin, Karl Nunes, the West Indies skipper opened with George Francis and Learie Constantine. Both fast bowlers had toured with the previous West Indies side in 1923 and some pundits had suggested they were as quick as Gregory and MacDonald were in '21. Both possessed fast speeds approaching 90 mph. Francis bowled at the stumps and had proved a thorn in the side of the MCC during the 1925/26 tour. Constantine had a lethal slower ball. Apart from Larwood, the West Indies had the three fastest bowlers on the planet. Francis and Constantine ran to the wicket like 100m sprinters then leapt upwards in their delivery strides with terrific intent, to hell with energy consumption. Neither Sutcliffe nor Hallows looked to be enjoying the initial encounters; struck on the arms and chest the pair of them clung on.

Though the West Indians, especially Learie Constantine, fielded with razor-sharp agility, the catching proved a disaster and Hallows enjoyed two lives. Nunes changed his bowlers with Herman Griffith replacing Francis, pace for more pace, and Cyril Browne for Constantine, medium-paced leg-breaks for pace.

Sutcliffe looked ill at ease, especially with Browne's variations, and Hallows hated those inswingers from Griffith that cramped his style but through grim determination the pair took England to 51 before Hallows fell by the sword, attempting to force the pace in

Constantine's second spell. Sutcliffe laboured to 48 before being drawn into an indiscretion against the returning Francis. As the day wore on so the fast men became spent forces. Tyldesley (122), Hammond (45) and Chapman (50) took England into the second day before being dismissed for 401.

Although Hobbs missed the first Test against the West Indies (thigh strain picked up whilst chasing a ball to the boundary), his absence appeared not to matter as England won by an innings and 58 runs. In Francis, Constantine and Griffith, the West Indies had the pace to terrorise moderate batsmen, especially through their waywardness, but their batsmen played with too much flair and insufficient grit. 'Tich' Freeman, Kent's five-foot four leg-break bowler enjoyed match figures of 6/77, and Vallance Jupp 7/103 as West Indies achieved totals of 177 and 166.

England versus West Indies 2nd Test Old Trafford 1928

The West Indies dug in with greater character at Manchester, where Hobbs returned to the England team with Hallows banished from Test cricket for evermore. The Surrey and England veteran started his game by running out Challenor with a surprisingly agile pick-up and throw-in from mid-on to Elliot, the keeper. Tich Freeman's googlies proved too much for the inexperienced batting line-up and by half way through the last session on day one, the West Indies had been despatched to the pavilion for 206. Hobbs and Sutcliffe faced a potentially torrid last hour against Francis and Constantine but neither were hit, the pitch remained true in bounce, the bowlers' lines lacked consistency so the great pair picked up some easily acquired runs and walked off at the close of play unruffled on 84 for no wicket.

Hobbs (53) failed to add to his score as next day he edged the medium paced leg-break bowler, Browne, to Winston St Hill in the slips. Nevertheless Sutcliffe (54), Hammond (63) and Jardine (83) handed England a first innings lead of 145. Tich Freeman (5 for 39) swept through the same bewildered bunch to hand England another innings victory, this time by 30 runs.

England versus West Indies 3rd Test Oval 1928

Hobbs profited from the sun beating down on that 45-year-old body, warming his joints, and in the interim the 'master batter' fine-tuned his batting repertoire with 560 runs at 93.3 before turning his attention once more to the West Indies, this time on home turf at the Oval.

The West Indies had the luck of the toss and batted first on a breezy day under a predominantly blue sky on the last of the three-day Tests that summer, August 11th 1928. They might not have had much backbone to their batting, but Challenor and Roach performed their jobs as openers with resilience once again and scored freely to reach 91 in the first seventy minutes of the fixture; in doing so the pair set up the prospect of a competitive game. However, Larwood and Tate blasted out six wickets between them to dismantle the West Indies innings, and the Caribbean cricketers had to close on 238 all out.

Chapman held four catches including two dazzling, quick-as-you-like snatches in the slip cordon.

For the last two hours Hobbs and Sutcliffe struck their eleventh century stand and raced to 155 before Sutcliffe fell for 63, 'yorked' by Francis. Hobbs gave no chances, struck especially well on the leg-side and executed one or two commanding drives in reaching 89 not out by the close. To place his innings into proper context, only the day before he had taken 200 not out against Warwickshire so the veteran looked tired by the close.

He dug in on day two but gave two chances, a caught and bowled to Francis went begging on 95, and Nunes the keeper put him down on 99. A shower at 12.20am allowed some respite and Hobbs walked off looking haggard and pale as though he yearned for sleep. Upon resumption at 2.30pm Hobbs flashed his bat recklessly and a couple of edges flew over the slips for four apiece. He did pretty much as he liked to the bowling, running for those stolen singles and outpaced Tyldesley two to one. On 159, Hobbs pulled Francis to short leg where Small held the unlikeliest of chances. To illustrate the value of Hobbs, after his dismissal, Griffith tore through England's middle order to extract Tyldesley (73), Hammond (3), Leyland (0), Hendren (14) and Chapman (5) before a thrilling counter-attack from Tate (54) and Larwood (32) took the score to 438. Another innings victory followed in this one-sided series and Hobbs averaged 106 from his two innings.

The team selected for the 1928/29 Ashes series seemed to involve a look at the first-class averages. Hobbs with 2,542 runs at 82 could not be ignored, second only behind Douglas Jardine's 1,133 runs at 87.15. He had to go despite turning 46 during the series and even though England had so much batting talent. With Woolley's 3,352 runs at 61.03 controversially ignored, the comfort blanket of Hobbs and Sutcliffe at the top of the order allowed the selectors to sleep at night.

No England team in Australia has been so packed with batting talent as those components that made up Chapman's Ashes squad of 1928/29. As if to illustrate the great strength of England's batting resources, let us visit the Oval in mid-September 1928: the Champion County against the Rest. Lancashire enjoyed the privilege of Ernest Macdonald, the former Australian fast bowler, now in his mid-thirties. After Lancashire posted a respectable 296, taking their innings into the second day, Hobbs fairly climbed into the bowling, hooking Macdonald's bouncers as though they were fired from a pop-gun. The capacity crowd looked on in rare awe as Hobbs and Sutcliffe raced to 212 in two hours twenty minutes before Hobbs, appetite for runs suitably quenched, hoisted a catch to long on for 150 extraordinary runs – outstripping his younger partner at a ratio of three to one. As so often, Hobbs paved the pathway for lesser lights to follow. Sutcliffe (136) and Hendren (174) cashed in on the bowlers' sagging confidence to post 603 and allow the Rest to win by an innings.

Chapter Six Thrashing Australia in the 1928/29 Ashes

The 1928/29 Ashes tour would be the sixth and final one for Hobbs as an active cricketer. Once again Hobbs was allowed to bring Ada although Minnie Hendren thought it smacked of favouritism and held the opinion that husbands do not need their wives to score runs.

Nonetheless, Hobbs remained not only England's premier batsman but the greatest in history to date and his selection remained the first name on the team sheet. He had friends developed from the four previous years, his son Jack could run the business and this time, the voyage would be made on the SS Otranto, a vessel built in Barrow during 1925 that weighed 20,000 tonnes and was capable of carrying 1,700 passengers. The sheer size reduced the prospect of seasickness.

Two thousand well-wishers waved the MCC tour party off at Victoria station even though the only cricketers present at Victoria, that morning, were the amateurs: Douglas Jardine, Surrey's prolific, young middle-order batsman with a conspicuous shark-fin nose, and Jack White, the wily 37-year-old Somerset slow left-armer who had previously played just a couple of Tests in the disaster of 1921. The only professionals present were: veteran Phil Mead, bit-part player on the triumphant 1911/12 tour, now embarking on his second tour after the 17-year interlude; Leicestershire's all-round seam bowling workhorse George Geary and Nottinghamshire's Sam Staples, destined to return injured before the Test series started. All of the other members still played out the final fixture of the season: the Champion County versus the Rest. Lancashire had Ernest Tyldesley and wicket-keeper George Duckworth, while the Rest had Hobbs, Sutcliffe, Hammond, Leyland, Hendren, skipper Chapman, Ames, Tate and Freeman.

Frankly, the Lancashire versus the rest fixture at the Oval – the final curtain of the gloriously dry summer of 1928 – could not have gone better for several of England's top guns, ten of whom were on the tour party, Woolley the only one not to be.

Lancashire's Ernest Tyldesley scored 45 and 63 against Tate, Larwood, Freeman and Hammond. Charlie Hallows (95 and 17) reached his 3,000 runs for the season but England had no need for a reserve opener. For the Rest, Hobbs and Sutcliffe put on 221 before Hobbs fell for a glorious 150; Sutcliffe at this stage had 54. Though Woolley (22), Hammond (9) and Leyland (29) played only cameos, Hendren took Lancashire's attack to the cleaners. Sutcliffe (139) played every shot in the book over the course of four and a half hours but he was upstaged by a frenzy of spectacular hooking and driving from Hendren who thrashed 174. With Leslie Ames (58*) the pair put on 60 in three overs. Ernie McDonald, one of Armstrong's spearheads from 1921, had been pulverised; his 30 overs cost 183 for the scalps of Hammond and Chapman. The Rest won by an innings and 91 runs.

While England's batting department looked to be the strongest of all-time, the bowlers also took key wickets as the match figures reveal: Larwood 5/100; Tate 4/94; Freeman 6/177; Hammond 5/78.

After the game, they all high-tailed it by train to London, then across to Dover, over the Straits of Dover in a ferry, aboard a train in Calais that eventually transported them to Toulon, whereupon they picked up the Otranto.

The five-week voyage went uneventfully, but joyfully. Chapman could be seen in the ship's smoking lounge from mid-afternoon chatting amicably with Sir Frederick Toone, the fascist Yorkshire Secretary and - third Ashes tour in succession - England Manager. Toone never played first-class cricket but did represent Leicester at rugby union, back in the 1890s. A superb organiser, a details man, profound racist and highly regarded ambassador for the MCC abroad, Toone made white friends everywhere.

They guffawed with laughter, Chapman laughing from his socks up, face flushed red as though the pair shared some outrageous joke. Every afternoon after the Suez Canal, Chapman and Toone interviewed each member of the party, to cover expectations, targets and to understand what made them tick.

Let us imagine what the conversation might have been.

''Watch out for that Hammond fellow, dark horse you know'' muttered Chapman to Toone.

''Really?'' replied Toone, bushy eyebrows raised as though pointing to a pyramid.

''Eye for the ladies'', winked Chapman, striations of laugh lines flanking both eyes with mischievous gain.

''Oooooh'' mused Toone.

''Got clapped in the West Indies'' winked Chapman in hushed tones. ''Put it about a bit with the daughters and wives of dignitaries on Plum's recent tour and it took the whole of the 1926 season away from him, as he recovered from some grim form of VD''.

''Thought that was due to a mosquito bite?'' retorted Toone.

"Yes" smiled back Chapman, "that's the official line anyway".

A knock at the door of Toone's stately cabin and in came a broad shouldered 25-year-old athlete looking in his physical prime though with a facial complexion older than his years and with sunken eyes, residue features from the mercury treatment involved in removing the venereal disease. It was Walter Hammond, the Gloucestershire all-rounder, making his first Ashes tour after a steady first year in Test cricket.

Toone held a newspaper cutting from the Daily Telegraph with the 1928 First-class averages. Hammond had scored 2,825 runs at 65.69 and captured 84 wickets at 23.10.

"I hear you are to be married to Dorothy next summer, is that correct?" asked Toone.

"Yes Mr Toone," replied Hammond.

Chapman cut to the chase.

"I see you as batting in the top four and being our third or fourth seamer".

''Very good Mr Chapman'', replied Hammond, displaying those similar soldier-like qualities of servitude and subordination as his father must have done, serving and dying in the Great War.

Toone took notes and Chapman interviewed each and every member. The batting line-up looked, on paper, as solid as the Rock of Gibraltar but there was a sense that the bowling line-up in comparison placed a hefty reliance on Tate's reputation, Larwood's speed, and Freeman or White in an otherwise unheralded spin department. Geary and Hammond augmented the seam department and Staples could contain effectively with his patient off-spin.

Wisden Editor: S.J. Southerton attended the tour and reported, from start to finish, the most smoothly run tour. Time and again, Toone's schedule held firm. Five full weeks of voyage gave the MCC Tour Party of 1928/29, time to gel. Ada Hobbs provided all the companionship Jack desired. Ada liked to wear bob-hats, her favourite on the voyage out was the white hat with pink laced bow. She always wore skirts or dresses and she always sat to Jack's left at the meal table, a deeply contented couple. For their age, mid-40s, it is not hard to imagine that over the course of the voyage they may have copulated half a dozen times.

SS Otranto

Larwood spent much of his time sun-bathing, resting up, wearing a cheap pair of shades and admiring the opposite sex. He told management he needed to recover from the arduous season. Allowing his aches and pains time to dissipate seemed sensible to Chapman. Kent's wicket-keeper batsman, 22-year-old Leslie Ames, youngest member of the party, looked wide-eyed and bushy-tailed, soaking up life as an international cricketer, and he loved informing anyone within ear shot that Wally (Hammond) ''liked a good shag'' and Herbert ''could always be found near beautiful women''.

The average age of the 17 England cricketers equalled 34 and Hobbs (46), Mead (41), Freeman (41), Hendren (40) and Tyldesley (40) would all return honorary members of the Forty Club.

Undoubtedly, the late 1920s became the era of the middle-aged cricketer. Think about the reasons for a while. A complete lack of first-class cricket from August 1914 to April 1919 stifled the progress of emerging cricket talent. The public schools still played a full fixture list and it was possible to play competitive club cricket up North in the Yorkshire league, brushing shoulders with the likes of Hobbs, Hendren and Barnes. Like vintage motorcars locked away in a dry barn going nowhere for five years, the engines of normal 40-year-olds benefitted from the rest – less mileage on the clock than one might assume given the anno domini.

On landing at Perth, Hobbs looked pale, as though seasickness had been a daily endurance throughout the whole voyage. Hammond and Sutcliffe wore designer sunglasses as they trotted down the gangway, Leyland and Ames smiled into the middle-distance. Chapman wore a blazer and Panama as he strode off the vessel with a hearty swagger and a good couple of stone heavier than the slimline athlete of 1924/25. A docker shouted out a wager on the Ashes and Chapman took him up on the offer, for 'a quid'.

Toone had already heralded taxis to the hotel and there was a *Welcome to Western Australia* banner up above the porch. One taxi driver told Mead he remembered picking up his father back in 1911 from the exact same spot. Also sat on the same back seat Jardine felt the presence of thousands of flies and appeared infuriated by them. They seemed to hone in especially on Jardine, singling out for special treatment the sweat globules now pouring from the upper-class gentleman's forehead. Mead informed the driver that, yes, he was indeed the very same fellow and, remembering he offered the cab driver a cigarette 17 years earlier, handed him one after which Mead sat heavily back in his seat and lit himself one for good measure.

''For heaven's sake blow that smoke into my face'' pleaded Jardine, ''anything to deter these FUCKING FLIES'.'

The taxi driver who drove Jack, Ada and Herbert spoke a lot of bullshit about how he was the bastard son of Ernie Jones, the fastest Australian bowler W.G. ever faced. Born in 1896 on the very day his father bowled a bouncer that tore through the Champion's beard, Ritchie Jones was allegedly the love child of Ernie, in his bull-prime, and a carpenter's daughter.

Hammond, Leyland and Ames stared at all the fit young women, drinking in the images, chirpy and excited at the prospects.

Staples had pulled a back muscle badly, he spent most of the voyage lying in agony and his mobility had become a serious issue. The sudden decimation in the spin department would place more burden on the seamers, and especially the two remaining spinners: Freeman, who took a minor savaging last time round, and J.C. White, an ageing Somerset slow left-armer with rosy red cheeks who oozed the rural outdoor stereotype of a Somerset farmer. This theme dominated the conversation in the seamer's taxi, as big, wise Maurice Tate voiced the opinion that a lot more would have to come from George and Harold over the next few weeks. The only back-up was Wally. Larwood listened with furrowed brow. George had to stay fit this time. The elephant in that taxi was the injury to George mid-series against South Africa over the previous winter. Geary had taken 12/130 in the first Test, helping England to a 10-wicket win. He broke down after playing only a minor part during the second Test, that England also won. His absence for the last three Tests proved a major factor in reversing 2-0 to 2-2. England needed Geary to stay fit this time, otherwise the burden on Larwood and Tate would be immense. Larwood frowned the most; he knew that Tate had not yet fully recovered from his highly publicised arm injury towards the end of the season just gone. That left Larwood with injury prone George, *coming back soon from injury* Maurice, and the *I don't really feel like bowling* Wally.

At the hotel Chapman ordered a bottle of whisky at the bar and insisted on the tour party drinking a toast to the successful outcome in the Ashes. Sir Frederick Toone thought it a good idea. ''Best give the buggers the leadership they want'' he winked.

Shorn of his marital obligations to Ethel, 'Tich' enjoyed his down-in-one toast so much, he developed a taste for it. A second bottle surfaced not long after, held in the hand of a stunning young lady in a low-cut top. She filled Freeman's glass while answering Wally's brash question on whether she was married. Before long Freeman had swallowed more alcohol than he would normally consume in an entire season of domestic cricket. Just about everything and everybody was funny to him. He told Percy Chapman how much he loved him, laughed to a howling decibel when Ames inform him how Wally liked to shag the ladies and left the premises in a rare state, arms around Leyland and Hendren for support.

That night Freeman's head fell out of his bed. When he awoke in the morning it was unusually difficult to open his eyes. An intense throbbing pain to the head arrived followed by an altogether different magnitude event as Freeman tried to move his head. He reported late to breakfast and informed Chapman of his stiff neck and inability to rotate it.

Western Australia played precious little first-class cricket at a time when only New South Wales, Queensland and South Australia competed in the Sheffield Shield. Nonetheless, Western Australia's young talent had been sent off to New South Wales to receive a thorough coaching on the basics and they had successfully completed some decent signings, including the tall and imposing fast bowler Reggie Halcombe while Arthur Richardson, a 1926 tourist under Herbie Collins, had become player-coach.

England had just the one net session during which Freeman struggled to bowl the ball straight and his first delivery bounced four times before reaching the side netting. He soon slithered off with left hand holding the left side of his neck as upright as possible. Staples received a diagnosis of febritis, Hobbs looked shorn of timing, Larwood bowled on one cylinder, presumably to keep his powder dry for the long tour ahead, and Tate bowled accurately but very much within himself.

Chapman omitted Hobbs, Larwood, Freeman, Duckworth, Staples and Tate for the game against Western Australia. Before the start, the players assembled for the photograph below.

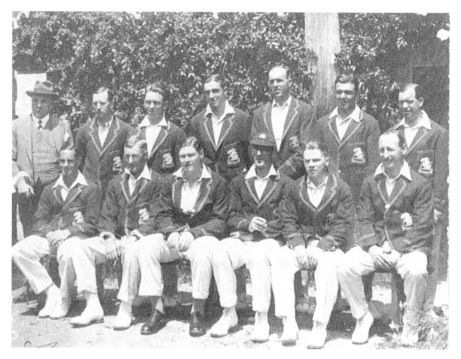

Standing: Major Toone, E. Tyldesley, Leyland, Hammond, Geary, Ames, Hendren.

Seated: Sutcliffe, White, Chapman, Jardine (smoking), Duckworth, Mead.

Sutcliffe made 28 before playing down the wrong line to Halcombe, Tyldesley stroked an immaculate 66, Jardine an off-side dominated 109 and Hendren a couple of sixes in a hard-hitting 90. England totalled 406.

Western Australia replied with 257 during the course of which the heavens opened and, despite Chapman's pleas, the umpires insisted on the match continuing until the rain intensified into a torrential cloudburst.

''How the hell will our clothes dry in our suit-cases on a three-day train journey to South Australia?'' queried Jardine, with more than an expression of disbelief.

With nothing to play for except general practice, the Englishmen went in again with Chapman promoting George Geary as a makeshift opener with Leyland. This proved a mistake since Halcombe bent his back and sent forth a viscous lifter that struck Geary a painful blow to his head. Big George had to visit a hospital that evening and the blow put him out of action for a month.

The immensely tiring and uninspiring three-day train trip from Perth to Adelaide allowed just 48 hours of much needed practice before being exposed to the strongest State bowling attack in Australia. At least that is what spectators were overheard saying. South Australia had the services of J.D. Scott, the fastest but most erratic bowler on the Australasian continent. Opening with him was the 24-year-old fast bowling prospect born with the name Thomas Wall, but he enjoyed being called 'Tim'. Wall had risen to the attention of the

Australian selectors with nine wickets at 22.7 in his first and only two Sheffield Shield games at the end of the previous season. He bowled with a high arm and kicked off like an angry colt in his delivery stride. Whitfield ensured a supply of accurate military-medium, Williams bowled useful leg-breaks and googlies and so, too, did the world's number one spinner Clarrie Grimmett, also an exponent of accurate leg-breaks and googlies.

Chapman established a broad church to his selection policy. He set up a tour party Selection Committee including professionals Jack Hobbs and Ernest Tyldesley, while also including fellow amateurs Jack White and Douglas Jardine. Jardine's century in the Western Australian game already established his credentials, and Hendren's 90 came from a man already in form. Their positions in the top six for the Test more or less secured, the selectors picked the remaining contenders to battle it out amongst themselves. The team against South Australia still had the trunk of a strong batting line-up. The top five of Hobbs, Sutcliffe, Tyldesley, Hammond and Mead would all complete their careers with over a hundred first-class hundreds to their names; following this, Leyland would finish his career with a

Test batting average of 46 and Chapman, in his great moments, could exceed the strike rates of all the others and change the course of a game in an hour.

The bowling relied upon Larwood and Hammond as seamers, Freeman's leg-breaks, White's slow left-arm, and Leyland's less accurate slow left-arm. England were obviously a seamer light but the South Australian tail began with Grimmett at seven.

For the 1928/29 season, while the Tests were to be played out in six ball overs, state cricket - including England State games - were to be played in eight ball overs.

The pitch at Adelaide played out as a featherbed. There was no malice in the turf whatsoever. The bounce was slow, and low. Chapman won the toss and Hobbs and Sutcliffe batted through to the over before lunch. Hobbs, while not exactly mishitting the ball, had yet to find his golden touch of yore. He reached 26 in largely unfazed manner, robbing singles as was his want, but Sutcliffe out-scored the master batsman by two to one, and went into lunch 52* while Hobbs got himself bowled by moving too far to the off while attempting to steer Scott's full-length ball to fine-leg.

After lunch Tyldesley (8) groped at Grimmett and looked uncomfortable. The Lancastrian delicately cut Grimmett for two through gully but got snaffled next ball, caught at the wicket. Out came Hammond, bristling with intent, skin like worn leather, wide and handsome, like a galleon in full sail, a young Emperor. Out of his trousers he had a blue handkerchief, neatly folded.

After Sutcliffe (76) came the pear-shaped left-hander Mead, Hampshire's most prolific batsman of all time. Mead looked scratchy. At the start of his innings, he usually did. Difficult to dismiss, Mead had the solidity of a mature oak while never thrilling the spectator with fireworks; one of those where the spectator glances at the scoreboard, sees Mead on 30 and wonders where the hell those runs had come from.

Perhaps it was that Mead appeared laboured compared to the most brilliant swordsman of his day: the gladiator Hammond. Folk had heard the reputation of some brilliant new cricketer who batted with panache, caught pigeons in the slips, ran like Hendren in the outfield and could, when sufficiently provoked, bowl with genuine pace.

Sutcliffe unstrapped himself from his gear, showered, changed his shirt and prepared to sit out the day watching the rest of the innings. He had outscored Jack two to one and felt in good order. When he sat next to Jack on the Adelaide pavilion balcony Mead and Hammond had settled in. Mead played a couple of cracking cover drives in amongst all that twisting and fiddling ritual he went through before facing every ball. Broad of rump, narrow of eye, sloping shoulders, in the squad in place of Woolley, Mead needed to lay down a marker.

Hammond spread the majesty of his wings, like a great eagle new on the scene, he clipped Scott off his hip and danced down to Grimmett, treating his bowling like cannon fodder. Off Wall he cracked a cover drive so splendidly it bounced back some forty yards into the arena. At 293/4 after the first day, with Hammond sleeping on an undefeated century, and 58 from Mead following Sutcliffe's 78 - England were in a strong position.

Next morning Hammond (145) smote a six off Grimmett wide of mid-on, head height that whistled over the very long boundary without any evidence of exertion in the shot save for the pace the ball travelled. Chapman caught the mood eclipsing even Hammond's performance in a display of cavalier abandon, festooned with aerial swipes into the deep country. Chapman's own 145 came at more than a run a minute. England reached 528 but South Australia came within four of that, raising the question over the quality of England's bowlers when deprived of Tate's services. Freeman took five wickets but they cost 180 runs, White 3/103.

When England batted again there was nothing in the game; the result was bound to be a draw. Nonetheless all cricketers played for their pride and professionalism. Hobbs (64) and Sutcliffe (70) put on 131 in 75 minutes. Both looked at ease. Leyland (114) nudged the selectors, so did Mead (58*). England finished on 341/4; only Tyldesley (21) failed, appearing too anxious to succeed.

The squad took the overnight train to Melbourne for the Victoria game. The cricketers had overnight cabins with bunk beds. Professionals shared up to eight per room, Jack and Ada in another, Toone in a single, Gentlemen all in singles, everything going tickety-boo. Post cards were written ready to be sent, bridge played, crosswords attempted, books read then the rhythmic sounds of train-on-track cast deep sleep all around.

The game began in murky Melbourne conditions. Victoria batted first, a couple of showers came and went with the groundsmen failing hysterically to put the covers either in place or on time, looking like fools when gusts blew the tarpaulins around, and attracting derision from the disappointed crowd. The breaks in play allowed Larwood time to recover properly from spell to spell and as a consequence the Nottinghamshire spearhead ripped through the batting to claim 7/51. Woodfull (67*) carried his bat but Larwood took out numbers two to eight, including Ponsford, Hendry and Ryder. Tate returned with a respectable 1/45 from 19 overs.

Sutcliffe and Hammond were considered dead certs for the first Test so both were rested for this game. Monte Noble was quite scathing of Jack's 51 He wrote:

Hobbs gave an indifferent display for 51. He was in for more than two hours. Before he was stumped off Hartkopf he was twice badly missed. On each occasion he ran out to Ironmonger and skied the ball. The first came easily to Scaife's hands and was dropped;

Hendry was in time to attain position for the next, which dribbled through his hands. Shocking fielding – but equally shocking strokes. They were not those of the master batsman who seemed after his first fault to be indifferent to his fate.'

Jardine (104) spent over four hours at the wicket. A terribly correct batsman with the straightest of blades, Jardine obeyed orthodox laws to the letter. England's eventual 486 included the ever-popular Patsy Hendren (100) scoring his hundredth hundred in first-class cricket, before perishing in what looked a deliberate run out to give someone else a chance.

Chapman (71) handed out another swashbuckling assault and Larwood (79) displayed several fine drives in front of the wicket. Rain affected the result but Victoria, 322 behind on first innings, reached 135 for no wicket before the game ended. Australian judges reckoned England's bowling looked if not innocuous then certainly threadbare once Tate and Larwood were through their spells.

The team travelled up to Sydney by train and the six-day interval between games helped niggles die back. Becoming more accustomed to the stronger light it looked as though the England batting line-up may become a legendary one. So many inform batsmen, so few places. Hobbs missed the game against New South Wales, preferring to net his way back into form. Sutcliffe (67) showed his usual qualities of cautiousness and watchfulness but appeared 'not so safe or impressive as usual … short of a gallop' according to Noble.

Charlie Kelleway, now 39 and one of the stars in the 1912 Triangular Tournament, actually beat Sutcliffe for pace. Normally a little above medium and no more, Kelleway hurled one down with surprising pace that cannoned into Sutcliffe's pads and on to his wickets. Tyldesley fell later in the over and Hammond was all but dead meat with one that whistled past his off stump.

Jardine (140) scored his third century in consecutive innings, a new record, while absorbing the best that Kelleway and Gregory could fire at him. After Jardine departed the action, Wally Hammond demonstrated another Apollo-like performance at the crease. His driving along the ground smacked of peerless power and Hammond cut with precision. The Gloucestershire right-hander struck 30 fours and a meaty six over extra cover in a monster knock worth 225 in a little under five and a half hours. Half a dozen boundaries were glanced to fine leg. Hendren (167) enjoyed himself like a schoolboy robber in a sweet shop, filling his pockets when the old lady isn't looking. He drove, pulled and cut with conspicuous authority and was certainly not going to be outshone by Prince Wally.

Hammond and Hendren put on over 300, doing as they pleased. New South Wales skipper, Alan Kippax, brought a 20-year-old called Bradman on to bowl. Bradman bowled innocuous teasers in order to buy a wicket. Hendren's eyes lit up and he thundered a four past Bradman's outstretched hand first ball, almost yorked himself second, stroked the third into the ladies stand at long on for six, stroked the fourth into the ladies stand for six, then died on the fifth, trying to repeat the stroke, but being held several yards in from the ropes. With Leyland (47*) also looking good and young Ames (25) playing attractively the score mounted to 734/7 when Chapman declared. The run rate was 3.3 per over, when adjusted to the equivalent of six ball overs. Gregory, who ran in like a great shire horse, delivered 29 eight ball overs and went wicketless for 130. Kelleway, who started so promisingly, bowled 37 overs 2/140.

Kelleway made amends by top-scoring with 93* in the New South Wales first innings. Bradman (87) crisply announced himself and Kippax (64) helped the score to 349, 'Tich' Freeman clean bowled Bradman and took 5/136. Tate (3/98) and Hammond (2/64) collected the rest. Second time around New South Wales reached 364/3. Ominously for England, the last chapter of the game saw Kippax (136*) and Bradman (132*) indulge in an undefeated 249 run partnership. It may have ended with joke bowling from Hendren, Jardine and Sutcliffe, but the partnership began with New South Wales staring at an innings defeat.

Two rest days followed with the team remaining in Sydney giving a chance to see the sights. Leyland, Freeman, Duckworth and Ames took a cab to King's Cross and spent the evening goggle-eyed at the streets of women standing around in short dresses smoking. Down the backstreets sat the down-and-outs supping sherry. What went on tour, stayed on tour.

Duckworth and Ames had struck up a life-long friendship on the boat over, during the course of which they agreed that, whoever was not selected as wicket-keeper for the Tests, would help the incumbent in any way they could. The choice for the Selection Committee boiled down to the age-old conundrum: batting skills or keeping ability. Ames had the makings of a fine batsman and knew how to keep wicket to Freeman. Duckworth flung himself further and took miraculous catches, but had the batting average of a number eleven.

Once all returned from their various activities over what essentially became a 36-hour pass, the whole squad returned for a team meeting prior to the fixture at Sydney against an Australian XI.

Because the game had been moved to Sydney, it was up to the Sydney selectors to pick the team. This was supposed to be a chance for the National Selectors to fine tune their choices. Noble expressed strong disapproval at the omission of Oxenham. Are they preserving him in brown paper? No Victorian was selected, winding up the Victorians. Ponsford, Ryder and Hendry were unavailable. Woodfull and Grimmett nursed niggles so were rested.

Chapman rested himself and stood Hammond, Leyland, Freeman and Ames down. J.C. White captained the team and lost the toss to Victor Richardson, grandfather to the Chappell brothers. Though it was cloudy, the light looked good, the pitch firm and full of runs. Despite this, the Australian XI faced a tight quartet of Tate, Larwood, White and Geary. Every time it looked as though England needed a wicket to remain on top, they got one. The Australian XI made 231 but left Bradman (58*) stranded having entered at five.

Hobbs and Sutcliffe reached 20 without loss before the close of play. On the second morning the great pair received hearty applause from the Sydney faithful and Hobbs played with consummate ease. Defence impregnable, he scored runs from fine leg round to third man. Sutcliffe by contrast looked off colour yet they still compiled a stand of 93 before Hobbs (58) fell LBW to fast bowler Scott, and Nothling caused Sutcliffe (42) to edge behind. Jardine (6) failed for once but Mead (58) and Tyldesley (69) rescued the situation. On the third day Tate (59) and Geary (33) helped stretch the lead to 126.

Tate removed young guns Archie Jackson (61) and Don Bradman (18) and the Australian XI set England 118 to win. Hobbs (67*) and Sutcliffe (31) put on 80 and though Jardine (13) fell for a second low score, England won by eight wickets with Wisden recording that Hobbs batted 'in delightful fashion'.

The itinerary had some common sense attached to it. From Perth to South Australia to Victoria, to New South Wales and now up to Queensland, first for a game against the newest elected state in the Sheffield Shield, followed by the first Test on the same ground. Though in Brisbane, the ground was the Exhibition Ground, not the Gabba.

England powered to an innings victory. Queensland collapsed to 116 all out on a rain affected track, much to Freeman (5/51) and White's (4/26) delight. Hobbs and Sutcliffe responded with a stand of 62 during which the Brisbane crowd excitedly cheered the stolen singles they had heard so much about. Hobbs (30) recklessly gifted his wicket slashing outside the off-stump but then Northling, the rugby union player and medium pacer, removed Sutcliffe (34), Hammond (0), Tyldesley (8), Chapman (35) and Ames (10) and then, in between time, Mead (1) got himself run out. Thankfully, Leyland (114), Geary (32*) and Freeman (17) helped build a first innings lead of 177.

Geary (5/47), White (2/45) and Freeman (2/47) ensured an innings and 10 run victory by removing Queensland (160) without the need to bat again. All was therefore set up for the first Test on the same ground, three days later, November 30th 1928.

So there the Selection Committee sat. Chapman with whisky, tobacco filling the air on the balcony of his hotel suite overlooking Brisbane, a pleasant sea breeze wafting it away before the wretched fumes made J.C. White's eyes redden. Ernest Tyldesley had already approached Chapman with his request to step down from consideration for the first Test, his form not so productive as those of Mead and Leyland. Given that skipper Chapman was left-handed and the dead certs for selection: Hobbs, Sutcliffe, Hammond, Hendren and Jardine were right-handers, the consideration to pick another left-hander, purely to spoil the field settings and bowlers' lines, looked valid.

Chapman, Jardine, White, Hobbs and Tyldesley opted for Mead, who had no pretensions as a bowler, ahead of the youthful Leyland who enjoyed administering left arm chinamen; perhaps this was due to Leyland's inability to take more than one first class wicket for 180 runs so far on tour. Hobbs liked the barrier of Mead coming in at three, an immoveable object and the only other member of the

1928/29 squad who also played in the victorious 1911/12 side. Mead had stood up heroically to Gregory and Macdonald at the fag-end of the 1921 series. If anybody beyond Hobbs and Sutcliffe could blunt Gregory, it was Phil Mead, another already in the hundred hundreds club.

Duckworth received the vote for wicket-keeper; the Lancastrian deserved the spot for his extraordinary diving abilities, especially to his left side. Duckworth did not leap with feline grace but he dived to where he needed to get often enough, and despite the shirt hanging out, and sunhat fallen by the wayside, Duckworth caught and stopped the ball at distances few others, even Ames, could reach. The Tests were to be timeless and comprising six ball overs, the shorter overs thought to be fairer to the bowlers on what were likely to be over-prepared pitches.

Much debate centred on whether to select just three bowlers plus Hammond, or four bowlers plus Hammond. In the end, the committee took the massive gamble of going in with Tate, Larwood, White and Hammond.

Geary, Ames, Freeman and Leyland all had cause for feeling distraught at missing out. Geary could bat and had just taken a five-wicket haul in the last game. Ames kept tidily to Freeman, his Kent colleague, and shown some prowess with the bat. Freeman had come off the back of 304 first class wickets in the 1928 season - an all-time record (still is) - and had bowled at least as accurately as White. Leyland had scored two centuries and in six dismissals so far on tour averaged 60.2.

It rained a lot in the 48 hours before the Exhibition Ground's first and, in fact, only Ashes Test; 50 mm fell in a twenty-minute deluge. On the morning of the match, the pitch looked well grassed with durable binding qualities. Both the infield and outfield were a lush green, superbly carpeted in Indian couch grass.

No representative of Queensland was selected for Australia. Jack Ryder, the tall and slender Victorian batsman who scored a double century against England on Gilligan's tour, was now the Australian Captain. Gone were Bardsley, Macartney, Collins and Mailey. In at number seven, making his Test debut, was the 20-year-old Donald Bradman from Bowral, New South Wales; the other debutant was

Herbert Ironmonger, a left-arm medium paced bowler, who carried some surplus flesh and could not run too quickly because he was a couple of months short of his forty sixth birthday; however, 'Dainty' was a bowler of international standard and a batsman about as good as you or I.

Australia versus England 1st Test Brisbane 1928/29

Chapman won the toss and elected to bat. He gesticulated to the team with his right hand from out in the middle, a flowing cover drive. Hobbs and Sutcliffe, both fresh from some throwdowns, gathered their box, pads, gloves and caps. Sutcliffe had applied suncream around face, ears and neck and let the comb place the surplus through his hair. He hit a cricket ball repeatedly upwards a hundred times before stopping. The umpires and Australians ventured on to the turf amidst polite clapping, followed by the famous England pair who strode off towards the middle with an enthusiastic ripple of applause from the discerning section of the crowd. From an Australian point of view so much depended on the fitness of Jack Gregory.

Act one: Gregory versus Hobbs. Ryder includes a deep fine leg and a forward short leg to cut off the famous pair's tip-and-run tactics. Gregory pounds up to the wicket like a galloping stallion, full of endeavour, already exuding the intense expression of competition. The experienced warhead who emerged during the 1919 Australian Imperial Forces team, peaked during Armstrong's tour of 1921, and had been a constant threat ever since, looked faster than for several years. Fourth ball he dropped short and Hobbs hooked him smoothly for four.

Though Gregory delivered fire and brimstone, Hobbs absorbed it and from the other end, Charlie Kelleway seemed to play both openers in. Runs came and Ryder introduced Ironmonger, and brought Woodfull into forward short point to stem the flow of singles. Grimmett made it four bowlers in the first session and with the score already 85/0, Ryder chucked the ball to Gregory for a final fling before lunch. He bowled a long hop that Sutcliffe top edged down to fine leg for Ponsford to rush round and catch, just on the stroke of lunch too.

Shortly after the interval, Mead cut Grimmett nicely through the covers for an easy couple or three at a stretch. Hobbs ran a second run slowly and young Bradman hurled the ball in firm and flat to Oldfield who, seeing Hobbs dawdling along towards the non-striker's end, threw the ball at the umpire's stumps and ran the master batsman out for 49. On no previous occasion in his other 76 Test innings had Hobbs been run out.

When Mead (8) fell LBW playing back to Grimmett, England were in trouble at 108/3. Digging them out, Jardine (35) and Hammond (44) put on 53. Fortunate not to have been stumped by Oldfield - the ball got lodged in the wicket-keeper's pad – Hammond lacked the aggression required to take the game by the scruff of the neck. At 217/5, the advantage of winning the toss looked to be slipping away but that was when the imposing, six-foot three-inch left-hander Chapman joined the five-foot seven right-hander Hendren - their only similarity, the caps on their heads. Ryder had already tried fourteen different bowling permutations. He loved giving them shorter spells so batsmen could never settle. Hendren and Chapman survived to the close of play when they successfully appealed against the light. At 272/5, the day delivered shared bragging rights.

On the second morning Hendren stole the honours. He cut, drove and hooked with relish. Chapman (50) lived dangerously, Tate (26) dominated for a while but it was Hendren's stand with Larwood (70), yielding 124 for the eighth wicket, that swung the pendulum England's way. Larwood cracked Gregory for four through point with a magnificent square cut that came off the bat like the sudden snap of an ageing plank. Then he danced down the wicket to Grimmett and slogged the wiry leg-spinner back over his head. All the while, stout 'Patsy' Hendren stood firm at the other end, disdainful of any width, pragmatic in defence, outstanding nous on shot selection and, aside from Hobbs and Sutcliffe's legendary knocks, the cheerful cockney executed the finest attacking innings by an Englishman since the War. The stand of 52 with White (14) for the ninth wicket took the total close to 500 and when Hendren (169) at last fell, caught long on, England had recovered to post a formidable 521.

Before the close of day two, Australia had sunk to 44/4. Larwood blasted out three top order wickets for nine, and if not mortally wounded, Australia had suffered a terrible day at the office. First there was the huge rearguard action delivered by Hendren and the England tail, then the short, sharp, shock from Larwood's machine gun. Chapman's catch at fine gully to dismiss Woodfull for nought and start the rot, flashed faster than the eye could travel and was taken at the furthest point his leap and outstretched hand could achieve. No one else on either side could have caught it. Terrified, Hendry and Ryder appealed against the bad light and, while the sun still shone with not a cloud in the sky, Umpires D. Elder and G.A. Hele upheld their decision with Chapman, face flushed in disbelief, walking off wide-eyed and eye-brows raised. Several of his team members followed suit in unity but deep down, the day had unravelled astonishingly well for England.

As they all sat down to a beer in the dressing-room, the England players could not quite believe their luck. Larwood got his back patted countless times throughout the day. A broad beam had remained in place since midday on Hendren's face. Everyone had a buzz of joy around them. There was a loud knock at the door.

In came big Jack Gregory, Australia's talisman since the War. He looked quite serious and silence descended.

''That's it guys, it's all over for me'' said Jack Gregory, tears welling up in his eyes. The gifted all-rounder had damaged his knee cartilage so badly, his career finished with a shuddering halt. The injury flared up during the Hendren-Larwood stand earlier in the day. Larwood bit his lip to stop himself giggling but for all the hard luck comments, 'sorry to hear that' phrases, there was genuine sorrow for a good man and a great entertainer. When Kelleway reported ill at the start of day three, unable to take the field again in the game, that left the Australians without their new ball attack.

On the third day, Hendry (30) and Ryder (33) played some 'sparklingly' good shots but Larwood (6/32) and Tate (3/50) shot the rest out for 122. With a first-innings deficit of 399, it may have been sporting to put the opponents in again to see if England could win by an innings. Monte Noble wanted England to enforce the follow-on. Yet the Tests were all timeless. What was the hurry? Larwood and

Tate put their feet up. England batted again and Noble roared his disapproval.

A storm was headed to Brisbane later that day so England batted and reached 105/2 before the rain came. Hobbs and Sutcliffe ran along to 25 in fifteen minutes before Hobbs (11) fell lbw trapped on the back foot by Grimmett. Sutcliffe (31) became the other casualty, lofting Ironmonger to the substitute Oxenham. The pitch looked good for a thousand more runs at the start of day four, and England plodded along at between two and three an over, killing off the game, relishing the job of wearing the Australian bowlers into the dust. Mead (72) bored the pants off everybody, Jardine (65*) looked stylish, Hendren (45) hurt a lady's hand in the seventh tier of the Grand Stand with one six, struck another and played to thrill and Larwood (37) threw the bat to fine effect once again, enabling Chapman to declare an hour before the close setting Australia the small matter of 742.

Out strode Bills Woodfull and Ponsford. Lest it not be forgot: Ponsford possessed the batting statistics of a heavy-weight run-machine. No one in first-class cricket had scored two quadruple centuries save for Ponsford. He made 429 against Tasmania to nail down his marker in 1922/23, creating a new world record score, then bettered this with 437 against Queensland in 1927/28.

In the event Larwood once more removed Ponsford; in the first innings the former miner had bowled the sturdy Victorian for two. Starting his second innings in the twilight of day four, Larwood bounced him on off stump causing the prolific flat-track bully to flinch and glove the missile to Duckworth behind, this time for six. To consign Australia's chances to the dustbin, it rained so much overnight that play could not begin until after lunch. The strong sun dried the pitch into a 'sticky dog' where the odd one kicked up from a length and the Australian batsmen crumbled to 66 all out. White achieved 4/7, polishing off the tail, Larwood and Tate two apiece and neither Gregory nor Kelleway fancied batting so England won the first Test by the colossal and still unsurpassed total of 675 runs.

By thunder the Australian batting received plenty of negative criticism, so too the selection policies. Only Bill Woodfull, carrying his bat for 30* in the second innings, could hold his head up high.

Simply put: Woodfull aside, the Australians appeared to capitulate like lambs to the slaughter. Where was the stomach for a fight?

England had all the luck, no question. They won the toss, batted first and the rain came to kill off the Australians quickly on the fifth morning, thus rewarding the highly risky strategy of picking only three specialist bowlers. Two Australian bowlers broke down with injury or illness. Yet the selection lacked foresight and relied too much on experience; only Bradman of the young was picked and he failed (18 and 1). All the headaches had their place at the table of the Australian Selection Committee while the England tour party headed to Warwick, upcountry, to play a jolly against a Combined Country XI composed of the best club cricketers in the region with one or two (like McCoombe) fringe players in the Sheffield Shield.

Chapman, Larwood, White, Hendren and Mead were rested with Tyldesley, Geary, Ames, Leyland and Freeman taking their places. The appointment of Douglas Jardine as captain raised some eye-brows, his imperialistic accent coupled with that Harlequins' cap highlighted the perception that Jardine looked down his long, thin and angular nose at Australians. Jardine had a deep-seated dislike of

Australians, especially their cricketers. The seed was sown back in 1921 in the Oxford University versus Australia match. Armstrong walked his players off the ground a little early because the draw had become a cast iron certainty. Jardine, on 96 at the time, felt cheated.

Back to the 1928/29 tour and Freeman (8/32) destroyed the Combined Country side in the first innings; Sutcliffe (77), Tyldesley (115), Hammond (110) and Leyland (67*) helped England reach 510. Ames (run out 22) showed some good form but Duckworth (40) eclipsed him. In their second innings the Combined Country XI chose to hunt Freeman down the track in a death or glory strategy designed to mangle the diminutive leg-spinner's lines and lengths. The policy was never going to change the outcome but they went down fighting Freeman nonetheless, trading blows so to speak, enjoying their moments of conquer but Freeman (7/74) enjoyed the last laugh. The innings and 169 run victory added further momentum to England's seemingly unconquering march across Australia.

The squad travelled by train to Sydney ready for the second Test. Chapman removed Phil Mead from the team and brought in George Geary to add more ballast to the bowling. From the Australian team

Bradman was relegated to 12th man duties with Victor Richardson taking the batting slot while 28-year-old Nothling and 46-year-old Blackie replaced Gregory and Kelleway. Dr Otto Nothling was an odd selection given that he was an Australian rugby union player and played relatively little first-class cricket. He did bowl useful medium pace and could strike the ball a great distance but Australia could not meet fire with fire. Why not Scott, Wall or Halcombe to provide a physical threat? As for Don Blackie, he provided medium paced off-breaks from a long curling run that started close to mid-off. Blackie only began his first-class career at the age of 42, in 1924; so, Blackie had little mileage. Even so, the Australians had little in the way of penetrative bowlers beyond the wiles of Grimmett.

Australia versus England 2nd Test Sydney 1928/29

Sydney was packed under a glorious day of sunshine, tempered by the cool north-easterly breeze coming from the Pacific - excellent spectator conditions in the shade or under a wide-brimmed hat.

Ryder won the toss and elected to bat, moving Ponsford down to four and opening with Woodfull and Victor Richardson. Given Richardson's brilliant 231 against England a matter of weeks earlier, his omission from the first Test seems erroneous.

40,000 spectators attended the first day's play and were treated to a decent opening partnership of 51 between Woodfull and Richardson before Larwood bowled Richardson (27) and Geary bowled Kippax off his pad sparking a controversial episode.

Kippax stayed his ground accusing Duckworth of sharp practice. Initially neither umpire gave Kippax out until Duckworth had persuaded the square leg umpire that he had not touched the ball. Hobbs also gave his account of what happened from cover. The square leg umpire concurred with England, so Kippax had to go. Kippax looked furious; heated emotions radiated from his exchange of words with the England team. His face flushed red and veins running up the sides of his neck became swollen. The situation simmered and failed to deescalate as quickly as one might have imagined because as Kippax strolled past Larwood on his way off, the Nottinghamshire ex-minor told him quietly - in the tone of hard-luck - a couple of words that the lip-reader with binoculars interpreted as ''fuck off''.

The Australian Board of Control asked both umpires for their accounts of the incident but no details were ever issued to the press. Monte Noble looked horrified and condemned the square leg umpire for giving Kippax out when the laws of cricket stipulate that such a decision can only be made by the bowler's umpire. Lunch was taken with Australia on 69/2 with Ponsford now partnering Woodfull.

Soon after, Larwood broke Ponsford's left hand while the Victorian used it to defend his facial features from a throat high bumper, consigning his season to an abrupt end and Geary removed both Woodfull (68) and Hendry (37) before tea was taken at 163/4. By the close Oldfield (40*) and Ryder had taken the score to 251/8; Geary grabbed the headlines with 5/35. Montague Noble assessed Geary's statistics as flattering while Wisden, though praising Geary, stating that he *bowled very well, especially the ball which came from his arm a little*, did also reckon that Geary's bowling looked *to be anything like so difficult to play as his figures would suggest.*

The next morning Australia's limping first innings died at 253, Woodfull (68) lived up to his reputation as the 'unbowlable' and Bertie Oldfield (41*) helped to extend the tail but the total oozed mediocrity and it would be no exaggeration to state that, from an Australian's perspective at least, the score was tinged with disappointment that it could not be double that.

Out strode the famous pair but both Hobbs and Sutcliffe were tied down with the accuracy of Grimmett's leg-breaks and googlies, as well as Dr Otto Nothling's irritating medium pace. Hobbs especially, lacked fluency against Nothling. With storms forecast for the afternoon Chapman fretted about whether England should be going for it, gathering in as many runs as possible before the heavens opened. At lunch Hobbs (25*) and Sutcliffe (11*) had survived but Percy Fender and Monte Noble felt they could have scored double that without taking too many risks. They allowed the bowlers to find their lengths. Both famous batsmen were criticised for scoring too slowly. Sutcliffe absorbed the mood of his peers over the long interval. Fourth ball into the afternoon and without addition to his score, Ironmonger delivered a wide half-volley; Sutcliffe executed a flowing cover drive that succeeded only in edging the ball to a comfortable catch for Hendry at first slip, 37/1.

The next man in was Walter Hammond, the ladies' man, in his young leonine days. Hammond had shown immense capabilities as a batsman, bombarding county crowds with mighty sixes, crackling off-drives, on his day even taking on and destroying county cricket's finest bowlers, including Ted Macdonald. He caught stupendous grabs in the slips and bowled brisk and accurate fast-medium seam. Hobbs reckoned the show pony was a flat-track bully. The pair, at opposite ends of their careers, batted together for the next half an hour in murky conditions until light rain brought the players from the field at around 2.50pm, Hobbs (36*), Hammond (12*).

It rained for the next couple of hours. During the enforced interlude, and unbeknown to Hobbs, Monte Noble made an awards presentation to him, handing Hobbs a wallet with 46 gold sovereigns in, and a gold mounted boomerang with the inscription: 'To John Berry Hobbs on his 46th birthday from friends and admirers in NSW'.

The crowd burst out singing, 'For He's a jolly good fellow'. Noble took Hobbs on a tour of the outfield where he waved to the masses who gave him three cheers. By the time the startled and, frankly, shocked and humbled England opener had completed his circuit, his team mates, many of whom had been the subject of a Hobbs prank, waited for him at the pavilion gates and manhandled him onto their shoulders, whereupon he was carried to the dressing-room amidst mass and prolonged applause from the crowd of over 58,000. The extraordinary event had shaken Hobbs up quite a bit. He never actively sought the limelight other than by using his bat. Occupying centre stage for a life time's achievement, at short notice, knocked Hobbs out of his comfort zone. At any rate he fell soon after the resumption for a hard-fought 40 before edging Grimmett behind to be both caught and stumped by Oldfield.

By the close, England were 113/2, Hammond 33* and Jardine 23*. In the three Test innings of the series to date, neither Hobbs nor Sutcliffe had made a fifty. The wicket was greasy although not rain ruined ('sticky'). Being 'timeless' the rate of scoring slowed.

England concentrated on keeping Grimmett out and taking their scoring opportunities against the others. The policy worked.

Jardine (28) ran himself out but Hendren (74) and Hammond opened out and flourished in a 145-run partnership. Hobbs and Sutcliffe looked on as the next England batting superstar began a gigantic run of form that broke all records. Hammond's back-foot shots through the covers sounded like the spanking from a Victorian school-master. No one executed a cover or off-drive harder than Hammond. By the end of the day Hammond (201*) had achieved what only R.E. Foster (287) had accomplished in 1903 - score an Ashes Test double century for England. For all the greatest and bow of reverence to Hobbs and Sutcliffe, neither of them would score a Test double century against Australia.

The famous pair watched all day long, this rising star of English cricket staking his territory in the England batting line-up for the next fifteen years. I wonder how Hobbs felt. Did he begrudge the Gloucestershire player his batting feat? One wonder did the famous pair have to fight a sense of melancholy envy, watching this young adornment to the game not only herald in a new chapter but break their records? The pair had dominated allcomers, creating records left, right and centre. Their Test records up until the 1928/29 series were unparalleled and in their own right, colossal. True, Sutcliffe enjoyed the perfect pitches upon which 'timeless' Tests depended. Hobbs, in his long career, played mainly three-day Tests where the emphasis on batting lay in getting a move on. No other player or combination had threatened their shared kingdom; they had enjoyed an astounding run of success. Now, in the blink of a day, when both batted below their capabilities, they saw the arrogance and swagger of the next generation. Wally was a quiet, brooding type; he appeared normal enough but kept his thoughts and his private life very much to himself. He hit the ball harder than both openers and his defence had all their hallmarks. A bigger and broader man than both, still only 25, Hammond had much for others to envy.

''He's gone past your top Ashes score now Jack'', exclaimed Maurice Leyland.

''Indeed Maurice'' replied Jack, smile planted on his face, ''Wally's playing wonderfully well isn't he''.

Goodness the bowling attack looked tired. Hammond played the percentages. 86 not out at lunch, 150 at tea and 201 not out at the close. He kept Grimmett out and plundered the rest. On he went into the fourth morning, picking up exactly where he left off the day before, feasting off the ravaged Australian attack, complete with 45-year-old Ironmonger and 46-year-old Blackie.

When Hammond (251) departed he was a little miffed at not breaking the Foster record but soaked up the praise and adulation. An avalanche of female attention descended upon him. Back to the Test, Geary (66) and the tail took the total to a record 636, every single player reached double figures. Australia (397) batted well in their second innings in the absence of Ponsford. Woodfull (111) and Hendry (112) scored centuries but England only needed 15 to win. Curiously, Chapmen rested Hobbs and Sutcliffe and gave the opening slots to Geary and Tate. When they were both dismissed, White and Duckworth came in to finish the job in an eight-wicket victory.

The only cricket before the 3rd Test in Melbourne was a two-day fixture against Newcastle and Hunter River, not first class and it ended in a draw. All England's top four batsmen were rested.

Christmas came and went and Chapman lost the toss at Melbourne

and had to field first on a gorgeous batting strip. Australia made one

forced change following the Ponsford injury and brought back young

Bradman, while they freshened up the bowling attack with an

infusion of youth: 21-year-old fast-medium bowler Edward

A'Beckett; and 28-year-old medium pace swinger Ronnie Oxenham.

Out went Ironmonger and Nothling. England remained the same

team.

Australia versus England 3rd Test Melbourne 1928/29

Starting on the 29th December 1928, the Melbourne Test turned into

a seven-day marathon. Ryder won the toss and on a wicket that

looked superb chose first use. Winning the toss counted so much

more in olden days. Whoever batted last had to battle the worst of

the conditions. Monte Noble assessed the value as the equivalent of a

100-run bonus but also believed the bonus to be at least that much at

Melbourne. With the ruling at the time forbidding the use of covers once the Test commenced, batting first on a hard, true surface was a given. Should it rain and hot sunshine follow, batting would become virtually impossible. In the annals of the first-class game, a drying 'sticky dog' at Melbourne was considered the most desperate wicket for batting on the planet.

The Melbourne wicket is never a batsman's paradise on the first morning regardless of weather conditions. The ball came through at a variety of heights and multi-paced. One delivery from Tate rose alarmingly, took the edge of Woodfull's bat and sailed high over the slip cordon for a boundary. Soon after Woodfull fell, edging Tate to Jardine and Larwood made short work of Vic Richardson by supplying Duckworth with an easy catch. Hendry fell soon after lunch but Ryder (111*) and Kippax (100) scored centuries to leave the hosts healthily positioned on 276/4. Duckworth made a name for himself as a compulsive appealer, screaming out pleas of approval to the umpire, and the mighty crowd jeered his impudence as nothing more than jiggery pokery.

Ryder added only one run on the second morning but Bradman (79) and A'Beckett (41) helped Australia post 397. Their progress was too slow to thrill with only 121 runs in 200 minutes, either side of lunch, so there was no pressure on England's openers.

Hobbs and Sutcliffe walked out to bat at 4.00pm in front of over 60,000. A'Beckett and Hendry opened the bowling without alarm so Ryder brought on Grimmett and Hobbs swept him through square leg to reach 3,000 Test runs but, having reached 20 in thirty-five minutes, Hobbs drove loosely at a wide half-volley from A'Beckett and handed Oldfield a catch. *The Times* wrote disparagingly that '*he is clearly nothing like the Hobbs of four years ago either in his fielding or in his batting*'. England reached 47/1 by the close.

Sutcliffe and Hammond batted on the third morning in front of far fewer spectators; many were put off due to the slow scoring the day before when, over the full four and a half hours of play, the crowd endured the secretion of only 168 runs. The first few overs needed careful play but Sutcliffe and Hammond soon blossomed in a stand of 133 before Sutcliffe (58) played on to one of Blackie's slow off-breaks. The rest of day three showcased another superb performance from Hammond as England closed on 312/4 with the Gloucestershire right-hander still dominant on 157* and the Australian fielding ragged from leather chasing.

On the fourth day Hammond (200) reached his second successive Test match double century and fell immediately afterwards with the score 364/5. England fizzled out for 417, a lead of only 20. By Noble's estimation, Australia looked ahead on points at the halfway stage. When Woodfull (107) and Bradman (112) built up a winning lead on day five in the absence of Larwood (strained right heel), the Australian score of 347/8 looked ominous, pendulum swinging towards the hosts.

Plenty of overnight rain cooked England's chances. After a delayed start, with groundsmen, both umpires and Jack White depositing handfuls of saw dust over bowlers' foot-holes, play commenced at 12.30pm. Put off by the weather, the morning crowd totalled around 25,000. After the resumption, one from White bounced an astonishing amount given the good length and genial pace. It missed batsman, stumps, wicket-keeper, the lot and ran off for four unhelpful byes to the England cause but White clean bowled both

Grimmett and Blackie without a run from the bat to record durable match figures of 113.5–50–173-6 but, with England requiring 332 to win, all sage judges foresaw the inevitable England collapse such that a fourth innings total of around 80 would be par for the course. Indeed, the likes of veteran Australian bowler Hugh Trumble commiserated with the England players as they walked in.

According to Hobbs: 'We considered we didn't have a chance of getting the runs''.

Hobbs and Sutcliffe negotiated the three overs prior to lunch and during the interval the sub-tropical sun dried the Melbourne pitch into a veritable monster.

Percy Fender assessed the situation thus: *'The only speculation was whether England would get over or under 100; no one dreamt she would get any more and the game was counted as being all over bar the shouting'.*

Lunch was a sober affair around the England table. Amateurs and professionals sat together subdued into silence. Massive queues formed as local folk rushed to witness the thrill of the kill and during the 40-minute period of lunch a further 15,000 paid entry fees. The hand of the weather God had turned the wheel back towards Australia. Despite being 0-2 down, Australia already had Woodfull (twice), Hendry, Kippax, Ryder and young Bradman score centuries and the exciting Archie Jackson in reserve. Given England's lean bowling stocks, after Australia bounce back to 1-2, which they were all but certain of accomplishing, the fear for England came in the form of injury or illness to Tate, Larwood, Geary and White. With only Freeman in reserve and given the timeless nature of the Tests, it was quite conceivable for Australia to clinch the series.

Sure, enough a lifter from A'Beckett soon after lunch touched the shoulder of Hobbs's bat and lobbed invitingly to the tall, lean figure of 'Stork' Hendry at second slip. Normally a reliable fielder, Hendry grassed the chance and the ball plopped to his feet. The crowd, subdued up to this point, broke out into a howl of protestation.

Ryder soon replaced Hendry with Blackie and Grimmett with Oxenham. To Noble's intense exasperation Blackie chose to bowl his off-breaks from round the wicket with two short legs and a leg slip, a direct copycat strategy of Arthur Richardson's failed attempt at the Oval in '26. Noble held his head in his hands.

That afternoon session both batsmen suffered countless bruises.

Eye-witness Fender claimed:

'The wicket behaved as badly as it possibly could, brought out every trick in its bag, yet England's opening pair fought on without flinching in the face of tremendous odds. About three balls in five hopped up head or shoulder-high, some turning as well and all stopping almost visibly as they hit the ground. The batsmen were hit all over the body from pads to shoulder, and in two or three cases even on the neck and on the head, all from good or nearly good-length balls'.

They stole singles where they could under that hot sun and only played at deliveries aimed at the stumps, anything off target entirely abandoned. In defence both employed soft hands to kill the ball dead on the turf. As soon as his bat made contact with the ball, Sutcliffe twisted his wrists upwards in a flourish, a noted idiosyncrasy. Hobbs displayed impeccable footwork. When forced at the last moment to alter his stroke, he did so with utter technical correctness.

For 1¾ hours Hobbs and Sutcliffe survived that afternoon session on the sixth day; between the overs they met regularly in the middle, spoke a few words while gardening, and on at least one occasion, both spanked the wicket on the underside of their bats to flatten down pitch bumps. They conquered all that Ryder could assault them with. By the tea interval Hobbs (36*) and Sutcliffe (32*) had taken England to 75/0. Chapman and the rest stood on the players' balcony clapping long and hard in appreciation and awe, humbled and privileged at being handed this gift of attestation, this birth and imprint of a life-long memory to genuine greatness as the peerless pair walked off. A contemporary newspaper wrote that the accomplishment of surviving under such pitch trickery *'deserves to be inscribed in letters of gold in the annals of cricket'*.

The wicket eased in the evening session though still held the occasional terror. Hobbs called for a new bat just before the century partnership. As Maurice Leyland picked up several bats, curiosity impelled Jardine to take them out himself. Before he finished congratulating Hobbs, the old man whispered that Jardine should come in next and not at number six. Hobbs reasoned the if England could defend successfully before the close, the wicket would roll out better tomorrow, runs would be easier, and Hammond could be unleashed to finish the job, especially given his purple patch. Jardine relayed the news back to Chapman, having walked off with the same bats. Chapman concurred and with the score on 105, Hobbs (49) fell lbw to Blackie for arguably the most decorated under-50 score in England's entire cricket history. Wisden loved it: *he* (Hobbs) *hit only one four in his 49, but the value of his innings could not be measured by the mere runs he made. Remarkable footwork, masterly defence and unerring skill in a difficult situation were the memories this innings left'.*

Sutcliffe had 42 at the time, with byes and leg-byes making up the other 14 runs as even Oldfield had trouble with the erratic bounce.

According to Sutcliffe:

There were balls that had to be played because they threatened the sticks, and there were balls that had to be left alone because the batsman, who was relieved when he got his bat out of the way of them, knew that three-quarters of the Australian XI circled him....no

one could tell what it (the ball) was going to do until it hit the turf

which had so much help for the spinning ball.

The ''glue-pot'' pitch, as Sutcliffe called it, was worse than the drying Oval wicket of '26. The Melbourne glue-pot had more variable bounce. Indeed, on many occasions the bounce rocketed upwards from a good length. Both openers carried multiple bruises on the torso, shoulders and thighs, big blue ones that lasted longer than a week.

Just as Hobbs suggested, Douglas Jardine, Harlequin cap radiating an imperial snobbery, lasted out until the close with the straightest of England middle-order bats, as did Sutcliffe who spent over four hours accumulating mainly through pull shots and snatched singles.

Defying the impossible England closed on 171/1, Sutcliffe 83*, Jardine 21*. The wicket had eased considerably in the evening session, drying and dying. Oxenham and A'Beckett were according to Noble: 'quite ineffective', 'straight up and down bowling'. With more than a hint of alacrity Noble rounded on the Australian attack, labelling his compatriots the 'weakest within memory'.

Jubilation and excited chatter embraced the England dressing-room, the mood of the game u-turning over the course of two sessions. Hobbs had already showered but soaked in the ambience with a contended smile. On multiple occasions Sutcliffe announced that he loved a ''good dog-fight, I love a good dog-fight'', fists clenched in intent, towel around his midriff, hair combed into place, quite the man at home. No one cracked open the champagne as the job still had the mileage for a collapse but the funeral mood in the Australian camp contrasted the momentum swing in the game.

There was no rolling of the pitch prior to the start of day seven. England required a further 161 with nine wickets left. After a while, Grimmett bowled Jardine (33) off his pads with a wrong-'un; that accounted for Australia's sole success in the morning as Sutcliffe, with unwavering concentration, took his score to 105. He struck only one boundary in front of square on the off-side and only one behind, all the other seven boundaries had come from hooks off Hendry or glances. After lunch Hammond and Sutcliffe took the score to 257 when Hammond had the misfortune of being run out while dancing down the track to Grimmett. The prolific Gloucestershire batsman, deceived by the flight, came down hard on the ball and succeeded only in jamming it into the ground, whereupon the ball spun like a top conveniently within range for Oldfield to complete the run out.

Hendren joined Sutcliffe, filling him with encouragement to see the job through, and added a mix of exuberance and class. Outscoring Sutcliffe two to one, Hendren received a life on 21 when Bradman dropped him at long on as England sauntered towards the finishing line. At 318, Sutcliffe's (135) monumental achievement came to a close, lbw to Grimmett. Hendren (45) got bowled trying to finish with a six. Chapman (5) skied one to Woodfull off Ryder attempting much the same outcome and Tate (0) ran himself out backing up too much when Bradman – making amends for his earlier blunder – swooped in like a swallow in the covers to stop a Geary drive and threw the stumps down to leave England 328/7, still four short with Duckworth to rely on.

Let's go there. The crowd screams and roars encouragement, demanding a hat-trick as Ryder runs in to bowl. The field is clustered around Geary, all saving the single, only Larwood and White to come. Geary rocks forward into a mighty drive sounding like a rifle shot. Bradman chases in vain but the ball hammers into the cover boundary wall and England have won by three wickets, to go 3-0 up after three Tests and, most importantly, retain the Ashes.

Toone, ever one for details, had pre-ordered a crate of champagne. Chapman gave an interview, extolling the virtues and issuing hearty gratitude to his famous opening pair. He paid tribute to the great battle and fine spirit the game was played in, mentioning the young Don Bradman as one for the future. By the time he returned to the England dressing-room, all were present to cheer the inspirational and hugely popular leader. Chapman had by now won his first four Test matches as captain. Glasses got poured quickly. Several overflowing in bubbles. Chapman glugged it like spring water, others followed suit. Enveloped in the cloud of success, that warm and mellifluous moment, how they fed the fuel of joy, loving each other's companionship, imprinting the memory. Chapman gave a short, impromptu speech stating how proud he was that this England team had already won back the Ashes and implored his team to celebrate big-time.

Hendren cracked the Vallance Jupp joke once more. War wounds were proudly shown off, Sutcliffe's torso displayed a pock-mark of bruises that won a round of applause from all. Amidst the genial hour or so, wallowing in their successes, Hobbs quietly told Chapman that, as the Ashes had now been won, he would stand down and allow someone else to open.

Toone knocked again on Chapman's door, this time louder.

''Enter!'' instructed Chapman, frowning deeply at the headache, eyes puffed, hair misshapen from the pillow, the pile of cold vomit beside the bed a crapulous reminder from the previous evening.

Toone entered, eye-brows pyramidally raised. The old Yorkshire Secretary and England Manager had previously worked alongside J.W.H.T. Douglas and Arthur Gilligan, men who were broadly sober but imbibed regularly and with moderation. Chapman, by contrast, liked to imbibe during a game and seek out social settings in the evening for some late-night parties.

''We need to pick the teams in the run up to the fourth Test and give Jack some time off, the old boy is exhausted'', implored Toone.

But before he could quite finish, Chapman opened his mouth very wide and yawned out fumes that spoke strongly of the night.

''Can't do the Geelong fixture Fred old boy'', muttered Chapman, now lying back on his bed, left hand clutching his forehead, eyes shut. ''Bout of food poisoning, must have been the frightfully red chicken breast in my lunch sandwich yesterday'', proffered the England Captain.

Before Toone could get a word in edgeways, Chapman waved him off with his right hand and the following parting words: ''Tell the chaps I'll be back for the Bendigo game when, all being well, this nasty little stomach bug has worked its way through''.

Loyalty to England captains was Toone's strong suit. It kept providing him with winters away in the sun. Another good review and who knows? He might get asked again. He closed the door, cursed under his breath and strode off to inform the rest of the

Selection Committee of the Captain's present indisposition – a stomach bug.

''So, you see gentlemen, our Captain will be laid low for a couple of days while (he coughed) the bug works his way out of the system''.

''Was that from the same chicken we ate?'' enquired Hobbs, smile adorning his face.

Tyldesley guffawed, unlike him, but he did. Jardine smiled tolerantly. White gave a short cackle of a laugh. The simple fact was that good old Percy had gone on a bender. First champagne lubricated his throat, then cocktails, whisky, more wine, more whisky until he had gone around most of his players either informing them amicably that he loved them, or that he f****** well loved them, as indeed he announced to Hobbs. He picked Freeman up off the ground with his large hands on the lapels of the Kent spinner's blazer, while the spinner had been otherwise engaged in animated conversation with the pert breasts of a waitress. When elevated to eye-level Freeman's nervous grin fuelled a kiss from his England skipper on his right cheek before gently lowering the Kent man down again to resume his life.

''Go fetch me a maiden Tich!'' yelled Chapman, before bursting into hysterics at his own humour.

At one stage he took to calling Herbert Sutcliffe by another name, Rudolf. He insisted that Harold Larwood down a glass of whisky with him ''for victory'', flicked cigar ash into someone's sherry glass and sung with some gusto the first verse of God Save The King.

Jack White tolerated Chapman's nickname for him: 'Al' could be short for Alexander. However, Chapman's nickname referred to 'albino' which made fun of his rosy red country cheeks and shock of blonde hair. White was white and whiter than white but not actually an albino. It appeared Chapman had, as yet, no nickname for Mr Ernest Tyldesley, the other professional on the committee. All this a melange of fresh memories seeping back into the selectors' minds as they all smiled, giggled and roared at the behaviour of their outrageous skipper. 3-0 up and the Ashes retained, all could afford to laugh.

Eventually, when the laughing at Chapman's latest antics had died down, Hobbs suggested he vacate his position in the side for someone younger, now that the Ashes were won. He looked drained, in need of recuperation. So did Herbert. Both were allowed to travel to Adelaide ahead of the South Australia fixture followed by the fourth Test. Before then the famous pair performed professionally against Geelong, sealing another century partnership at the top of the order before Hobbs (50) was bowled in the over before lunch, 107/1. Sutcliffe (56) retired himself and the rest of the order thrashed around in entertaining manner to declare at tea on 289/7. Geelong hung on.

Hobbs took a break from the game and spent the week with Ada, missing the two-day fixture in the old mining town of Bendigo. Bendigo played thirteen against England's eleven. Sutcliffe (30) still ached from his Melbourne dogfight and got himself bowled.

Chapman returned all cheerful and accompanied the team to Tasmania for a couple of first-class fixtures against the state. Tasmania was not part of the Sheffield Shield tournament but had produced Test cricketers in the past such as Ted McDonald. Hobbs and Sutcliffe remained on the mainland, making their way across to Adelaide at their leisure.

Jardine (214) and Mead (106) took advantage of some pleasant offerings and Freeman enjoyed match figures of 8/91 in an innings victory in the first game. Ames (100*) came of age in the second fixture, again won by an innings.

Just as the players were becoming fed up with so much cricket Toone pulled a masterstroke and organised an entire week off with no fixture obligations, rather like a half-term holiday.

Hobbs recuperated well. He returned after an extended break to put on 155 with Sutcliffe, in the first 145 minutes, against a South Australian attack containing Clarrie Grimmett and quick guy J.D. Scott. On 75, the old man connected with a meaty pull, only to be held at mid-wicket. Sutcliffe (122) showed excellent shot selection and was fourth out at 243 having struck nine boundaries over almost four hours, most of them on the on-side but Hendren stole the show and drove with style to record ten boundaries in a run-a-ball 90.

It rained. South Australia (178) succumbed meekly to Jack White (7/66), all except Victor Richardson (82), the superb athlete about to be dropped from the Test team. Chapman batted again, this time Sutcliffe (27), going for quick runs, fell to Scott's bouncer from a mistimed hook shot. The pair had put on 44. Tyldesley failed again but Jardine (114) recorded his fourth century of the tour and Hobbs (101) his first; the Surrey pair put on 146 but the game finished a draw under a blanket of rain. Two days of intermittent net practice and stretching exercises, and England kept an unchanged team for the fourth Test played conveniently at Adelaide.

Australia versus England 4th Test Adelaide 1928/29

Adelaide buzzed with Test fever, thousands of folk driving in from the country. Hotels, guest houses, caravan parks and camping sites heaved with tourists. The ground authorities had issued free parking to attract the crowds from a greater sphere of influence. New batting sensation and teenage wonder-boy Archie Jackson, the New South Welshman with six first-class centuries already, had been selected in Vic Richardson's place. Together with Don Bradman, the Australian batting line-up looked to be shaping up well for the future.

In front of a crowd of 21,380, Adelaide looked no more than half full. Frankly with extra seating having been installed for a capacity of 50,000, the first day attendance figure was a little disappointing. Chapman won the toss and chose the obvious course of action which was to bat first. The Australian folk had seen enough of England batting. They wanted to see Jackson and Bradman conquer England's attack.

Hobbs and Sutcliffe strode out once more and the first ball from Ted A'Beckett rose from short of a length, flew by Hobbs's nose and Oldfield had to jump as high as he could and only got a touching glance. The batsmen ran three byes yet immediately after that unnerving start, the pitch calmed down and neither opener looked in the least hurried or bothered and after only twenty minutes Ryder centralised his options around Grimmett's leg-breaks and googlies, with Hendry, A'Beckett, Oxenham and Blackie executing their bowling skills from the other end.

The famous pair ran plenty of quick singles. In fact, they were lucky not to be run out on three separate occasions. Building a foundation as Hobbs and Sutcliffe were in the process of establishing, did not excite the crowd. They looked on subdued, silenced by the polish and professionalism of Hobbs and Sutcliffe. After an hour Hobbs hit his first boundary, an off-drive off Grimmett and at the interval, after a ninety-minute opening session, England lunched contentedly on 77/0, Hobbs 41, Sutcliffe 31.

In the afternoon, both players gave an excellent demonstration of reliable run gathering. They delayed their strokes superbly, killing the ball dead on either side of the wicket and scampered like hell to the other end. Hobbs tucked away another single to reach his fifty with the score on 94/0 and the crowd clapped with cordial respect. However, when Blackie dropped a sharp return chance from Hobbs, not long after, the crowd groaned. By 2 pm the pair had added their ninth century partnership against Australia, and thirteenth as England's opening pair. After 145 minutes at the crease, Sutcliffe reached his own chanceless fifty, again to applause. On these batsmen went about their journey and just as it seemed to ordinary folk that they would bat forever, Hobbs (74) played a cut shot off Hendry too close to his body and Ryder held a good catch at slip, low down to his left. The great opening pair had put on 143.

Enter Mr Jardine. Jardine played his cricket as though it were a battle of wits, deadly serious, a ploy to emphasis the distinction between imperials over plebs. Not one for witty remarks or small talk with batting partners, especially in between overs, Jardine never looked anything other than wholehearted, short-fused and intent at the crease.

Grimmett came on for a new spell and second ball Sutcliffe attempted to hit him out of the ground by hunting the great leg-spinner down the track. Stumped by yards, Sutcliffe (64) walked off red-faced having committed a rare but cardinal sin. When Jardine (1) fell to Grimmett England had slumped to 149/3. Jardine refused to accept the decision. Umpire Elder had given Jardine out lbw while gliding Grimmett off his pads down to fine leg. Jardine had hit the ball audibly and rather obviously, so he felt. It was the last ball before tea and as they all trooped off Jardine did not know whether he had been given out or not; he only determined this once back in the pavilion when he asked for confirmation from Elder himself. As he spoke Jardine had the look of superiority over Elder; he chose his words with diplomacy yet radiated a strong aroma of disapproval at the umpire's verdict without actually stepping over the red line.

Hendren lit up faces with his brilliant running between the wickets with Hammond. All Australian crowds loved Hendren but Blackie bowled him an absolute beauty for 13. Chapman (39) hung around for a while, lashed a few boundaries then edged a wide one. Aside from Hobbs and Sutcliffe only Hammond (119*) with a hard-fought century in 263 minutes had contributed significantly in England's 334.

The crowd had swollen to 37,700 in time to see Woodfull and boy-wonder Archie Jackson reply for Australia. Woodfull (1) fell in Tate's first over to a miraculous take by Duckworth, diving to his left to catch a leg-glide. Larwood removed Hendry with a much simpler catch for Duckworth and when Kippax yorked himself against White, Australia had collapsed to 19/3. One of the most memorable innings of all time came from that wreckage. Teenager Archie Jackson weathered the storm like the frail and slender boy holding on for dear life. By his side, captain Jack Ryder drove powerfully and the score soon ticked over. Hammond was exhausted after his long innings. Geary nursed a leg strain and could not be over bowled. That left Larwood, Tate and White.

Jackson brought up his half-century with a leg glance off Geary and had reached 70 by the close, Ryder 54 and Australia 131/3. After the rest day, Monday witnessed the glorious flowering of Archie Jackson, in front of 23,800 spectators. He stormed to a century, reaching the milestone with an exquisite square drive off a wide half-volley from Larwood with the first ball he faced after lunch. The shot became etched into thousands of people's minds. The fluency of Jackson reminded folk of a freer version of Kippax with shades of Victor Trumper and more than a suspicion of Ranjitsinhji. White bowled Ryder (63) early on but Jackson and Bradman embarked on an 82-run partnership either side of lunch. Shortly after Jackson's century, Bradman (40) edged Tate to Larwood and this signalled a plunder of the bowling by Jackson.

Batting with the lower middle-order for support, Jackson square cut repeatedly wide of second slip being especially severe on Hammond. Jackson brought up his 150 with a late cut for three off Hammond, then stroked the next three deliveries for four, two and three. Australia took a lead of 35 on first innings. Of Australia's 369, Jackson made 164.

Hobbs (1) and Sutcliffe (17) both failed but England replied with Hammond (177) scoring a century in each innings coming off the back of double centuries in each of the two previous Tests. Jardine (98) put on 262 with Hammond but Oxenham (4/67) and Blackie (2/70) pegged England back to 383 all out with only Tate (47) wagging the tail.

Australia failed by only 12 runs to reach 348 and this fourth consecutive victory in four Tests during the series was mainly due to Hammond (119* and 177) and White (13/256). There is no doubt though that Jackson (164 and 36) won the hearts and minds of the spectators.

That evening the team hopped on the train back up to New South Wales and on route, left the train at dawn to honour a fixture against 12 of Ballarat. Sutcliffe (6) failed against a medium pacer called Bennets who finished with 7/127. Hobbs, batting down at number 10, scored a masterful 82 not out. England ran out of time in their quest for an innings victory, not that they were taking the game all that seriously. Chapman could not be bothered to play so Jack White captained the team and he thought Herbert Sutcliffe should open the bowling.

Sutcliffe had been given precious little warning about White's left-field decision. He marked out his run and bowled six overs of surprisingly accurate right arm medium pace for just eight runs. That spell of bowling, coupled with the very wet and miserable few days spent in the rain in New South Wales, caused Sutcliffe to strain his shoulder. Either way, as a possible consequence of opening the England bowling, a sporting act for which Herbert had received no training or coaching, Sutcliffe spent the rest of the tour an invalid, unable to take part in any more cricket.

The fifth Test saw Hobbs (142 and 65) open the innings with Douglas Jardine (19 and 0). England 519 (Hobbs 142, Leyland 137, Hendren 95, Hammond 38) and 257 (Hobbs 65, Leyland 53*, Tate 54, Wall 5/66) lost on the eighth day by five wickets to a youthful Australia 491 (Bradman 123, Woodfull 102, Fairfax 65, Geary 5/105) and 287/5 (Jackson 46, Ryder 57*, Bradman 37*, Hammond 3/53).

Sutcliffe's loss may go some way to explain England's defeat; the rock-like reliability at the top had gone. The fact that Chapman felt unable to play and handed White the captaincy on the morning of the game may also explain the loss. Apparently, Chapman might have been partying too hard the night before. At any rate, on the plus side, England had unearthed another batsman of obvious international class in the left-handed Yorkshireman, Maurice Leyland. Jack Hobbs recorded his 12th Ashes century and attended his last Ashes tour as a player. The 46-year-old managed 451 Test runs at 50.11, Sutcliffe 355 at 50.71, Hendren 472 at 52.44 while Hammond enjoyed the world at his feet with 905 at 113.12.

Hobbs missed the first Surrey fixture of the season because after the long voyage home, he needed time to get his land legs back. Besides, being Jack Hobbs, he could pick and choose his games. In his forty seventh year, Hobbs needed to manage his body. He played for Surrey in the first game of the County Championship season, against Hampshire at the Oval and, on the first day, sailed into the Hampshire bowling to the tune of 154. He stroked 17 fours and eleven threes and in doing so gave a rare exhibition of his full repertoire across three and a half hours of pulsating perfection. Wisden describes his innings as being created *in masterly style*. The veteran Kennedy toiled for 37 overs to take one for 118 as Surrey hit up 490/8 in the day. Rain drowned out the rest of the game.

It is obvious that Hobbs picked his fixtures according to distance. He could not be arsed to travel far. At the Oval for Surrey against South Africa he failed twice with 15 and 1 and he scored 55 and 33 against Warwickshire just a couple of days later, also at the Oval.

He conveniently missed all away trips. For instance, he declined to visit Nottingham to face Larwood and Voce and also absented himself from the home game against Sussex, so declining an examination from Tate.

He returned to action for the home game against Essex and helped himself to 6 and 102*. Nicely warmed up for the season, he rested for a week to ready himself for the Test Trial match, pitting the victorious Ashes winning team against the Rest.

Herbert meanwhile went where he was bloody well told. None of this namby-pamby 'only-play-at-home' nonsense up North. Yorkshire sent him to Leyton in Essex where, in Sutcliffe's single innings, he failed with 11. Then he had to go across the Pennines to take part in the Roses match and played a fine, defensive innings with technically correct forward defensive prods played often enough to rile at least one Lancastrian supporter into shouting out: ''What d'you think you are a war memorial?''

Despite being heckled, Sutcliffe's 69 - adding 124 with Leyland against Macdonald and Richard Tyldesley - won praise from Neville Cardus who was moved to write:

''Again, he proved himself, for three hours, a batsman for a big match. I find it hard to believe that England would have lost the fifth Test match last winter had Sutcliffe been there to go in first with Hobbs''.

Roses matches tended to be slow, dull draws like both fixtures in 1929.

Sutcliffe scored 43 in Birmingham against Warwickshire then in Sheffield only 4 and 41 - knocked over by Freeman of Kent in the second innings. Sutcliffe was doing the county circuit all right. Still with Yorkshire he took a timely 113 from the South African attack and then had to travel to Cardiff to fail (6) against Glamorgan, bowled by a Mr Trevor Arnott. At any rate, Herbert Sutcliffe had performed adequately in his first half dozen games and made his way to Lord's to open the innings once again with his great England partner Jack Hobbs, for England against the Rest. Never one to show emotion, Herbert was a little peeved at what he thought was a certain amount of disrespect shown by one or two of the younger Yorkshire players. Arthur Wood, the wicket-keeper, had just knocked Herbert's two top front teeth out diving across him to take a catch. Maurice

Leyland had taken to calling him 'beautiful Herbert', an adjective Herbert presently felt inaccurate to the extent of sarcasm.

The country had a general election on 31st May 1929. Sutcliffe and Hobbs both registered their votes: Sutcliffe almost certainly a Baldwin Conservative vote, Hobbs probably. The news was agog of a Labour Government. The Tories had won most votes, but Labour, under Ramsay MacDonald, – buoyed by the flapper vote – had won most seats. This meant the leaning vote went to David Lloyd-George of the Liberals. Now the funny thing about Lloyd-George, aside from a legendary libido that earned him dozens of bastards, was that he was 'Welsh' and both Baldwin and MacDonald had prayed for a decisive election result one way or the other rather than the pyrrhic victory of having to court Lloyd-George's approval. On 7th June MacDonald became Prime Minster simply because Baldwin stood down too bitter about the prospect of parleying with DLG.

Engrossed in the daily paper on the train down, Sutcliffe's eyebrows rose in surprise at MacDonald's announcement that, for the first time in history, a woman MP was appointed: Minister of Labour Margaret Bondfield. Baldwin had reduced the age for which women could vote from 30 to 21. That brought in six million more voters than in 1924 yet the flapper vote went to MacDonald. Back to the cricket.

The Test Trial, one of Warner's initiatives, had been set up to unearth fresh bowling talent. Relying on Larwood, Tate, Geary and White was all very well until injury struck. Who were the next best? The Selection Committee watched as Jack White won the toss and elected to bat. Chapman had still not returned from Australia and once he did, he soon became injured for the season. The ground was almost three quarters full as Hobbs and Sutcliffe walked out to bat once more. Up against them was Bill Voce, Larwood's partner from Nottinghamshire, who bowled fast-medium left-arm, Bob Wyatt (right-arm medium swing), Percy Fender (liquorice all-sorts), Tom Goddard (off-spin) and Walter Robins (leg-breaks and googlies).

If Warner had wanted to be inspired with fresh talent, then the first day became a palate puckering disappointment though the spectators loved it. England caned the Rest to reach 487/8 in a little under six hours. Hobbs (59) had shaped well. Given two lives, Sutcliffe played forcefully for 91 and everyone in the top seven reached at least 30 with Tyldesley (68), Leyland (76) and Tate (79) the highlights.

Over the weekend, Hendren had finished reading a copy of Lady Chatterley's Lover by D.H. Lawrence. The novelist had a keen sense for pornographic literature and had just made the headlines once again, for painting nudes. His book was banned due to its obscene material involving an adulterous affair between an upper-class lady and a gamekeeper. Lawrence used sexual swear words liberally, dropping the c-bomb to fine effect, and compiled 13 different sex scenes, including a reference to anal sex. To Hendren, the book represented a comedian's delight. He would read extracts to the chaps before play to keep moral high. Hendren mimicked amusingly but his high-pitched lady's voice and unsuccessful attempts to hide a cockney accent added extra hilarity.

''Oh, you earthy gamekeepers, well I don't know…oh alright… but only if you mention my private parts in a rough yet tender manner and clasp them enthusiastically betwixt your craggy extremities.''

Perhaps it was the way Hendren 'scrunched' up his face as he uttered the word 'betwixt' that provided the catalyst but the dressing-room, door diplomatically closed, guffawed nonetheless. This England team had grown used to success; Freeman for Geary provided the only change from members of the recent touring party. Freeman bowled magnificently but the Rest put up a good fight.

Fender, batting for the Rest, sent a catch to Hobbs at cover point but the veteran fell heavily and tore a ligament in his shoulder. In all, he missed the first four Tests against a rejuvenated South African team and seven games for Surrey.

The England bowling and fielding reached superb standards but the Rest batted pluckily in the face of Larwood's searing pace and Tate's relentless accuracy. In the end Freeman 'tickled' them out with 5/132 in an all-out total of 370 but not before Fender (100*) had struck 14 boundaries.

England's second innings started mid-way through the morning session on the final day. Leyland opened with Sutcliffe in the absence of Hobbs but gloved an early one. Sutcliffe (52) and Hammond (59) put on over 100 but Robins (5/53) and Goddard (3/36) helped dismiss England for 169, the lowest total this England team had achieved since they first played together in Perth back in

October. The game finished as a draw with much for the England selectors to discuss, not least who would open with Sutcliffe.

The selectors could have chosen Andrew Sandham or Percy Holmes, even George Gunn. In the end the Rev Edgar Killick took the place of Hobbs for the first two Tests of the South African series. Still at Cambridge University, the fresh-faced reverend scored 31, 23, 3 and 24 and was never seen or heard of in the England team again. Moreover, Killick died suddenly a week after turning 46 while playing cricket for the Diocesan.

For the third Test Edward Bowley of Sussex received his promotion to open the innings with Sutcliffe and made 31 and 46, followed by 13 in the fourth Test and was subsequently ditched to make way for the return of J.B. Hobbs. The great Surrey and England legend had announced a return to full fitness and form with scores in his previous three first-class innings of 97, 134 and 48. Indeed his delay in returning to the England fold had attracted negative publicity in the press with several pundits questioning whether Hobbs was hiding from representative cricket. He reasoned that turning out for Surrey did not require such agility in the field though for England Hobbs had to be at or close to his fittest.

Meanwhile Sutcliffe had scored a couple of centuries in the first two Tests, but in the second two had actually scored fewer runs in three innings than Ed Bowley but the famous partnership was rekindled for the final Test at the Oval. By this stage England had an unassailable 2-0 lead.

Arthur Carr had returned as captain for the fourth Test at Old Trafford, taking over the leadership from Jack White who had complained of a tired bowling arm. Carr, that blood and thunder hunting type with a hairy back and balding prematurely, believed fast bowlers operated better with beer for lunch and tea. England under Carr won handsomely by an innings in the 4th Test at Old Trafford. Woolley (154) played a remarkable innings, flogging the South Africans in the manner of a severe Victorian schoolmaster and Tich Freeman whittled out 12/171 to hand England an innings and 32 run victory.

England versus South Africa 5th Test Oval 1929

Deane won the toss at the Oval and, with sunshine on a rain-soaked wicket, sent England in. Hobbs played pitifully for him and ended up miscuing full tosses and his general timing seemed to have deserted him. His adoring Surrey fans glanced at each other with worried expressions, the ravages of time at last having caught up. He fell for 10 attempting a pull shot to a rank longhop and being caught at short leg. Sutcliffe (104) held firm but England could only reach 258. South Africa thrashed an England attack shorn of Tate, Larwood and White to the tune of 492/8 declared.

On the third and last day, Hobbs and Sutcliffe strode to the wicket with the luxury of that 2-0 lead and for an hour Hobbs turned the clock back to his pre-war heyday and thrilled the crowd with an avalanche of extravagant shots that smacked of someone already with appetite sated. He lasted an hour, a golden one at that, and made 52 from 77. The more sedate and correct Sutcliffe lasted to the end of the drawn match with his second century (the first player ever to perform the feat twice in the same Test). The Yorkshire cricketer finished undefeated on 109 with Wally Hammond, in bludgeoning form, likewise unconquered on 101 in a total of 264/1.

Hobbs and Sutcliffe took the winter off. So did Larwood, Tate, Freeman, Hammond, Geary and White. Hobbs could afford to winter in contented relaxation. Though 46 years old, the Master once again topped the first-class averages with 2,263 runs at 66.55. Sutcliffe came eighth with 2,189 at 52.11.

Two England tours of 1929/30 ran concurrently to New Zealand and the West Indies, a chance to spread the gospel of Test cricket far and wide, a chance to reward fringe England players with international experience and, bizarrely, an opportunity to exhume two ageing England stars. George Gunn had not represented England since before the Great War and had turned 50. Good old Wilfred Rhodes, aged 52 and still the oldest Test cricketer, was another veteran selected. Both went to the West Indies. The 39-year-old Andrew Sandham opened with Gunn and returned to England in April 1930 with the Test record score of 325. Hendren (693 Test runs at 115.50) played himself back into England contention, after a disappointing 1929 season that saw him lose his England place. While in New Zealand, Frank Woolley's batting slipped under the radar in the

Tests but 13 Test wickets at 20.07 promoted his cause nonetheless. Meanwhile Hobbs ran his sports shop and Sutcliffe kept himself trim with press-ups and sit-ups, regular jogging, star jumping and hiking on the moors.

Chapter 6: Bradman's Ashes

The Australians arrived at Tilbury Docks armed to the front teeth with young batsmen including the prolific Don Bradman fresh from breaking records in the Sheffield Shield. Across the Australian domestic season, the 21-year-old New South Wales right-hander amassed 1,586 runs at 113.28, statistics puffed up by a second innings 452* against Queensland, a world record score in all first-class cricket at the time. Having made a name for himself in the wreckage of the previous Ashes (468 runs at 66.85), Bradman blazed a trail in the early stages of the 1930 tour, confounding experts such as Percy Fender and Archie MacLaren who assumed he would struggle in foreign conditions. Batting in thermals under miserably wet and cold weather, Bradman began his conquest with 236 against Fred Root and Worcestershire, slammed 185* against George Geary and Leicestershire, played brilliantly for 78 out of 107 against

Wilfred Rhodes, Bill Bowes, George Macaulay and the rest of the Yorkshire attack, before calming down with 9, 48*, 66, 4 and 44. Bristling with intent against arch critic Percy Fender, Bradman thrashed the Surrey attack for a chanceless 252* in a little under a day's cricket under the watchful eye of Jack Hobbs. In the game against Hampshire in which Phil Mead collected a pair, Bradman made 191. Before the first Test at Trent Bridge the little bastard had 1,230 runs in his back pocket at an average of 111.8.

Hobbs, beefed up by a century in each innings against Glamorgan, had compiled 725 runs at 65.9 but in a hint that the tide of anno domini had turned against the Master, he had been run out twice and bowled in his only innings against the sharp speed of Larwood for 5. Sutcliffe had 642 runs at 58.36, including 69 against Australia, his only visit to the crease, during which he witnessed Clarrie Grimmett capturing all 10 for 37. Both Hobbs and Sutcliffe had turned in their usual immaculate and professional performances but Bradman looked on a different level. He was raising the bar.

That 1930 summer saw 'Shrimp' Leveson-Gower elected as Chairman of Selectors with Jack White and Frank Mann making it a triumvirate of former England captains. Jack Hobbs and Wilfred Rhodes were once more invited to impart their considerable knowledge and they sat at the table in an office above the Long Room at Lord's picking the team for the first Test at Headingley.

"Welcome gentlemen and thank you for making the trip over" announced Leveson-Gower, shuffling some papers replete with ink and calculations of up-to-date seasonal averages. Smiles radiated back, Wilfred's the thinnest and least natural. Percy Chapman had already been picked to continue as captain. The friendly and sociable Kent left-hander did have five consecutive Ashes Test victories even if he had to drop out from the last Ashes Test after a binge on the whisky.

"Sandham did well in the West Indies, my goodness" uttered Hobbs.

"No" replied Wilfred.

"Hasn't made a score above 65 since he returned" uttered Leveson-Gower.

"England still needs you at the top of the order" voiced Jack White.

''Well, if England still needs me'' replied Hobbs and a chorus of affirmation echoed back.

The England batting resembled a gigantic cruise liner with so many top-quality parts it proved almost impossible to agree on the finest middle-order. Hobbs and Sutcliffe's places were, of course, agreed within a minute. Hammond and Hendren were obvious choices and also approved unanimously.

Then the debate kicked off as each selector voiced his opinions for the fifth specialist batsman. Hobbs and Rhodes both wanted Woolley, desperately unfortunate not to have been selected on the previous trip and what good did Phil Mead do then? Besides, Mead had harvested himself a pair against the Australians a couple of weeks earlier. Frank Mann and Jack White thought Maurice Leyland, going with youth. Leveson-Gower mentioned Duleepsinhji and spoke of his delightful footwork in compiling 92 for the MCC at Lord's against the full-strength Australian bowling line-up. Ernest Tyldesley had struggled for meaningful runs, Duleepsinhji had flair with the bat but added nowt with the ball and looked too slow in the field. Woolley received the nod.

''Bowlers'' said Leveson-Gower.

''Larwood'' voiced Hobbs.

''Tate'' reasoned Rhodes.

Silence. Hobbs and Rhodes stopped there to give others a chance. A few seconds later Mann cleared his throat.

''Richard Tyldesley got Hammond in both innings and has been hoovering up county batsman all season.... always seems to get four or five wickets an innings''.

White kept quiet, knowing he must surely be on the short list for the spin bowler slot having been ignored for the captaincy.

''Aye put 'im down an all'' instructed Rhodes in his quiet piercingly penetrative Kirkheaton drawl.

''Isn't Richard Tyldesley a little too fat these days?'' remarked White, face a rosy red, shock of white hair a contrast, the lean features of a fit, earthy outdoor type.

''Catches everything, opens cages at 'ome, lets pigeons fly out and catches 'em as they fly at 'im'' replied Wilfred in a slow, whisper but enough to draw complete attention.

Hobbs smiled and said nothing. Mann looked at White, then at Levenson-Gower, and volunteered: ''Good contrast to Larwood and Tate, I admire the facility of his top spinner''.

Two more places up for grabs: wicket-keeper and spin bowler. Leveson-Gower tapped his fountain pen on the desk.

''Let's discuss the keeper'' announced Leveson-Gower.

''Duckworth'' said Hobbs.

''Ames'' reckoned Rhodes, ''remember he got that 149 in the West Indies…. could keep wicket to Freeman and there's two slots already''.

White felt narked, ''but he's not even the best keeper in his own county''.

''Let through 36 byes in that Test, is he Test standard?'' questioned Leveson-Gower.

''Duckworth has the energy and is the best keeper I've seen since Strudwick'' responded Hobbs.

''Duckworth'' and a nod from Mann.

''Duckworth it is then'' scribbled Leveson-Gower ''and now to the spinner''.

''I do rate Walter'' stressed Mann.

''Why?'' quizzed White.

''He can go through any side on his day with those googlies'' continued Mann before being briefly interrupted with a guffaw from Hobbs, a little too loud for his station.

''They've got a lot of right-handers these Aussies, good to have the ball spin away from 'em'' added Rhodes with the clout of an expert. ''If Mr Robins can bowl decent leg-breaks, pick 'im''.

White went pale as Leveson-Gower wrote Robins down.

''J.C.'' announced Leveson-Gower as though the world should bow at his feet, ''you can be in the twelve, vice-captain in case Chappers goes on one of his benders again, sound good?''

White had silage to sort back in Somerset but supposed he could readily get his farmhands to manage that and the prospect of a few days in Yorkshire hobnobbing with the cricketing elite conquered his qualms at being overlooked.

''Sure'' was all he could muster.

England versus Australia 1st Test Trent Bridge 1930

At Trent Bridge, venue for the first Test, Hobbs batted like an ageing oak scattering its last remaining acorns before the tempest of time. He top-scored in England's first innings with a studious and diligent innings crafted out whilst Fairfax defeated Sutcliffe through an edge to slip and then Grimmett, the highly accomplished leg-break bowler, sliced his way through Woolley (0) Hammond (8) and Hendren (5), sending the once indomitable middle-order back to the pavilion having ransacked their egos. Hobbs never looked flummoxed, totally in control despite rain breaks, and lasted until Fairfax induced an edge to second slip on 78.

England's 270 looked modest until rain came to ruin the Australian's chances and Tate sent back Woodfull, Ponsford and Bradman for miserable single-figure scores and they never recovered. England

took a 126-run lead into the second innings then Hobbs and Sutcliffe

walked out to bat a second time ...

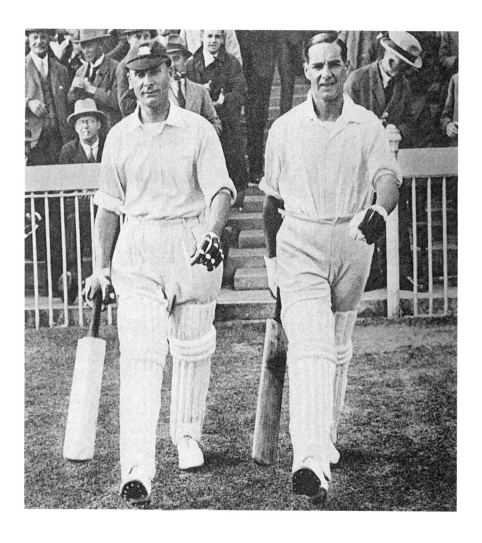

and put on 125 together at over a run a minute. Hobbs struck ten

boundaries and reminded folk of his prime. After having danced down the wicket to Grimmett and struck him sweetly for a straight driven four, Hobbs attempted the same stroke, missed and Oldfield stumped him for 74. It looked to all the world as though Hobbs had given his wicket away, drunk with too many runs, like he so often did for Surrey to allow the others a chance. With a lead now over 250, Sutcliffe retired with a split thumb, Woolley and Hammond failed again but Hendren (72) ensured Australia had to get 429 to win. Bradman took them close with 131 before Robins deceived him with a googly, and McCabe's forceful 49 ended only with a spectacular diving catch at mid-on from Copley (substituting for Sutcliffe), some unknown yet to play a first-class game. That stunning catch allowed an England victory by 93 runs.

After five Tests across the 1928/29 and 1930 Ashes series, it is interesting to compare the veteran Hobbs, England's greatest batsman of all time, with Bradman, the 21-year-old spring chicken from Bowral, who became the game's greediest plunderer of huge scores. Hobbs (49 and 11) scored more than Bradman on debut (18 and 1); Bradman returned after being dropped to score 79 and 112 whilst Hobbs could manage only 20 and 49. One all. Bradman went

2-1 up in the fourth Test of the 1928/29 series with the narrow victory of 40 and 58 when Hobbs made 74 and one. The fifth Test of that series let us call a draw: Hobbs 142 and 65 versus Bradman's 123 and 37 not out. At Headingley, Hobbs hit 78 and 74, marginally ahead of Bradman's 8 and 131. Over five Tests the 47-year-old still held his own against the 21-year-old.

The atmosphere in the England dressing-room was akin to euphoria. It seemed the doubts of age had rescinded once again on Jack. What is more, Percy Chapman had now won his ninth Test on the trot. A crate of ale arrived and toasts made.

Again, the England dressing-room erupted into laughter as this time Hendren gave his rendition of the gamekeeper, complete with wink.

''Afternoon m'lady – do you fancy a quick one over yon five barred gate?''

Larwood loved it and demanded more, a request emphatically endorsed by several of his colleagues; Hendren continued, reading with laughter himself now uncontained:

''She lay still, feeling his motion within her, his deep-sunk intentness (pause while laughing) ... the sudden quiver of him (pause again) ... at the springing of his seed (complete breakdown) ... then the slow-subsiding thrust'' (prolonged jubilations).

Therein lies the very summit of Hobbs and Sutcliffe and the scene of their last England Test victory in partnership together. Australia would very soon benefit from the talents of cricket's most extraordinary phenomenon. Change was in the air.

Hobbs kept delighting his Surrey fans, never more so than the soothing 173rd first-class century, against the Australians between the first and second Tests. Sandham (20 and 10) failed to prosper in company with Hobbs (10 and 146*), against Australia's first-choice attack. Sutcliffe had three weeks off waiting for his thumb to heal, all the time confining his activities to rousing hikes in the hills around Pudsey and three mile runs against the clock.

The Australians had played out draws against Surrey and Lancashire, with Wall, Fairfax and Grimmett claiming the bowling honours, Woodfull and Kippax scoring centuries with Bradman (5, 38 and 28*) relatively quiet.

England versus Australia 2nd Test Lord's 1930

England made several changes for Lord's. Woolley and Hammond were shunted one place up the order with Duleepsinhji coming in at number four. Incidentally Sandham's drought finished with a masterly four hour 176 just days before the Test but the team had already been announced. George 'Gubby' Allen came in for the injured Harold Larwood and Jack White for Richard Tyldesley who failed to nail his spot in the first Test and underwhelmed (2/87) for Lancashire against the tourists at the time the selectors convened.

The sun shone for the full four days at Lord's, indeed the first one reported on by new cricket journalist, E.W. Swanton. Overnight queues of spectators slept rough, hurled up in blankets or playing cards. Thousands poured into the ground before play. Lord's heaved with Panama hats, wide caps and almost exclusively jacketed gentlemen interspersed with the odd schoolboy earning or skiving a day off school. Just occasionally one caught the glimpse of a woman.

Let us go there now. Lord's is bathed in sunlight. The Great Depression had been sweeping around the globe since Black

Tuesday (04/09/29) had signposted a significant fall in US stocks. Productivity fell, industries closed, a global phenomenon, and in Britain unemployment soared to one and a half million. The Labour Government rejected a channel tunnel between England and France only a fortnight earlier due to lack of funds and with ordinary folk losing their jobs, most of those who attended the game as spectators were the professional classes, office workers, the fortunate middle-classes, those who could both afford to miss a day's work and sport a new Panama hat. A small concentration of clothe hats could be seen studying Chapman's body language, out in the middle, from in front of the Tavern. Standing several inches taller than Woodfull, Chapman exuded charisma and hearty jollity. Up he spun his sovereign in a proper flick rotating the coin heavenward as a blur.

''Heads'' called Woodfull, down the coin fell.

Tails. Chapman wins the toss and bats, signalling with his right hand a flowing drive which, in itself, sparks a roar of approval from the crowd. Why would he do otherwise on such a flat pitch with good bounce and carry? Out strides Hobbs and Woolley, two living monuments of the game, throwbacks from a bygone era, Hobbs 47 years old, Woolley 43, still plying their trade at the highest level, both selected on merit. Woolley walks out, much the taller, with that ramrod straight back, left shoulder slightly but conspicuously higher than the right.

Hobbs takes guard to Tim Wall, the Australian spearhead. Pipes puffing, folk in deep concentration, absorbing the initial overs, considerately silent as the bowler runs up. A single to both in the first over opens their accounts. Woolley shapes up to Fairfax at the start of the second over who runs in to bowl his customary in-swingers and away-swingers. He bowls a length delivery on off-stump that Woolley dispatches through mid-off. Next ball the Kent left-hander glides a couple behind square and a meaty cover drive is partially stopped with stinging hands at extra cover; they scamper a single.

Wall roars in like a charging stallion, all hustle and bustle and chest puffed out. He bowls fractionally short and Woolley sails into this with a sledgehammer square cut that fairly rockets to the boundary down the hill towards the Mound Stand. The rest of the over Woolley plays with due respect as Wall recovers his line and length.

Hobbs is not used to being out-gunned at the crease. The thunderous roars of approval from the capacity crowd are kindled by his new partner. In comparison the greatest England batsman of all time looks subdued. Woolley fails to notice a sharp single to get the agitated Hobbs off-strike and next ball Hobbs edges behind to keeper Oldfield, and England are one down for 13. Had the more sedate and safe Sutcliffe been at the other end, or in his absence Hobbs's Surrey partner Sandham, Hobbs would not have felt the pressure to push at one obviously wide of off stump. The old man's pride had cost him.

A ripple of applause greeted Hobbs as he walked up the pavilion steps. As he walked through the Long Room the old pranker remembered Walter Robins stuffing three brand new England Cricket caps into his cricket bag from the box of caps in the Gentlemen's dressing-room. Allegedly three former England cricketers (Nigel Haig, Jack Durston and Jack Hearne) had approached Walter Robins before the game to bung them fresh new caps to replace their faded ones at home. All three had been slaughtered in previous Ashes encounters during Armstrong's time. Durston only had the one England cap. Anyway, Hobbs walked into the Gentlemen's dressing-room and stuffed the remaining thirty or so new England caps into Robin's cricket bag; he managed to close the bag up and leave the scene before any of the Gentlemen could notice.

The Lord's test of 1930, Sutcliffe-less as it was, proved irrefutably that a new superstar had emerged to challenge the supremacy of England's great reservoir of batting talent. This new phenomenon was to shake world cricket like nothing before or since: the Bradman effect.

England reached 405/9 at the end of an exhilarating day's play, ignited by Woolley with his glorious cameo (41) before the Pride of Kent fell to one of the great gully catches in Ashes history: hard-hit; off the full face of the bat; hit downwards while executing a sledgehammer square cut to a Fairfax long-hop; straight into Wall's outstretched right hand. Woolley lit the path and no-one on the 27th June 1930 batted with greater splendour, though Kumar Duleepsinhji (173) made by far the largest contribution before throwing his wicket away recklessly having a heave at Grimmett. Tate (54), Hendren (48) and Hammond (38) all contributed and a last wicket partnership of 38 helped swell the score to 425 on Day Two but so far, and including the 162-run opening partnership between Woodfull and Ponsford in Australia's reply, the main incident of the game had yet to take place.

Don Bradman (254) played what he reckoned to be his greatest ever innings. Every single shot was executed perfectly from start to finish. He only raised one shot above the carpet throughout his record-breaking innings – the highest Test score in England – and that was a catch struck to within Chapman's vicinity. Australia totalled a record 729/6 declared and Hobbs (18) failed again in the second innings, scratching around like a has-been. Despite a heroic rearguard action from the captain Percy Chapman (121) and Gubby Allen (57), Australia won by seven wickets. The return of Herbert Sutcliffe could not come soon enough.

Hobbs wanted to retire from Test cricket there and then.

Walter Robins had a moment of idiocy so crucial to the outcome. Batting with Jack White and building a lead for England to have some total to bowl at, the pair had put on 18 with reasonable ease to take England into a lead of 69. Yet Robins ran himself out much to the horror of the crowd at Headquarters. Folk were agog at his stupidity as he walked through the Long Room. Leveson-Gower reproached him for his stupidity and Robins told him where to get off before hastening towards the Gentlemen's dressing-room.

After England's defeat, Robins did not make a habit of entering the Players dressing-room but, frankly, a red line had been crossed. Robins had endured a cross-examination during the aftermath of a thrashing. Having suffered horrific first-innings figures of 42 overs 1/172, Walter Robins had at least picked up 2/34 as Australia reached 72/3. He did not know whether he had praise or admonishment coming his way when Shrimp asked for another word. 'Shrimp' Leveson-Gower had noticed with some concern the theft of 31 brand new England cricket caps from the box in the Gentlemen's dressing-room. He had also seen how Walter's cricket bag had swollen to twice the size. Robins had thus endured a cross-examination during the emotional aftermath of a record-breaking defeat, from a gentleman of the cricketing world whose integrity was beyond reproach. Robins, who many professionals regarded as rather full of himself, opened the door, entered, hands on hips and totally lacking in comedy. The players listened with eyes flitting from player to player, searching for any sign of the guilty party. Hobbs, Woolley, Hendren and Tate knew all right. Newer members, those not there on the 1924/25 Ashes trip, may not have known Hobbs the pranker. His pranks may have become rarer with maturity but this one worked to perfection and helped Hobbs continue his England career to the end of the series. In the end, with Chairman of Selectors emerging behind Walter Robins, both with distraught expressions, Hobbs confessed his folly. Made to feel a thief, Walter Robins failed to see the funny side.

Rather than stand shoulder to shoulder with Walter Robins, Percy Chapman stood with Hobbs. It was only a prank, played at a time when Duleepsinhji and England appeared to be doing well, not during or after his pummelling at the hands of Bradman. Both Hobbs and Chapman made a mental note not to pick Robins for the next Test.

The first ten days of July gave time for Sutcliffe's thumb to heal, have the three stitches taken out, have dead skin flake off and the wound dry out beyond all possibility of infection. He returned to light nets from 4th July while Jack Hobbs helped himself to 75 and 38 against Derbyshire, at Derby.

Yorkshire faced Surrey before the third Test at Sheffield for Emmett Robinson's benefit game. Macauley removed Hobbs (17) lbw but Surrey went on to win by an innings. First game back from injury, Sutcliffe (95) gave staunch resistance as Yorkshire subsided to 206 all out in the first innings but was bowled by Allom for a duck as Yorkshire folded second time round for 210, held together by Maurice Leyland (98).

After such a savage beating at Lord's, Leveson-Gower demanded change and the selectors dropped both Woolley and Hendren for the third Test at Headingley. Not since the Old Trafford Test of 1909 had England gone into an Ashes Test with neither Woolley nor Hendren. Woolley's game was more for the three-day game of yore, Hendren was unlucky and he felt the pain acutely. He hoped the decision was based on sound cricketing judgement. Sutcliffe returned to join Hobbs, Hammond remained at three, Duleepsinhji at four, Leyland brought in at five. Geary came in for his all-round qualities instead of Gubby Allen (0/115 at Lord's, despite the second innings 57), and Robins found himself cast away into the wilderness and replaced by Richard Tyldesley, the very fellow whom Robins had remarked recently was 'very fat'. Instead of Jack White's slow left-arm (3/166 at Lord's), the England attack armed itself with sharp pace from the returning Harold Larwood.

England versus Australia 3rd Test Headingley 1930

Australia won the toss and England fielded all day under a barrage of scorching drives, pulls and hooks as the bowlers toiled while Don Bradman beat all existing Test records with 309 not out overnight, having scored 105 before lunch so emulating Macartney on the same ground four years earlier. Mainly due to the 21-year-old batting sensation, Australia reached 458/3 at the close.

The England dressing-room took on a sombre mood after play ended. The Headingley pitch had played immaculately, bounce even and pace nicely coming onto the bat. What a toss to lose. As for Larwood, Tate, Geary and Tyldesley, none of them spoke, they sat weary limbed licking their wounds. The unit had been tamed, overwhelmed, ravaged, with egos plundered.

"Well, played chaps, better luck tomorrow", quipped Chapman, glugging from his lemonade bottle. For once the bonhomie of the team failed to ignite, the responses subdued.

Next morning the last seven wickets fell for the addition of 98 runs with Bradman (334) getting 25 of them to overhaul Sandham's infant record as the highest score in Tests. Only Maurice Tate (5/124) could take solace from his performance. Larwood looked drained, Geary innocuous, Tyldesley leaked runs but at least Hammond (1/40) kept his end quiet. In response to 566, Hobbs and Sutcliffe reached 17 without loss at lunch on day two.

The score mounted without alarm to 53. Hobbs then played a forward defensive prod to a good length Grimmett top-spinner and the ball stayed long enough in the atmosphere to invite a dive forward from a'Beckett, fielding at silly mid-on, who rolled over and came to rest on his knees, claiming a magnificent catch. Hobbs was not so sure and later on said Bertie Oldfield, the Australian keeper, had told him that a'Beckett had *not* made the catch. The bowler's umpire, Tom Oates, blinded by a'Beckett's dive, referred the decision to the square leg umpire, Bill Bestwick, who hesitated, then gave Hobbs out. The incident veered towards tarnishing the good sportsman aroma Hobbs had acquired over the previous two decades. The pressure of responding to Bradman's superhuman run machine was starting to mount.

Sutcliffe (32) fell soon after but England grafted hard to reach 212/5, with Hammond 61* overnight. England required a further 205 to save the follow-on, Heavy rain came to England's help and erased most of the third day's play, the umpires not commencing play until 5.45pm. Neither Hammond nor nightwatchman Duckworth forced the pace and both survived until the close. Hammond (113) produced his only decent score all series while Duckworth (33), Chapman (45) and Tate (22) helped the score to 391.

Following-on for a nervous last three hours of the game, Hobbs and Sutcliffe began well but a dark cloud came over. As they patted the wicket, Herbert commented: ''what do you think about the light?''

''Not very good'' answered Hobbs, ''and if Clarrie Grimmett goes on at the dark end we will appeal''.

Grimmett sometimes bowled with a low arm, one that gets hidden in the shadows of the stand behind. Woodfull put Grimmett on at the dark end and the openers appealed against the light and succeeded. The Headingley crowd booed the openers, a crowd reaction neither batsman had felt before. Five minutes later the umpires brought everyone back on and both openers showed enough composure to calm the nerves of the crowd until Sutcliffe drove gently to mid-off and started on a run. Mid-off happened to be Bradman who had lulled Hobbs into thinking he was asleep to the threat. Exactly the opposite was the case; Bradman had laid a trap and the old boy fell into it. Sauntering down the wicket without a care in the world, Hobbs ground his bat like he had done tens of thousands of times before, in the correct manner. Bradman accelerated at the ball, scooped down and threw with Hobbs still a full yard short when the stumps broke. The event brought out loud squeals of delight from several young members of Woodfull's team, in contrast to the crowd's silence from disappointment.

Sutcliffe chiselled out 28*, bat low to the ground. Hammond (35) fell once more to Grimmett but the umpires took the players off for bad light to end the game at 5.50pm. England had escaped thanks only to the weather. A further week and a half went by without either opener playing for their counties.

Anxious about the Bradman factor, the selectors made several changes to the bowling department in a desperate shuffling of weapons. Larwood needed resting for the Old Trafford Test; in his place Morris Nichols of Essex was chosen through his eye-catching performances with the ball. Taking regular wickets all through the season, pace bowler Nicholls had captured 25 Championship wickets for Essex at home since the start of July at a cost of 7.88 each. What is more against Glamorgan he scored a century so could bat at number eight.

Richard Tyldesley had underwhelmed at Headingley so Tom Goddard, an off-spinner from Gloucestershire, made his debut several months shy of his thirtieth birthday. Though given an ordeal at the hands of Yorkshire with figures of 4/153 immediately prior to the fourth Test, Goddard had picked up plenty of wickets and, having altered from an out-and-out fast bowler only two seasons earlier, Goddard had a lethal faster ball that pinged full and into the batsman's pads; Goddard also enjoyed a massive breakback from his off-spinners. George Geary moved aside in favour of Ian Peebles, the tall Middlesex leg-spinner and googly bowler, of Scottish ancestry, educated at Oxford. Perhaps Bradman might be susceptible to googlies bowled by a more accurate bowler than Walter Robins?

England versus Australia 4th Test Old Trafford 1930

The fourth Test at Old Trafford in 1930 ended a draw because only 45 minutes play was possible on the third day, with the whole of the fourth day washed out completely. In what play took place, Ian Peebles had Bradman beaten by turn and unconvincing against googlies. Put it this way, Peebles beat Bradman for turn, had him dropped by Hammond in the slips then caught by Duleepsinhji for 14. Australia pottered along, inflated by an eighth wicket partnership of 87 between Fairfax (49) and Grimmett (50), to 345.

Hobbs and Sutcliffe scored 29 in the 35 minutes before lunch on day two. During this time Tim Wall unleashed a vicious breakback that struck Hobbs in the bollocks, a proper broadside-blow. He fell like a shot stag to the ground and uttered an ungodly comment best lost for good in the silence of history. After a couple of minutes of writhing around on the ground clutching his genitals, Hobbs slowly dragged himself back on to his feet and noticed all the young, grinning faces under their baggy green caps. Even Sutcliffe wore a broad smile. The pain lingered on after lunch but Hobbs refused to buckle. Sutcliffe, for once, comfortably outscored Hobbs and when the younger man reached his fifty, Hobbs had but 13.

The contrast in tempo could not be more marked. Sutcliffe *'gave a brilliant display of driving, pulling and hooking. He might have been caught directly after lunch if Hornibrook, fielding in the slips, had not baulked Richardson but that was the only mistake in a dashing exhibition of strong and certain forcing cricket.' (Wisden 1931)*

The century partnership came up for the eleventh and final time for Hobbs and Sutcliffe in Ashes Tests. Hobbs (31) edged Wall to Oldfield, trying to force the pace with a cut shot. Hammond (3) played on to Wall and Sutcliffe (74) was held brilliantly by Bradman, right on the mid-wicket boundary fence. Duleepsinhji (50) and Leyland (35) helped take the score to 251/8 before rain ended the contest.

Eighteen days stretched ahead before the final Test, now upgraded to timeless because the conclusion would decide the Ashes. It rained heavily for the time of year. Australia managed to win by an innings over Somerset at Taunton. Archie Jackson (118) found some useful form at last with his first century of the tour and Bradman (117) had not yet stopped feasting. The forgotten Jack White (4/91) had some reward for his efforts. Glamorgan (93) were despatched by the noble presence of Grimmett and menacing pace of Wall but rain prevented a result. Warwickshire (102/3) against the tourists ended in a rain-soaked draw without Australia even batting. Then they succumbed to the off-breaks of Northants and England cricket legend Vallance Jupp (6/32, including Bradman) who caught the tourists on a sticky-dog and bundled them out for 93. Woodfull (116) and Vic Richardson (116) dug them out of trouble to ensure a draw.

Sutcliffe spent the time in between showers playing second fiddle for much of the time with Percy Holmes, who carried his bat for 132 against Gloucestershire while Sutcliffe (13) failed. Sutcliffe (15) failed again on his one visit to the middle in the Old Trafford Roses match and scored a duck against Leicestershire when Holmes made

81. He recovered some form with 52 against Derbyshire in Leeds and followed this with 132* in Sheffield against Glamorgan during a 235-run partnership with Holmes (130 run out).

Hobbs picked and chose his fixtures. The 47-year-old volunteered to face Larwood and Voce on his Oval pitch and scored 36 before Larwood removed him, caught by Staples. Some fresh air down on the South coast with Ada brought Hobbs down to Hove to face Sussex whereupon he struck 106 before Tate bowled him. Haig bowled him for 40 in a friendly against Middlesex at the Oval. When Hobbs had reached 16, he overtook Dr W.G. Grace's record first-class runs with 54,921. Hobbs declined to visit Birmingham and Cheltenham, instead he rested up and popped in to his sports shop.

'Dodger' Whysall raised the selectors' eye-brows with 120 against the Australians and had scored heavily in the last few years. In the last three weeks he had made 128 against Kent and 'Tich' Freeman, then his highest career score of 248 against Vallance Jupp's Northamptonshire team. The trouble with Whysall was his age of 42 which meant that this most solid of batsmen was also slow on his feet.

The selectors convened once more before Jupp's 6/32 against the Australians so the earthy amateur remained in the international wilderness. The sensation erupted when news filtered out that Percy Chapman had been removed from office. Warner noted he had lost his edge as a captain and his field placements had become too static. Chapman's drinking had also ruffled feathers and his batting looked too simplistic, based too much upon a swashbuckling see-ball-hit-ball mentality. Though an excellent close-in fielder, in fact arguably the best in the world, Chapman had lost his athletic youth before time and carried a buoyant amount of timber. Bob Wyatt received the call-up to captain England because he was a steady batsman and a tidy medium-paced swing bowler, more suited than Chapman for the balance of the team. The nuances of a timeless Test demanded a higher price on one's wicket.

Hobbs hid his look of horror as best he could. Rhodes stared out of the window and into the distance, so as to remain calm. What had they done? All five selectors came to the decision although Hobbs, in retrospect, admitted their error. The horror on Hobbs's face came from the bowling attack. Tate remained the spearhead but had already put in a huge shift. Larwood was returning having cleared up his niggle. Ian Peebles bowled 55 overs in the fourth Test and purchased his three wickets at the cost of 50 each, conspicuously more than Goddard, 2/49 from 32 accurate overs, more than Hammond 2/24, Nichols 2/33 and Tate 1/39. Three wickets for 150 would have done for many a bowler, his dismissal of Bradman alone earned him another Test. The problem was that Hammond had to be the first change seamer, Wyatt bowled his military medium and Leyland some exotic chinamen. That was it.

Hobbs had wanted his Surrey teammate Andrew Sandham instead of Dodger, Leslie Ames as a batsman-keeper instead of Duckworth and Tom Goddard, Tich Freeman or Charlie Parker instead of Peebles. The press had a field day. Wyatt even received a death threat if he dared take England team on to the Oval field.

Bob Wyatt displayed a face at rest that settled into a natural frown hinting at disapproval. He looked like someone not worth knowing yet no one ever had a bad word to say about him. His batting had a solidity about it that made one drift into an afternoon nap. He could hit the ball hard but no one ever reminisced about the glory of Bob's batting. He bowled useful medium pace bowling that could potentially break stands but it was the dependability of his batting, to add a spine to the middle-order instead of the happy slapper Chapman, that planted the England captaincy into Bob's lap. A little uneasy at supplanting good old Percy amidst the storm of protest, Bob gave Percy the freedom of the England dressing-room throughout the Test.

Once more queues formed the evening before the great timeless Test, England supporters hoping for a repeat of 1926. Men wearing caps and smoking fags sat on boxes playing cards under street lights, urchins came forth asking for pennies, rats scuttled around the pavement across the road, a conversation on the merits of Wyatt against Chapman wafted over as tired folk gave up on the night and lay down under blankets to snatch a few hours kip. As sleeping rough goes, the conditions on the evening of August 15th 1930 were benign, warm and dry. With dawn at six and traffic belching out vehicle exhaust fumes most in the queues woke up early. The queue appeared to be composed of groups of people, between two and ten in number, so that one of them could buy refreshments from the pop-up stalls or wander off to urinate against some wall not so easily seen by others, and return to their place in the queue. Public toilets existed at the tube station but that was a ten-minute walk.

England versus Australia 5th Test Oval 1930

In 1926 the scoreline of 0-0 from three-day games prompted that famous timeless Test, now the scoreline of 1-1 from four-day games delivered the next. After the crowd made their way in, Wyatt and Woodfull walked out to toss the coin under a cloudless sky. Wyatt read out his team sheet:

''Hobbs, Sutcliffe, Whysall, Hammond, Duleepsinhji, Leyland, Wyatt, Tate, Larwood, Peebles, Duckworth''.

Woodfull responded with his:

''Woodfull, Ponsford, Bradman, Jackson, Kippax, McCabe, Fairfax, Oldfield, Grimmett, Wall, Hornibrook''.

Conversations closed as the coin fell, Wyatt looked down, that frown seemed to disperse and it came up heads. He shook Woodfull's hand and both walked back to the pavilion, the crowd straining to interpret any sign. Eventually Woodfull looked up to his balcony and signalled a bowling action that raised an immense cheer.

Ten minutes later out strode the Hobbs and Sutcliffe. Hobbs blue cap on head walking as always to the right of his younger partner, himself, short-back-and-sides dark brown hair neatly parted. With Oldfield at the far end and Hall marking his run-up at the Pavilion End, Hobbs walked to the far wickets, noting the three slips, gully, point fielder some twenty yards away, square leg a similar distance, just a ring of fielders saving the single and Fairfax at deep fine leg.

A great monument of the game, hero-worshipped by man and boy alike, who straddled the era from W.G. to Bradman, still exudes comfort and class. There he is, back in behind the ball with time to spare. He lets two go by the off-stump then taps a full one, too straight, down to fine leg to get off the mark, inducing a ripple of appreciative applause.

Fairfax holds no surprises for Hobbs at the far end and he dominates the stand as Sutcliffe prepares himself for the long haul. The sun is out, the wind light, the temperature already into the mid-seventies Fahrenheit, the wicket easy paced, bounce even: perfect conditions.

Both are circumspect, realising the need for crease occupation and after an hour 24 runs have been added. Woodfull shuffles his attack and replaces his opening bowlers with Grimmett and McCabe and it is off a wide swinging McCabe half-volley that Hobbs drives sumptuously through the covers for four. Sutcliffe meets in mid-pitch just as the ball bounces over the ropes.

"Marvellous shot Jack", he exclaims.

"Just warming up Herbert" the legend winks.

Sutcliffe bats as Sutcliffe does. He gives the appearance of not timing the ball, especially when essaying his favourite hook shot. Sutcliffe exudes strength, Hobbs exudes class and the score ticks along in steady fashion until Hobbs square cuts Grimmett emphatically for four to induce a spontaneous and rousing cheer from his beloved and faithful home crowd.

Woodfull removes McCabe and brings on left-arm medium pacer Percy Hornibrook who Hobbs glances to long leg for another boundary. Wall comes on for a second spell and immediately unleashes a head high bouncer that Hobbs hooks with mature and ravishing brilliance for four. Within the first hour sufficient memories are etched to satisfy the entrance fee. The crowd come alive in rapturous applause, enveloping them all in the warm womb of wonderment.

How cruel the dismay that immediately descends is tangible as Hobbs attempts a repeat hook to another bouncer, slightly faster than the one before but Hobbs hideously mistimes the hook so that it lands in short leg's hands and the Surrey and England champion has to walk off for 47, from a total of 68. At least Hobbs had performed better than in his first innings here four years earlier. Whysall (13) missed a straight one from Wall (97/2) but Duleepsinhji (50) cut, drove and pulled with delightful effect, dominating a stand of 65 with Sutcliffe. Yet when Hammond (13) and Leyland (3) were both bowled by Grimmett and McCabe respectably, England had slumped to 197/5.

Sutcliffe batted superbly in the evening session. He had batted four and a quarter hours until tea for 68, then advanced this to 138 not out by the close. Wisden records:

'He (Sutcliffe) and Wyatt added 119 and before Sutcliffe was out on Monday morning the stand had realised 170 runs in two hours thirty-five minutes. Sutcliffe batted for six hours and three-quarters and scored exactly the same number of runs as he had done in the corresponding match four years previously. The situation compelled him to play a restrained game until he and Wyatt had definitely settled together but from tea-time on the opening day his cricket was first-class. ... Sutcliffe brought off some splendid hits to square-leg and to the on, while his off-driving was admirable. As far as was seen he did not give a chance...'

England reached 405 (Sutcliffe 161, Wyatt 64, Duleepsinhji 50, Hobbs 47) but that proved insufficient in the shadow of Australia's 695 (Bradman 232, Ponsford 110, Jackson 73, McCabe 54, Fairfax 53*, Peebles 6/201).

Larwood (1/132) and Tate (1/153) had figures to forget but there were crumbs for comfort. Jardine watched footage of Bradman's 232. A heavy shower had spruced up the wicket for a time during Australia's mammoth innings and Bradman appeared to flinch in the face of several thunderbolts from Larwood that rose wickedly from the surface. When Bradman had 175, Larwood struck him a painful blow above the heart and Duckworth noticed hesitancy in Bradman's batting. Jackson (73) suffered a dozen body blows from length balls that rose. The concept of 'bodyline' had its origins here, in a courageous fourth-wicket partnership of 243 between the two youngsters that decided the result. Indeed, Archie Jackson had a life even before he got off the mark. He drove Peebles to mid-off, Hobbs bounded in all 47 years of him, scooped up the ball and lobbed it underarm to the umpire's end only for the ball to bounce past with Jackson yards short. The pair quickly realised they could run singles to Whysall all day long, the mobility of the 43-year-old short of Test standard, speed of foot waning through two days in the field, despite weather interruptions.

At any rate, heavy rain and a drying sun had turned the pitch into a hazardous wicket by the time Hobbs and Sutcliffe walked out to bat in the gloom of the evening session on day three. For the final time in Test cricket with the crowd on their feet applauding the final chapter of a glorious era, the two famous players had 45 minutes to survive until the close.

Wyatt had asked Hobbs whether he might like to bat tomorrow and have a nightwatchman open instead but Hobbs was adamant. Hobbs, to the right of raven-haired Sutcliffe, looked nervous in the glare of prolonged cheers abating only when the pair arrived at the wicket. Woodfull ordered his team into a circle and called Hobbs to the centre. Once surrounded by the old enemy, Hobbs received three hearty cheers with each Australian fielder doffing their caps in due reverence.

The Oval crowd had never seen the like before. Bewilderment turned to astonishment then an outbreak of delight and good cheer. The display of affection brought a tear to Hobbs and he never forgot their act of kindness, either way it softened him up.

The great pair even had the boost of genuine luck when Sutcliffe survived a dropped catch in the slip cordon. What is more, Hobbs tried to scamper a single from a defensive drop but Wall, following through, hurtled down the wicket and kicked the ball at the stumps with Hobbs obviously short of his ground. The ball missed. Everyone wanted Hobbs to sign off with some wondrous century that defied the odds but it was not to be. Hobbs (9) played on to a short delivery from Fairfax that he tried to pull for four. Under the circumstances, starting out 290 behind, the ball was too full to pull. The end for Hobbs hung a melancholy cloud over the Oval, Peebles later wrote: 'He paused sadly for a moment, then walked quietly back to the pavilion and out of Test match cricket. He took with him much of England's hope of recovery in the current match, and a quarter century of glorious memories'. England closed on 24/1.

Rain wiped out the entire day's play on Thursday 20th August and once play started up again on the Friday, Whysall (10) failed again. Sutcliffe (54) and Duleepsinhji (45) added 81 and Hammond (60) also went down fighting but the unfancied Hornibrook (7/92) largely cleaned England out in the second innings but 251 under those conditions looked a commendable effort despite the innings and 39 run defeat.

Sutcliffe had a superb series, second only to Bradman - although day-light exists between the two achievements: while Bradman had 974 runs at 139.14 (still a world record for a series), Sutcliffe came in second in terms of runs (436) and average (87.20). Hobbs came in sixth in the England averages with 301 at 33.44. He would dearly have liked to make more runs and finish his career on a high but, even so, no one had more than his 5,410 Test runs, no one who had finished his Test career had a higher average (56.94) than Hobbs and no one had scored more than his 15 Test centuries.

Chapter Eight: Warm Embers

As the shadows lengthened in the Autumnal sun, so Hobbs and Sutcliffe were reunited once again through their creator, 'Shrimp' Leveson-Gower, who still ran the end-of-season Scarborough festival, a proper three-day fixture against the Australians. Vic Richardson captained the Australians in the absence of Woodfull and Leveson-Gower gathered together eight of the England team who lost at the Oval, and played: Andrew Sandham in place of Dodger Whysall; 52-year-old Wilfred Rhodes on his final first-class game, instead of Hammond, and Charlie Parker in place of Peebles. In some ways, Shrimp showed his preferences at selection meetings. It seemed he had sensibly lined up Sandham in case Hobbs flagged during the Ashes; he rated Charlie Parker's left-arm medium pace, even though the Gloucestershire bowler was 48.

On the same ground eight years earlier almost to the day, Hobbs and Sutcliffe had started out for Shrimp's eleven against the MCC Touring Party to South Africa and they put on a century partnership with Sutcliffe going on to a century. It seemed long ago.

The pair gave Shrimp a solid start until Hobbs (24) snicked Fairfax to Oldfield; Sutcliffe (45) saw the century up before being caught in the covers. Rain lost too much time but despite Sandham (59) responding well at number four, Mr H.D.G. Leveson-Gowers XI totalled 218.

Australia replied with 238 and though Bradman scored 96 before Parker bowled him, Wisden claimed *'Bradman should have been caught at mid-off first ball and just after reaching 60 was twice missed, all three chances being off Rhodes.'*

The wily old Yorkshireman still grabbed 5/95 on his final first-class appearance. He took a wicket with his first ball on Australian soil, and a wicket with his last on English soil. Rhodes finished with a world record 4,187 first-class wickets and 58 centuries. His achievement outshone Hobbs (59) and Sutcliffe (27) who both made contributions in the second innings before the match ended in rain.

Hobbs still loved batting so carried on playing for Surrey. The 1930 season as a whole proved above average for Hobbs. He made 2,103 runs at 51.29 and came sixth though Sutcliffe, with 2,312 runs at 64.22, topped the chart.

When Hobbs and Sutcliffe disbanded at Test level, Sutcliffe had 3,231 Test runs at 67.31. Hobbs rested up, ran his sports shop and collected £500 from a shilling fund set up by the Herald. The newspaper had done the same for W.G. Grace, at the same age, after his glorious summer of 1895. They raised far more for the Doctor. The cloud of Ashes defeat had been too painful for ordinary folk to dip into their pockets.

Hobbs had two options for the winter of 1930/31: mooch about in his sports shop all winter; or take Ada to India on a private tour with the Maharajah of Vizianagaram's XI. Hobbs chose the latter, especially when he knew Sutcliffe was going. The pair played a series of matches against fledgling Indian State sides and Sri Lanka (then Ceylon). Hobbs scored two centuries but the games at the time were not considered first-class. Sutcliffe's finest shot all tour appears to have been a direct hit on a panther while out big-game hunting near Benares.

The famous pair were, at one time, guests of the Maharaj Kumar and further accompanied by a couple of princes. Proud of his kill, Sutcliffe dashed from his platform to run over and inspect the felled beast before being warned not to. Hobbs shot a sambur, rather a large deer weighing in at over 200 kg. According to Sutcliffe: 'Jack was quite excited about the success of his shot until he saw the dead beast. The ''look'' in his eyes – I cannot describe it – upset him greatly, and, though he did not say anything at all about it. I am sure he made a vow there and then never to kill again. At all events, his part in that hunt ended with his first shot. He never lifted the rifle to his shoulder again'.

Next day with Hobbs playing golf, Sutcliffe went off into the bush in search of further large animals to shoot. He had the company of a weapon-less guide and recent tales of a large tiger on the prowl ringing in his ears from the evening before. He soon shot a sambur and was hot on the trail of taking a bear out as well when his guide heard a rustle in the undergrowth to their left. Sutcliffe heard the wish to hush and, no doubts some carnivore had crept up stealthily, snapping branches intermittently, the timings between each snap indicating a deliberate attempt at stalking. Sutcliffe raised his rifle in readiness, heart in mouth, praying the rifle would oblige if required. Images of newspaper headlines screamed across his face: England legend devoured by tiger. For all that caution out came a tiny fox just as scared of Sutcliffe. He vowed never to enter the bush again with only one gun.

1931

In that sunset year of 1930, Don Bradman piled up 3,170 first-class runs at 99.06. In 1931 Herbert Sutcliffe delivered a handsome imitation with 3,006 at 96.36 while the venerable Surrey and ex-England opener managed 2,418 at a respectable 56.23.

New Zealand came over for their second visit and played three Tests. Sutcliffe missed the first Test but played the last two where an innings victory and rain meant he only batted twice, centuries on both occasions, one a not out and an average of 226. Hobbs, of course, had retired from international cricket but the two great pals were reunited on three occasions, twice representing the Players (in the Gentlemen versus Players fixtures) before they both ended the season turning out for their creator's XI against the touring New Zealanders.

In the second week of June, Hobbs and Sutcliffe turned out for the Players in a fixture that had relapsed the previous year but aside from that had been a regular fixture at Lord's (Great War excepted) since 1806. To compensate, three fixtures were set into the calendar with the first, at the Oval, heavily depleted of cricketers on both sides due to ten counties involved with the County Championship. From the Players team and apart from the great openers, only Leyland, Verity and Bowes were - or were to become - successful

Test cricketers. The Gentlemen had Wyatt, Jardine, the ageing Percy Fender and a giant of a fast-medium right-arm bowler in Maurice Allom.

Foul weather made for spectator discomfort and boredom on the first day since only two hours and forty minutes play took place in between three stoppages. However, within the four periods of play, Hobbs and Sutcliffe achieved their twenty-fourth opening stand together and by the close had reached 193/0. Scrutinising their innings, Wisden wrote: *'In this way the batsmen had to play themselves in some four times yet they always succeeded in so doing. Sutcliffe, it is true, was at fault once or twice, putting up on the off side a ball from Palmer that fell between the fieldsman and, when 21, skying another from Morkel on the leg side where Wyatt, running some distance, judged the catch well but failed to make it. On the whole, however, Sutcliffe played extremely well, bringing off some very pretty strokes on the leg-side and some fine clean drives. His batting, however, did not reach the standard of that of Hobbs who was quite at his best, thoroughly master of the ball however much it rose and using the pull with particularly good effect. Hobbs had made 60 and Sutcliffe 43 when, with the total at 105, there came the delay of nearly two hours.*

After the break the bowlers had to use a wet ball and two such experienced batsmen took full advantage. Hobbs made shots all-round the wicket and reached the 179th century of his career before the close. When an inswinger from Allom had him trapped on the crease Hobbs had 110 in a partnership of 203. Sutcliffe (120) got stumped and the rest of the innings folded for 329. There was never any prospect of a result in three rain interrupted days. Arthur Wellard (5/45) and Bill Bowes (3/55) removed the Gentlemen for 205 and Hobbs (31) and Sutcliffe (36) gave a satisfactory start to the second innings in the drawn game.

Months past and the pair next met each other at the Oval in the Surrey Yorkshire Championship match in late August. Inevitably, both players enjoyed great games but, also common in 1931, rain interfered to prevent a result. Sutcliffe (26 and 101*) batted excellently and scored his twelfth century of the season while Hobbs (133*) carried his bat and rose to great heights, putting on 82 for the ninth wicket with Allom (38) to hand Surrey a first innings lead of

67. The old maestro faced down the young, tall, bespectacled paceman, enjoying his breakthrough season, Bill Bowes, and his future England team mate, Hedley Verity, who seamlessly filled the void left by the retirement of Wilfred Rhodes. Sutcliffe and the rain had the last say.

Another anecdote hidden in the annals of time took place in the Grand Hotel at Scarborough where the amateurs stayed during the famous cricket festival. It was the evening before the Gentlemen versus Players fixture, one of Shrimp's three end-of-season cricket matches, nine days of cricket in all. After the hotel supper of beef and potatoes with blackberry crumble and custard for dessert, the Gentlemen convened around the bar in the Cricketers' Room for port and cigars.

Vallance Jupp, that earthy humoured chap from Northants, could be heard telling a joke about a pickled penis. Trouble was Jupp had his back to Shrimp, the Chairman of Selectors and long-term organiser of the Scarborough Festival. Shrimp was holding some photographs of the cricketers for them to sign. Shrimp coughed to announce his presence and curb Jupp's crude joke. So enthusiastic was Jupp in bellowing out his new joke that not only did he fail to hear the cough - out came an enactment of a woman being fucked hard by some new sex toy, the pickled penis, one sourced from abroad too impolite to mention in 2022. Apparently, after unscrewing the lid from the jar, the penis could perform at the following commands: ''pickle penis my fanny'' stirred the penis into bouncing out of the jar towards the woman to perform the required task; ''pickle penis back in the jar'' instructed the toy to stop, retreat slowly, then bounce back in the jar ready for next time.

After Jupp had enacted an unfeasibly loud female orgasm, complete with eyes clamped shut, face contorted into pulses of disfigured pleasure, the pickled penis failed to stop when commanded such that the woman-in-the-joke ran naked out into the streets in broad daylight being chased by the bouncing pickled penis; whereupon she ran around the corner and bumped into a policeman.

''Hello, hello, hello and what have we here?'' said the policeman-in-the-joke

''Help me officer! I am being chased by a pickle penis'' screamed the woman-in-the-joke.

''PICKLE PENIS?'' yelled the disbelieving officer, ''MY ARSE!''

Launching his punchline gave Jupp the opportunity to reveal the hilarity of the joke by embarking on a loud, raucous laugh that resonated from the belly and continued right to the purple face and wide-open mouth. Moreover, he thumped the table to further acclaim the comedy before eventually quietening down and replenishing his breathe.

Jupp failed to extract much in the way of audible laughter, just red faces and controlled titters.

''Would you gentlemen and Jupp care to sign these photos?'' enquired Shrimp.

Starting on the 5th September, the first day's play between the Gentlemen and Players ended in the disappointment of an abandonment. With two days left there simply was no chance of a result. Nonetheless Hobbs won the toss and elected to bat. The crowd sat back and watched the famous pair record their seventh first-wicket partnership of over 200; they saw Hobbs (144) score his ninth century of the season and the 184th of his career; moreover, it was their 25th century partnership in first-class cricket.

Sutcliffe benefitted from being dropped by Walter Robins off Nigel Haig when on one, with the score only nine. After that he hit splendidly well on the leg-side and played a *masterly innings* before edging Haig once more to Robins in the slips who made no mistake this time. The partnership of 227 took 160 minutes. Hobb's *batting in practically faultless fashion and bringing off some especially delightful strokes in front of the wicket, reached his hundred in two hours and three-quarters.*

Despite nursing a hangover, Vallance Jupp claimed the wickets of Hendren (28), Leyland (0), Paynter (6) and Larwood (11) with especially well flighted off-breaks to claim 4/74 before Hobbs declared overnight at 414/6. The Players bowled the Gentlemen out for 210 (Wyatt 92) before Leyland and Paynter reached 27 without loss; then came rain for the final say.

The next day the New Zealanders took on Mr H.D.G. Leveson Gower's XI, a team brimming with England stars past (Hobbs), present (Sutcliffe, Duleepsinhji, Wyatt, Leyland, Allen, Larwood,

Verity) and those who had once played for England but, despite being available, were never again picked (Vallance Jupp).

Perhaps the New Zealand bowlers were tired after a summer of general impotence. There were some easy Test runs on offer in 1931. Sutcliffe, remember, had averaged 226 against them: two innings, two centuries; one not out. Hardly seemed fair to pit them against such giants as Hobbs and Sutcliffe. The great pair delighted the capacity crowd in a wondrous partnership of 243 in 190 minutes, in response to New Zealand's 217. According to Wisden: *'Giving no chance and driving and pulling to great purpose, Hobbs registered his tenth hundred of the season and the 185th of his career. Sutcliffe, batting with much skill but lacking enterprise, took four hours and a half to make 126 – his thirteenth hundred in 1931.'*

Finding a new partner for Sutcliffe in time for the Ashes in Australia over the winter of 1932/33, had become a burning issue. Sutcliffe, now 37 years old, was still very much in his prime. Hobbs found himself excluded from Test Trial matches but in one of these, the North versus South game at Old Trafford, Sutcliffe performed outstandingly to ward off defeat for the North after the South had posted 447 (Woolley 50, Duleepsinhji 128, Hammond 130, Voce 5/106). First Sutcliffe made 96 out of 242; then - following on - the North made 307 with the dapper Yorkshireman, 110*, carrying his bat.

Only once were Hobbs and Sutcliffe reunited in 1932, the occasion at Lord's in mid-July for the Players against the Gentlemen. Hammond (110) batted superbly with powerful and well timed driving the hallmarks. Hobbs (24) had batted breezily before playing on to Gubby Allen and Sutcliffe (16) laboured for seventy minutes. The Players managed 301 thanks to contributions from Paynter (45), Voce (26*) and Freeman (31) but the Gentlemen took a hold on the match with a first innings lead of 129 thanks to centuries from Duleepsinhji (132) and the Nawab of Pataudi (165), bolstered further with 64 from England captain Jardine. Jardine declared overnight to force a result on the last day.

When the Players batted with such a deficit, Hobbs and Sutcliffe put on 62. Wisden pulls no punches here:

Hobbs from the start showed himself in splendid form. Sutcliffe, on the other hand, although helping to raise the score ... never seemed quite at home with the attack.

Sutcliffe (21) fell LBW to Freddie Brown who, twenty years later, would captain England. Allen removed Woolley (31) and Hammond (5) before the arrears had been wiped clean, then Hendren (14) soon after. Hobbs played delightfully and after three hours brought up the 189th century of his first-class career. With the game alive, three hours remaining and only 99 ahead and three wickets remaining, Hobbs put on 50 with Voce (27) and 42 with Duckworth (16) before carrying his bat for 161* - extraordinary performance considering Hobbs was in his fiftieth year. Wisden records:

Batting in masterly fashion for five hours, Hobbs gave no chance and but for slight lameness would, no doubt, have scored many more than 161. His great innings was made up of eleven 4's, thirteen 3's, thirteen 2's and fifty-two singles.

On hearing the news back in London, Pelham Warner broke down in tears of joy.

Only one Test was played during the 1932 season, against India at Lord's. This was the very first official Test played by India, then composed also of Pakistan and Bangladesh. Naturally, the inexperience of India led to their downfall although the 158-run defeat masked the fact that had the England captain, Douglas Jardine, not scored 79 and 85* - the result might have become nothing less than a national humiliation.

Sutcliffe (3 and 19) and his Yorkshire opening partner, Percy Holmes (6 and 11), had a miserable Test, one to forget. The selection of Holmes defied belief. The Yorkshire opener was 45 for goodness' sake. He may have won a contest for the size of his prostate gland but not for his reactions at the crease and most definitely not for his speed across the turf.

The first-class averages still showed no decline in the Master (1,764 at 56.90) who came fourth, behind Kent's exciting wicket-keeper batsman Leslie Ames (2,482 at 57.72), Ernest Tyldesley (2,420 at 59.02) and Herbert Sutcliffe (3,336 at 74.13). There was no shortage of middle-order batsmen with Hammond, Duleepsinhji, Jardine, Leyland and Hendren, established stars one and all, with batting averages over 50 for the season. The problem was Herbert's long-term England partner now he and Jack had separated amicably, citing the passage of time. Holmes had the next highest aggregate for an opener (1,208 at 44.74) but he had conspicuously notified everyone at Lord's of his own passage of time.

The Ashes of 1932/33 saw Jack Hobbs make a further visit to Australia, this time as a ghost writer. Hobbs proved a worthy writer insomuch as the detail of the cricket however his reports were so bland in terms of the controversy - the Bodyline Series. Hobbs felt unable to criticize Larwood's bowling nor Jardine's tactics. As former team-mates and Ashes winners, Hobbs felt duty-bound to sit on the fence. For this approach, Hobbs received much criticism. Many an Australian and one or two Englishmen wanted Hobbs to use his status and publicly condemn bodyline tactics.

Hobbs knew exactly what it felt like to receive bowling directed at his rib-cage and head. Bill Bowes, the tall, bespectacled Yorkshire opening bowler gave Hobbs a bouncer barrage in the Surrey Yorkshire game. Viewing this barrage, Warner felt outraged and wrote disparagingly about such intimidatory tactics in the press. That spell of bowling ensured Jardine's late approval of Bowes for the Bodyline series.

Sutcliffe played a lead role as a batsman in the Bodyline series of 1932/33. He starting off with 41 in the first Test at Sydney before the ball rolled onto his stumps. However, the bails remained unmoved and so the venerable Yorkshire and England opener went on to 194, then 1* in a 10-wicket victory. In the 4-1 series victory for England, he scored 440 at 55.00, exactly the same returns as Hammond; in one innings fewer, Bradman had 396 at 56.57. The extraordinary run-machine from the 1930 Ashes (974 at 139.14) had been successfully reduced to a mortal in the face of a barrage of fast bowling mainly directed into his rib cage, sometimes with a ring of close fielders behind square on the leg-side. Chief destroyer Larwood (33 wickets at 19.51) never played for England again, refusing to apologise simply for obeying orders from his captain, Douglas Jardine.

The two Tests on the New Zealand leg of the tour proved more productive for Wally Hammond (563 at 563) than it did for Herbert Sutcliffe (24 at 12) who also misfired in the first two Tests of the

1933 against the West Indies with scores of 21 and 20. Both Tests were won by an innings.

1933

Hobbs had turned 50 by the start of the 1933 season and he played no first-class cricket until the end of May when he turned out for Surrey, at the Oval against the West Indies. Stealing all the headlines once again, the Master stroked 221 in over six and a half hours - in response to the West Indies 480 - and was fifth out at 418. There were only 17 boundaries struck but many pleasing shots all-round the ground. The West Indian attack lacked Constantine but did include Martindale, one of the quickest, though he bowled only nine overs. In referring to Hobbs' 191st century, Wisden loved it … ''*his display was not only a triumph of skill, but no mean feat of physical endurance*''. He scored a further five centuries to winter on 196; his thoughts turned inevitably to the 200th, a feat of colossal magnitude.

Hobbs and Sutcliffe never opened together in 1933, nor did they ever oppose each other in the county game. Though Sutcliffe played in both county games between Yorkshire and Surrey, Hobbs absented himself from those games, preferring to recover from his aches.

For Sutcliffe, 1933 hinted at a gentle decline and the statistics fell short of his expectations. He came 15th in the first-class batting averages with 2,211 at 47.04 while old Jack with his 52-year-old reflexes weighed in with 1,105 at 61.38, third place behind 45-year-old Phil Mead (2,576 at 67.78) and Walter Hammond (3,323 at 67.81). Turning 39 over the winter, Sutcliffe declined to tour India for a three Test series, still under Jardine's captaincy. The selectors had ample opportunity to adjudicate Sutcliffe's potential opening partners for the 1934 Ashes.

Amateur Welshman Cyril Walters had a fine 1933 season (2,404 at 50.06) and followed with 284 runs in the Tests against India, in India, at 71.00. His place as Sutcliffe's partner at the top of the England batting order appeared a nailed-on certainty.

1934

Hobbs had high hopes of securing his 200th century. In the event, he scored his 197th in George Duckworth's benefit game at Old Trafford in late May, a four-hour vigil that released 116 runs. Wisden remarked that ''*His display, which created great enthusiasm, mainly accounted for Surrey securing the lead with six* *wickets in hand''*. His 51* in the second innings came from 149/3.

Hobbs hated his last century. He felt old. He laboured for hours; timing deserted. The only boundaries came from his pull through mid-on. The second innings fifty also brought home to him the passage of time. Common thought among his gargantuan number of middle-aged fanatics was that, had this been 1914, Hobbs would have doubled his tally. Hobbs could still defend like the best of brethren. He could no longer lace his finest knocks with the same assured driving as of old. He realised the passage of time and brought a halt to a still peerless first-class career with 624 runs at 36.70 for the 1934 domestic season. He tussled with the Australians (24 lbw bowled Grimmett) for Surrey at the Oval on a featherbed wicket at the end of May. A draw became inevitable when Sandham (219) for Surrey became eclipsed by McCabe (240) for Australia. On his last journey as a first-class cricketer, Hobbs caught the train to Folkestone where he played a final game against Australia for an England XI at Folkestone, making 38. Frank Woolley (66 and 1/28) and Lord Tennyson (1) were familiar faces from before the war with Chapman (5), Hammond (54) and Freeman (4 and 2/128) also there from his heyday. With less than three hours play on the first two days, a draw became inevitable. Sutcliffe declined to play, turning out for Yorkshire against the MCC at Scarborough instead.

Remaining in Folkestone, Hobbs turned out in his final first-class game for the Players against the Gentlemen, again no Sutcliffe. He made 24 and 18 in a low scoring encounter that saw the Gentlemen prevail by three wickets. As for Sutcliffe, fit for four of the five home Tests, his figures in the surrender of the Ashes (1-2) yielded a respectable 304 at 50.66, second behind county colleague Maurice Leyland (478 at 68.38) and fractionally ahead of Cyril Walters (401 at 50.12).

The closure of Jack's long and record-breaking first-class journey coincided with the end of Sutcliffe's Ashes career (not known at the time). There was to be a final Test match curtain call for Sutcliffe, who started the 1935 season in ominous form. A smug but aloof confidence spread through Sutcliffe's persona, buoyed by his considerable wealth accrued as a top professional. His accumulated wealth allowed Herbert to buy Woodlands, a luxury £2,000 detached house on the edge of Pudsey with commanding views of the surrounding countryside. When most of Yorkshire still used outdoor toilets, Herbert's family now had three indoor ones. That Sutcliffe could afford such a house owed almost as much to his thriftiness as to his abilities as a cricketer. His children remember a spartan existence in their early years, being forced to eat a Sunday roast in a draughty room with no heating. His accent had long since become aligned with those of an ex-public-school Southerner. As a hard-working social climber, Sutcliffe had plotted his path step by step of the way, like constructing one of those monumental knocks from his prime. He now called the Gentlemen by their first names, looking them squarely in the eye on level terms.

At any rate a century against Kent on a rain ruined surface, perfectly exploited by Tich Freeman, showed all of Sutcliffe's great qualities of concentration and willpower. That immaculate side-parting in his raven, perfectly combed hair could still be seen, at the non-striker's end, leaning on his bat, taking a breather from a dogfight.

The visitors in 1935 – the South Africans - had never been much of a force in England yet they were still unbeaten before the first Test at Trent Bridge. England batted first and Sutcliffe walked out with captain Wyatt (the Walters non-selection causing a minor outrage in the press) and the pair added 118 before Sutcliffe fell pads in front to the tall (six foot three) 23-year-old Arthur Langton, for 61. The Test ended in a rain affected draw, Sutcliffe only batted the once.

South Africa then beat a hitherto undefeated Yorkshire team, handsomely. Sutcliffe scored only 1 and 17 and had fallen in both innings to the fast-medium seamer, Arthur Bell. By the time of the second Test at Lord's, South Africa carried high hopes of defeating England at headquarters for the first time.

The Lord's pitch had become infested with a plague of leather-jacket insects, the outfield resembling a desert. The MCC had granted only three-day Tests to the South Africans in the belief they were a second-rate side. England and Sutcliffe in particular received a hiding. In the first innings Sutcliffe fell once more to Bell, lbw for a single. In the second innings, by which time the tide of the Test had swung markedly towards South Africa, Sutcliffe scored a laboured and fortunate 38. During the course of this innings Sutcliffe suffered a side strain and had to have a runner. When he fell, lbw to Langton, Sutcliffe walked off the ground for the last time in a Test, though few would have guessed.

Chosen for the Leeds Test, Sutcliffe had to pull out with injury; so, too, at short notice did Clark, Hollies and then Leyland. In one of the great romantic tales the call was sent out for Yorkshire's Arthur Mitchell. He had no idea of the problem until a car pulled up to drive him swiftly to the action. Mitchell, watering his broad beans at the time, hastened to his country's call, scored a brace of fine fifties and fielded magnificently.

Sutcliffe failed to make it back into the England side; some felt there needed to be games given to youngsters to construct a new batting line-up in time for the 1936/37 Ashes. Nobody objected too much, especially Yorkshire folk, who enjoyed watching their treasured opener score eight centuries in 1935, and his 2,494 runs at 48.90 were only fractionally less than Hammond and superior to all other batsmen in the land.

Sutcliffe did manage to score 1,000 runs in 1936 and batted to great effect with a double hundred in one Championship match, but his season's average of 30 bore a bleak shadow in comparison to his high-noon between 1924 and 1931.

He set up a Sports Outfitting company and took a managerial job in the paper trade where his efficient organisation was put to good use. For a while various cricketing administrative roles came his way, including that of England selector. He played a minor role in the Old England versus Surrey game in 1946 and took away 149 first-class centuries and a Test average of over 60; while in wider cricket he scored over 50,000 runs at 52.

Almost all of his greatest deeds were accomplished before middle age. Hindsight suggests Sutcliffe should have gone on Gubby Allen's tour in 1936/37. The series saw two England victories in the first two Tests, followed by three defeats as Bradman's form and confidence returned. No England opening partnership rose above 53 over the whole series, with those openers chosen to accompany Charlie Barnett - Fagg and Worthington – failing with wretched consistency.

Sutcliffe produced three fine seasons for Yorkshire running up to the war, hitting 15 more centuries whilst scoring around 5,400 runs at over 47; the neat, impeccable opener had proved that age had little barrier. Indeed in 1939 the veteran 45-year-old scored six centuries,

1,416 runs at 54.46. His Test average of 60.73 remains the highest for an England batter of all time.

Hobbs continued to score centuries in friendly cricket, his very last and 244th came in the Father's XI against Kimbolton School in 1941, aged 58. After WW2 Hobbs continued with his sports shop and became one of the 25 ex-England cricketers to be awarded life membership of the MCC. Elected onto the Surrey committee, Hobbs enjoyed the privilege of opening the Hobbs Gates at the Oval. He grew old gracefully, looking a dozen years younger with that brown skin, lean body and twinkle in those brown eyes. In Coronation year, 1953, soon after Her Majesty Queen Elizabeth II came to the throne, Her Majesty knighted him; in doing so, Sir Jack Hobbs became the first sportsman to be knighted for his services to the game, as a player. 'Shrimp' Leveson-Gower and Plum Warner had been knighted previously but for their administrative qualities, not skills as cricketers.

He played plenty of golf in his dotage, often with Herbert Strudwick and every year the Master's Club met up on Jack's birthday to wine, dine and remember the golden days. Strudwick, Hendren, Geary,

G.T.S. Stevens, Sandham and so forth, all local to London and the South East, were regular guests. He visited Lord's, the Oval and Hove whenever he could, this most humble, unassuming and much-loved man. Ada and he spent their last years living in Hove, near the seafront, spending their days taking in the bracing sea air. In his last years Jack cared for Ada who pre-deceased him by a year. To this day he remains the most celebrated England batsman of all time.

Hobbs passed away on December 21st 1963, just days after his 81st birthday. Sutcliffe wrote of his friend that Jack was the 'most brilliant (batting) exponent of all time, and quite the best batsman of my generation on all types of wickets, on good wickets I do believe that pride of place should be given to Sir Don Bradman ... A regular church-goer, he seldom missed the opportunity to attend church service on Sunday mornings both in England and abroad. He was a man of the highest integrity who believed in sportsmanship in the highest sense, teamwork, fair-play and clean-living. His life was full of everything noble and true'.

Hundreds of Surrey supporters and famous cricketers past and present attended a Memorial service in Southwark Cathedral, London Bridge, on February 20th, 1964.

Sutcliffe served for 21 years on the Yorkshire Committee, an ever-dependable member of the team. Brian Sellers, who served with him, reckoned '*Very few people realise what a great fellow he was. He was always courteous, kind and considerate ... you never saw him untidy; always chest out and chin up ... great gentleman ...astute businessman'*.

Sutcliffe lived until 83. Few questioned his judgement on a player and in his book 'For Yorkshire and England' (published before he played his final Tests) he wrote a page extolling the virtues of an unheard of 18-year-old batsman (who averaged only 29 that season), stating such bold phrases as: ''a batsman of a calibre quite unusual ... a certainty for a place as England's opening batsman ... a marvel – the discovery of a generation ... he has as many shots as Bradman ... technique that of a master...will be a power in the land ... his style and polished skill must triumph ...little chance of his equilibrium being upset''.

The comments were written of a teenager called Len Hutton.

Sutcliffe served as an England selector and as a sponsor for many good cricketing causes. His county and England colleague in the post-Hobbs era, Bill Bowes, wrote in his obituary that he *'never did anything mean or underhand'*. Yet Max Davidson (We'll Get 'em in sequins: Wisden Sports Writing; 2012) dug up some sad reflections on Herbert Sutcliffe. Known as a man with exceptional diffidence, it was as though Herbert's cornerstones had been shattered beyond repair after the horrors of the Great War. Emotionally, his only way to turn pointed to stoicism, stiff upper lip, fight back those tears. As unflappable as they come, Sutcliffe rarely laughed and only occasionally smiled. He could be abrupt and bristling, exuding inner strength and self-confidence. His son Billy (Mr W.H.H. Sutcliffe) captained Yorkshire in 1956 when the great broad acres fell to seventh in the County Championship and though they rose to third a year later, such was the disunity in a lax and toxic dressing-room, Billy fled first-class cricket. Yorkshire folk had shown frustration that he lacked the ability of his father and that parentage burden weighed heavily on the son.

Herbert became wheelchair bound in his last decade, riddled with arthritis and he celebrated his eightieth birthday in hospital, the same year his wife Emmie passed away. Last seen in public on the Headingley turf, Ashes Test of 1977, wheelchair bound, Herbert Sutcliffe posed for the cameras with the other two Yorkshire batters who had collected a hundred first-class centuries. Geoffrey Boycott, dressed in his England whites, had reached the milestone earlier that day, on-driving Greg Chappell for four in what turned out to be the deciding Test. Len Hutton, still holder of the England record Test score (364 at the Oval in 1938), was the other. Sutcliffe had had to be cajoled out on to the ground for the photograph, his regard for Boycott being one of 'cordial detestation' according to Don Mosey.

He moved to St Anne's nursing home in Crosshills. This did not stop him from flirting with the caring staff, often to open-mouthed surprise; the suggestions he made appeared rather explicit. Increasingly he relied on gin and passed away, apparently with no family members around him, on 22nd January 1978.

Statistical Comparisons

So much Test cricket has been played over the last century that, in some respects, many of the records of Hobbs and Sutcliffe have been eclipsed. Even the hallowed career partnership average of 87.81 has been surpassed (91.82 by Javed Miandad and Shoaib Mohammad). However, it is through scrutinising opening partnerships, those based on facing the new ball with its extra pace, swing and seam, where the greatness of Hobbs and Sutcliffe is most visible.

Table to show the highest average for opening partnerships in Test Cricket

Openers	Country	Average	Runs	100+ stands	Era
Hobbs and Sutcliffe	**England**	**87.81**	**3249**	**15**	**1924-30**
McKenzie and Smith	S. Africa	66.56	1664	5	2008-09
Brown and Fingleton	Australia	63.75	1020	3	1935-38
Hobbs and Rhodes	England	61.31	2146	8	1910-21
Lawry and Simpson	Australia	60.94	3596	9	1961-68
Majid Khan Sadiq Mohammad	Pakistan	60.47	1391	4	1974-78
Hutton and Washbrook	England	60.00	2880	8	1946-51

Sir Don Bradman is rightly considered the greatest run-machine of all time. No one compares to him. Yet, the disparity between Bradman's Test average (99.94) and second place for those with over 1,000 Test runs: is Voges (61.87). As the next table suggests, the gulf in run-making between Bradman and the rest is not *so* much more than Hobbs and Sutcliffe, as openers, compared to the rest.

Although Bradman is nearly twice as far ahead of his nearest rival

than Hobbs and Sutcliffe, both cases represent statistical anomalies.

The difference between Hobbs and Sutcliffe and their nearest rivals

is over ten times as high as between second and third.

	Test Batsman	Average	Diff	Test Openers	Average	Diff
1st	Bradman	99.94	38.07	**Hobbs and Sutcliffe**	**87.81**	**21.25**
2nd	Voges	61.87	0.90	McKenzie and Smith	66.56	2.19
3rd	R.G. Pollock	60.97	0.07	Brown and Fingleton	63.75	2.44
4th	Headley	60.83	0.14	Hobbs and Rhodes	61.31	1.44
5th	Sutcliffe	60.73	0.10	Lawry and Simpson	60.94	0.37

	Jack Hobbs	**Herbert Sutcliffe**
First-class career	1905-34	1919-39

span		
Runs	61,237	50,135
Average	50.65	52.00
Centuries	197	149
Century partnerships	166	145
Partners	Andrew Sandham 66 Tom Hayward 40 **Herbert Sutcliffe 26** Wilfred Rhodes 13 DJ Knight 6, CAG Russell 5	Percy Holmes 74 **Jack Hobbs 26** Len Hutton 15 Arthur Mitchell 6 Maurice Leyland 4
Test career span	1908-30	1924-35
Runs	5,410	4,555
Average	56.94	60.73
Centuries	15	16
Century partnerships	24	20
Partners	**Herbert Sutcliffe 15** Wilfred Rhodes 8 CB Fry 1	**Jack Hobbs 15** Bob Wyatt 2 Holmes, Jardine, Walters 1

Test Match Openers with a batting average of over 50

Test average	Batsman	Country	Era
60.73	**Herbert Sutcliffe**	**England**	**1924-1935**
56.94	**Sir Jack Hobbs**	**England**	**1908-1930**
56.67	Sir Len Hutton	England	1937-1955
51.12	Sunil Gavaskar	India	1971-1987
50.73	Matthew Hayden	Australia	1994-2009

If not quite so much as Bradman, the argument that Hobbs and Sutcliffe represent statistical outliers as opening batsmen as beyond reproach, even with a further century of Test cricket embedded into the data. Only one pair of opening batsmen have scored more century partnerships than Hobbs and Sutcliffe. The great West Indian side of the 1980s enjoyed 16 Test century partnerships between Gordon Greenidge and Desmond Haynes, one more than Hobbs and Sutcliffe managed for England. However, it is interesting to note that Greenidge and Haynes needed exactly one hundred more completed partnerships. Hobbs and Sutcliffe enjoyed one century stand every 2.47 innings; for Greenidge and Haynes, that meant a century stand every 8.56 innings.

Table below to show the ratio of century opening partnerships per completed partnership (one ended with a dismissal).

Batsmen	Era	100+ stands	No. completed	Ratio
Greenidge and Haynes	1978-91	16	137	8.56
Hobbs and Sutcliffe	**1924-30**	**15**	**37**	**2.46**
Hayden and Langer	2001-07	14	109	7.79
Cook and Strauss	2007-12	12	115	9.58
Gambhir and Sehwag	2004-12	11	84	7.64
Gavaskar and Chauhan	1973-81	10	56	5.60
Rogers and Warner	2013-15	9	40	4.44
McKenzie and Smith	2008-09	5	25	5.00
Rae and Stollmeyer	1948-53	5	19	3.80

Greatest Partnerships in English Cricket (Qualification: 2,000 Test runs)

Partnership average	Batsmen	Era
87.86	**Hobbs and Sutcliffe**	**1924-30**

66.61	Barrington and Dexter	1959-64
64.79	Barrington and Cowdrey	1959-68
64.69	Cook and Pietersen	2006-14
60.04	Collingwood and Pietersen	2005-10
58.82	Hobbs and Rhodes	1910-21
58.00	Hutton and Washbrook	1946-51
55.32	Cook and Trott	2009-15
54.07	Bell and Pietersen	2005-14
53.47	Gooch and Atherton	1989-95
52.35	Strauss and Trescothick	2004-06
51.19	Gooch and Gower	1978-92
51.17	Butcher and Hussain	1997-04
51.14	Trescothick and Vaughan	2000-06

Most prolific partnerships of all-time

Average	Runs	Batsmen	Era
91.82	2112	Javed Miandad and Shoaib Mohammad	1984-93
87.86	**3339**	**Hobbs and Sutcliffe**	**1924-30**
82.16	3451	Langer and Ponting	1998-06
78.42	3137	Mohammad Yousuf and Younis Khan	2000-09
68.36	3213	Misbah-ul-Haq and Younis Khan	2001-17

67.11	4765	Hayden and Ponting	2001-09
66.61	2265	Barrington and Dexter	1959-65
66.57	2330	Clarke and Ponting	2005-12
65.82	2304	Border and Jones	1984-92

Bibliography

Aside from the Wisden Cricket Almanack, the following books were referred to.

Arlott, John	Cricket: The Great Ones	1967	Pelham Books
Arlott, John	Cricket: The Great Bowlers	1970	Sportsman's Book Club
Arlott, John	Cricket The Great Captains	1971	Pelham Books
Arlott, John	100 Greatest Batsmen	1986	Queen Anne Press
Arnold & Wynne-Thomas	Illustrated History of the Test Match	1988	Sidgwick & Jackson
Arnold & Wynne-Thomas	An Ashes Anthology	1989	Christopher Helm
Arnold & Wynne-Thomas	Ultimate Encyclopaedia of Cricket	1997	Hodder & Stoughton
Barker, Ralph	Ten Great Innings	1964	Chatto and Windus
Batchelor Denzil	Book of Cricket	1952	Collins
Batty, Clive	Ashes Miscellany	2008	Vision Sports Publishing
Birley, Derek	A Social History of English Cricket	1999	Aurum Press
Bradman, Don	Farewell to Cricket	1950	Hodder &

Author	Title	Year	Publisher
		0	Stoughton
Brearley, Hussain & Baxter	Cricket's Greatest Battles	2000	Gen. Publications
Briggs, Simon	Stiff Upper Lips and Baggy Green Caps	2006	Quercus
Brookes, Christopher	English Cricket	1978	Readers Union
Brownlee, Nick	100 Greatest Moments in Cricket	1999	Gen. Publications
Cardus, Neville	English Cricket	1945	Collins
Cardus, Neville	Close of Play	1956	Collins
Cardus, Neville	Play Resumed with Cardus (Ashes 1930)	1979	Souvenir Press
Cardus, Neville	Roses Matches 1919 – 1939	1982	Souvenir Press
Cotter, Gerry	Ashes Captains	1989	Crowood Press
Davidson, Max	We'll Get 'em in Sequins	2012	Wisden Sports Writing
Doggart, Hubert	Cricket's Bounty	2014	Phillimore BP
Foot, David	Wally Hammond The Reasons Why	1998	Robson Books
Foster & Arnold	100 Years of Test Cricket	1977	Hamlyn PGL
Frindall, Bill	Wisden Book of Test Cricket 1877 - 1984	1985	Guild Publishing
Frindall, Bill	Wisden Book of Cricket Records	1986	Macdonald QAP
Frith David	Archie Jackson	1987	Pavilion
Frith, David	England versus Australia - pictorial history since 1877	1977	Book Club Associates
Gibson, Alan	Cricket Captains of England	1979	Cassell Illustrated
Giller, Norman	Ten Greatest Test Teams	1988	Sidgwick & Jackson
Giller, Norman	World's Greatest Cricket Matches	198	Octopus Books

Author	Title	Year	Publisher
		9	Limited
Gower, David	50 Greatest Cricketers of all Time	2015	Timpson
Green, Stephen	Cricketing Bygones	1982	Shire Publications Ltd
Grimmett, C.V.	Grimmett on Cricket	1948	Thomas Nelson & Sons
Haigh, Gideon	Book of Ashes Anecdotes	2006	Mainstream Publishing
Hamilton, Duncan	Harold Larwood	2009	Quercus
Hammond, Walter	Cricket My Destiny	1948	Stanley Paul and Co
Hayter, Peter	Great Tests Recalled	1990	Bloomsbury
Hill, Alan	Les Ames	1990	Christopher Helm
Hobbs, J.B.	Fight for the Ashes 1934	1934	George G. Harrap & Co
Howat Gerald	Plum Warner	1987	Unwin Hyman
Howat Gerald	Cricket's Second Golden Age	1989	Hodder & Stoughton
Hughes Simon	Cricket's Greatest Rivalry Ashes in 10 Matches	2013	Octopus PGL
Jardine, D.R.	In Quest of the Ashes	1934	Hutchinson & Co
Jardine, Douglas	Cricket	1945	J.M. Dent & sons Ltd
Keating, Frank	Gents and Players	1986	Robson Books
Kilburn, J.M.	In Search of Cricket	1990	Pavilion Library
Lemmon, David	Tich' Freeman	1982	George Allen & Unwin
Lemmon, David	Great Wicket-Keepers	1983	Stanley Paul and Co
Lemmon, David	Percy Chapman	1984	Queen Anne Press

Leveson Gower, Sir Henry	Off and On the Field	1953	Stanley Paul and Co
Mailey, Arthur	10 for 66 and all that	1959	Sportsman's Book Club
Marchant, John	Greatest Test Match	1953	Sportsman's Book Club
Martin-Jenkins, C	Top 100 Cricketers	2010	Corinthian Books
Mason, Ronald	Batsman's Paradise anatomy of Cricketomania	1955	Hollis & Carter
Mason, Ronald	Ashes in the Mouth	1982	Hambledon Press
Mason, Ronald	Jack Hobbs A Biography	1988	Pavilion Library
McKinstry, Leo	Jack Hobbs England's Greatest Cricketer	2011	Yellow Jersey Press
Moyes, A.G.	A Century of Cricketers	1954	Sportsman's Book Club
Murphy, Patrick	Fifty Incredible Cricket Matches	1987	Stanley Paul and Co
Noble, M.A.	Gilligan's Men	1925	Chapman and Hall
Noble, M.A.	Fight for the Ashes 1928/29	1929	George G. Harrap & Co
Peebles, Ian	Woolley The Pride of Kent	1969	Hutchinson & Co
Peebles, Ian	Patsy' Hendren	1971	Sportsman's Book Club
Peebles, Ian	Spinner's Yarn	1977	Readers Union
Porter, Clive	The Test Match Career of Sir Jack Hobbs	1988	Spellmount Ltd
Rice, Jonathan	One Hundred Lord's Tests	2001	Methuen Publishing Ltd
Rivers, James	England versus Australia	1949	T.V. Boardman and Co
Roberts, E.L.	Cricket in England 1894-1939	1946	Edward Arnold & Co
Roberts, E.L.	Test Cricket Cavalcade	1948	Edward Arnold & Co

Robertson-Glasgow, R.C.	Cricket Prints 1920-1940	1943	Sportsman's Book Club
Robertson-Glasgow, R.C.	46 not out	1948	Hollis & Carter
Robertson-Glasgow, R.C.	More Cricket Prints 1920-1945	1948	T.Werner Laurie Ltd
Streeton, Richard	P.GH. Fender	1981	Faber and Faber
Strudwick, Herbert	25 Years behind the Stumps	1927	Hutchinson & Co
Sutcliffe, Herbert	For England and Yorkshire	1948	Edward Arnold & Co
Swanton, E.W.	Gubby Allen Man of Cricket	1985	Stanley Paul and Co
Thomson A.A.	Cricket my Pleasure	1954	Sportsman's Book Club
Various	Cricket through the Pages	2000	André Deutsch
Various	Pick of the Cricketer	1967	Hutchinson & Co
Various	Boundary Book Second Innings	1989	Spring Books
Various	Double Century 200 years of Cricket in the Times	1985	Guild Publishing
Various	Double Century Cricket in the Times Vol 1 1785-1934	1989	Pavilion Library
Various	Guardian Book of Cricket	1986	Pavilion Books Ltd
Various	Picador Book of Cricket	2006	Picador
Various	Observer On Cricket	1987	Unwin Hyman
Various	Wisden's 50 Greatest Ashes Test Matches 1882-1999	2001	John Wisden
Warner, Pelham	Fight for the Ashes 1926	1926	George G. Harrop & Co
Wilde, Simon	Wisden Cricketers of the Year	2013	John Wisden
Woodcock, John	One Hundred Greatest Cricketers	1988	Macmillan

Wynne-Thomas, Peter	Complete History of Cricket Tours Home & Abroad	1989	Hamlyn PGL
Yapp, Nick	A Century of Great Cricket	1992	WHSmith

Printed in Great Britain
by Amazon

20544240R00231